Springboard and Platform Diving

Jeff Huber, PhD

Human Kinetics

Library of Congress Cataloging-in-Publication Data

Huber, Jeffrey J., 1953-
  Springboard and platform diving / Jeffrey J. Huber, PhD.
    pages cm
  Includes webography.
  Includes bibliographical references and index.
  1. Springboard diving. 2. Diving. I. Title.
  GV838.67.S65H83 2015
  797.2'4--dc23

                              2015022401
ISBN: 978-1-4504-2445-5 (print)

Acquisitions Editor: Tom Heine; **Developmental Editor:** Kevin Matz; **Managing Editor:** Nicole O'Dell; **Copyeditor:** Patsy Fortney; **Indexer:** Bobbi Swanson; **Permissions Manager:** Martha Gullo; **Graphic Designer:** Kathleen Boudreau-Fuoss; **Cover Designer:** Keith Blomberg; **Photograph (cover):** Rogan Thomson/Actionplus/Icon Sportswire; **Photographs (interior):** Neil Bernstein, unless otherwise noted; **Photo Asset Manager:** Laura Fitch; **Photo Production Manager:** Jason Allen; **Art Manager:** Kelly Hendren; **Associate Art Manager:** Alan L. Wilborn; **Illustrations:** © Human Kinetics, unless otherwise noted; **Printer:** Sheridan Books

Human Kinetics books are available at special discounts for bulk purchase. Special editions or book excerpts can also be created to specification. For details, contact the Special Sales Manager at Human Kinetics.

Printed in the United States of America   10 9 8 7 6 5 4 3 2 1

The paper in this book is certified under a sustainable forestry program.

Human Kinetics
Website: www.HumanKinetics.com

United States: Human Kinetics
P.O. Box 5076
Champaign, IL 61825-5076
800-747-4457
e-mail: info@hkusa.com

Canada: Human Kinetics
475 Devonshire Road Unit 100
Windsor, ON N8Y 2L5
800-465-7301 (in Canada only)
e-mail: info@hkcanada.com

Europe: Human Kinetics
107 Bradford Road
Stanningley
Leeds LS28 6AT, United Kingdom
+44 (0) 113 255 5665
e-mail: hk@hkeurope.com

Australia: Human Kinetics
57A Price Avenue
Lower Mitcham, South Australia 5062
08 8372 0999
e-mail: info@hkaustralia.com

New Zealand: Human Kinetics
P.O. Box 80
Mitcham Shopping Centre, South Australia 5062
0800 222 062
e-mail: info@hknewzealand.com

E5664

To my parents Hank and Sue Huber,
who provided the means, encouragement, and moral support
that fostered my participation in the sweet sport
of springboard and platform diving.

In Memoriam

In memory of Coach Morry Arbini,
who ignited a passion for the sport of diving
in hundreds of young athletes
and irrevocably changed our lives forever.

Contents

Preface

Some diving coaches and divers believe that great divers are born, not made, that natural talent determines success. After 37 years of coaching diving, I am certain that nothing is further from the truth. Let me offer you just a few of the many counterexamples I have witnessed during my career.

- A young woman contacts me and wants to transfer after her sophomore year of college. She was a high school gymnast who picked up diving during her junior year and decided to dive in college. But she was pretty bad—so bad, in fact, that two programs in the conference refused to consider letting her transfer even as a walk-on. I decided to take a chance. Two years later she becomes a U.S. National Collegiate Athletic Association (NCAA) national champion.

- A young man joins my team. He used a reverse somersault in his high school state meet and had no 3-meter experience. Three years later he is conference champion; conference diver of the year; NCAA All American on the 1 meter, 3 meter, and 10 meter; and after winning the 3-meter preliminary rounds, narrowly misses making the U.S. world team by a mere 6 points.

- A young female athlete decides to compete in college. As a high school diver, she qualified for the age group nationals, but never managed to make finals. Five years later she graduates as Big Ten champion, U.S. national champion, NCAA champion, and U.S. Olympian—in an event she did not compete in until her freshman year of college.

- A tall, lanky kid walks on, even though his age group coach suggested he has no talent and no courage for the sport. The kid is afraid of learning new dives, even afraid of simply standing backward on the 10-meter platform. Three years later he throws a 207C on a 10-meter platform cold turkey (without any preparatory warm-up) as a morning get-out dive. And he smokes the entry. Would you like more examples? I have plenty.

Great divers born, not made? Hardly.

Sure, some divers, such as Olympic champion Greg Louganis, are a rare and special breed of cat—phenomenal athletes who come along only once in a while. However, many athletes, through dedication, high effort, perseverance, and most important, proper training, become accomplished and successful divers. As the preceding examples highlight, diving is an incredibly teachable and learnable sport—if coaches know what to teach and how to teach, and divers know what to learn and how to learn. If you are a coach, this book will help you advance your divers to higher skill levels, no matter who you coach, where you coach, or what level you coach (e.g., summer league, age group, private club, junior high, high school, college). If you are a diver, this book will help you become the diver you dream of becoming. In simple step-by-step fashion, this book outlines the essential ingredients for effective springboard and platform diving.

Chapter 1 discusses how coaches and divers can work together. Specifically, it provides guidelines for how coaches can provide effective external feedback and how divers can receive and best use this information to improve their dive performance. The chapter provides suggestions for the type of feedback to give as well as how and when to give it, because sometimes how and when the feedback is presented are as important as or more important than what is presented. As legendary basketball coach John Wooden put it, "A coach is someone who can give correction without causing resentment." Chapter 1 also explains internal feedback and what athletes experience—and in many instances do not experience—during performance; divers can't always feel what they are doing. Also presented are some simple yet deceptively useful concepts and paradigms from learning research that I have found indispensable for effective coach instruction and athlete learning.

Chapter 2 tackles the beast of springboard diving—the forward approach. Former Indiana University and international hall of fame diving coach Hobie Billingsley once said, "The forward approach is the most difficult part of our sport." This chapter deconstructs the forward approach to reveal that it really isn't the difficult beast many make it out to be. The forward approach is composed of just a few simple and easily comprehended movements; once these movements are understood, coaches can teach and divers can learn the forward approach. The chapter concludes by outlining the basics of the forward platform approach. Similarly, chapter 3 deconstructs the springboard and platform backward press, breaking it down into a few simple teachable and learnable movements.

Chapter 4 demystifies takeoffs and connections by presenting the five essential positions for the forward, backward, reverse, inward, and armstand takeoffs and the three essential positions for connecting into tuck, pike, and twisting dives. Perhaps of even greater interest is the exploration of twisting mechanics. From my experience working with coaches and divers, many believe that twisting is a complex and somewhat mysterious and incomprehensible skill that is difficult to teach and even harder to learn. That is definitely not the case. A diver who can perform a forward jump with a full twist off the 1-meter board has learned how to do about 90 percent of what it takes to twist. In chapter 4 we look at the four easy steps for initiating a twist as well the progressions for teaching twisting with and without a twisting belt.

Chapter 5 covers the critical topics of dive positions, spotting, and come-outs. As you will see, dives are much easier to perform from a correct position. Also, after a poor takeoff, dives are more forgiving with a good position. In other words, it is possible to still perform an adequate dive after a poor takeoff, if a good dive position is established. Spotting refers to picking up visual cues or spots during dive performance. Athletes in other sports would never perform with their eyes shut, and diving is no different. The where, when, and how of spotting are presented, as is a simple progression for learning to spot. As with twisting, some coaches and divers believe that spotting is difficult. It is not. In fact, once divers begin spotting, it becomes automatic. Finally, chapter 5 looks at the actions for coming out of a dive. The come-out is critical for preparing for the all-important entry.

Chapter 6 addresses the line-up and the entry. The line-up is the body position attained immediately before entering the water. The entry is the action of the body moving through the water to create the big tamale of our sport—the rip! The rip (entering the water without a splash) is where it's at in diving, and it's one of the coolest parts of our sport. Ninety percent of performing a good dive is getting a good takeoff, but 90 percent of a diver's score often comes from the entry. Ripping is easy, and every diver can learn how to do it. Chapter 6 reveals the secrets of what divers do both above and below the water to attain a great rip. It also offers some simple but effective drills for learning to rip.

Chapter 7 is the fun part, in which we take the information in the preceding chapters and tie it together. This chapter provides the specifics for everything coaches should teach and divers should learn at each level of proficiency. For each level, I address appropriate concepts, the amount of deliberate play and deliberate practice required, types of games, practice frequency and duration, mental and cognitive skills, warm-up routines, coach reminders, and a skill progression checklist. As a coach, I was always on the lookout for new and improved teaching techniques that would give me the biggest bang for my buck—drills that accelerated the learning process. These checklists contain all of the drills I found most effective for helping divers find quick improvements.

Chapter 8 looks at four critical aspects for effective training and diver success that are often overlooked by coaches and athletes: strength, conditioning, nutrition, and recovery. Controlling these factors results in improved physical conditioning and dive performance; diminished risk of injury, sickness, and staleness; consistent seasonal training; and improved physical adaptation.

Chapter 9 explains how to create an annual individualized training plan (AITP), which serves as a seasonal road map for success. Although creating an AITP before the season takes some effort, it makes for a much more enjoyable and effortless coaching experience throughout the season. Employing the concept of periodization (doing different things at different times of the season), the chapter outlines exactly what divers should be doing during each training phase.

Many coaches and divers will find chapters 10 and 11 to be perhaps the most important. Without a doubt, the sport of diving is a mental game. At the 2008 Olympic Games, for example, U.S. Olympians were informally asked how much of performing well was mental. The typical response was 90 percent. Whether it involves battling the fear of learning a new dive, handling the stress of competition, managing the fatigue of training, maintaining the motivation to train, or building the confidence to perform, mental training is a critical component for effective skill acquisition and quality diving performance. Although there is no substitute for physical training, solid physical skills alone aren't enough to succeed. The missing ingredient is solid mental skills. Strong mental skills won't guarantee success, but weak mental skills almost assuredly will guarantee failure (USOC Sport Psychology Staff, 2006). Chapters 10 and 11 offer some simple but incredibly effective strategies and heuristics (i.e., simple rules of thumb) for developing strong mental skills in both practice and competition.

As a young coach working my way up through the ranks, I searched for printed forms, worksheets, drills, and practice plans that I could use to become an effective coach. Because nothing to my knowledge existed, I began developing them. Embedded throughout this book are items I created over the course of my career. Everything but the proverbial kitchen sink is provided. Also, throughout the book are sidebars called How to Teach that outline step-by-step directions for teaching specific skills. All How to Teach sections assume that the coach does not have access to a trampoline or other dryland equipment. However, the book also includes drills and skills that utilize both the trampoline and other dryland equipment for coaches with access to these types of equipment. Below are some guidelines for best utilizing the How to Teach sections.

Shortly before I retired from coaching, I was given perhaps the best compliment of my coaching career. At an international competition in Canada, a longtime observer of my career said, "Jeff, you took divers who never should have been great and made them great." I would slightly modify his observation by noting that those divers made themselves great; I simply facilitated the becoming-great process. Nevertheless, his observation underscores the point that great divers are not born great but, rather, become great by working closely with their coaches and by following a carefully crafted training program. My intent

Guidelines for Using the How to Teach Sections

- Coaches should begin all teaching sections with video review, verbal explanations, and slow-motion modeling so that divers have a clear cognitive understanding of skill requirements.
- Coaches and divers should use the drills listed throughout the book. These drills are proven to be reliable, efficient, and effective.
- Coaches should advance divers to a subsequent subskill after they have attained at least 80-85-percent mastery on the current skill.
- Coaches should keep in mind that divers progress at different rates of mastery attainment.
- Coaches should remember that divers differ in mental, emotional, and physical readiness.
- Coaches should avoid attempting to teach a skill, such as the forward approach, in its entirety. They should break these skills down and teach the essential elements and then piece them together.
- Coaches should remember that each skill requires a certain amount of physical readiness. For example, the hurdle requires leg strength, and the forward line-up requires core strength. Consequently, physical conditioning is a prerequisite for skill learning and mastery attainment.
- Please note that some photos of drills and techniques in this book were performed facing the side of the trampoline for photographic purposes only. Divers should always begin and end double-bouncing trampoline drills facing the long end of the trampoline bed.

from the outset of writing this book was to outline such a training program, a program that includes the essential diving skills and mental skills necessary to help aspiring athletes become great divers and aspiring coaches to become great diving coaches. I have endeavored to share with future generations of divers and diving coaches everything I gained during my 37-year coaching career. I wish you the best of luck in achieving your dreams.

Acknowledgments

I wish to thank Tom Heine and Kevin Matz for their experience and enthusiasm in keeping this book project moving forward. I especially appreciated their deft hands when it came time to offer suggestions and criticism and their support of the additional chapters, particularly the chapters on the psychology of training and competing. They recognized the value of these chapters. Thanks also to Nicole O'Dell for seeing the project to its completion.

I also wish to thank the models—Amy Cozad, Michael Hixon, Jessica Parratto, and Darian Schmidt—for enduring a grueling three-day photo shoot and for giving up a rare weekend's reprieve from training to spend it back at the pool and dryland center.

I would also like to thank Human Kinetics photographer Neil Bernstein whose patience infinitely exceeded mine and whose attention to detail and pursuit of excellence resulted in professional photos and better book. Thanks also to former diver Marc Carlton for his sketches, which helped immensely with the accuracy of the book's art pieces.

Many coaches influenced the information in this book and I would be remiss if I did not thank them. My former coaches: International Hall of Fame coach Glenn McCormick, University of Wisconsin coach Jerry Darda, and high school coach Morry Arbini. My colleague, USA Olympic head coach John Wingfield, whose ability to develop great divers is truly remarkable.

I also wish to thank all the divers I was fortunate to coach and to know not only as athletes but also as friends. We often learned together and invented new drills, techniques, and even new dives. Special thanks to two-time USA Olympian Christina Loukas for permission to use her photo on the front cover of this book. The photo recognizes her accomplished career and celebrates her parents, George and Patty, for their enthusiastic and unwavering support of the diving program.

I also wish to thank professors Richard Shiffrin, Robert Nosofsky, Robert Goldstone, Peter Finn, William Hetrick, Jim Sherman, Bennett Bertenthal, and the entire faculty in the Department of Psychological and Brain Sciences at Indiana University for their unanimous approval of my position as Professor of Practice, a position which has allowed me to continue working with students and to complete the writing of this book, which I view as a capstone to my coaching career.

Finally, I would like to thank my wife, Dr. Lesa Huber, for her understanding, patience, and enduring support not only during the writing of this book but throughout my 37-year coaching career.

CHAPTER 1

How Coaches Teach, How Divers Learn

There are 26 letters in the English alphabet, but no two letters are perhaps more critical to sport, particularly the sport of diving, than the letters X and O. Coaches and athletes focus relentlessly on the Xs and Os, which refer to the elements and mechanics that constitute dive execution.

However, as we get started, it is important to be mindful that, just as the English alphabet consists of more than two letters, coaching and learning diving consist of more than the Xs and Os. For example, although it is important to know the basic building-block skills (Xs and Os) to learn a difficult reverse optional dive, it is equally important to know such things as how to determine skill progression, assess athlete readiness, recognize individual differences, and provide good external feedback. For this reason, this opening chapter considers some of the ABCs (the non X and O factors) of coaching and learning—that is, *how* coaches teach and *how* divers learn.

The following sections discuss some simple but highly effective *hows* for teaching and learning the beautiful sport of diving.

Sending and Receiving External Feedback

Diving coaches spend most of practice time teaching, and divers spend most of practice time learning. Teaching means, in part, dispensing feedback about performance and instruction about improving that performance. And learning means, in part, attending to and processing that feedback and instruction and translating it into performance changes. Pretty basic, huh? A coach can be a valuable set of eyes for assisting athletes in seeing what they can't see for themselves. But feedback and instruction are most valuable—and most effective—when correctly sent by the coach and correctly received by the diver. What basic guidelines should coaches and divers follow for correctly sending and receiving external feedback?

First, however, a short story . . .

Around the midterm of my diving career, I had a terrible temper. If I missed a dive, I would come up from my entry and slap the water as hard as I could and yell some expletive. At the time, I was a somewhat accomplished diver, at least in my mind, and I thought what I was doing was natural and in some way actually helping me to become a better diver. It wasn't. In truth, my temper and bad behavior alienated me from my teammates, interfered with my performance, and most important, made me difficult to coach. This went on for some time until I began working with hall of fame coach Glenn McCormick.

Glenn was a calming presence on the team and highly respected by his athletes. He used a scientific approach to his coaching, but he also used an artful approach that included patience, sensitivity, and caring. One day during practice, I missed a dive and vigorously slapped the water and let out a few choice curse words. After that spectacle, Glenn waited a few moments and then calmly gestured for me to come see him. I got out of the pool and walked over and stood next to him. Without a hint of anger and without missing another diver's dive, he leaned into me and said softly so no one else could hear, "You know, when you do that, you look like a fool."

Now, if any other coach with whom I had trained had said such a thing, I would have gone ballistic, denied the accusation or, at the very least, defended my actions. But coming from Glenn, and said in such a nonthreatening and unemotional tone, it helped me see myself through Glenn's eyes—and the eyes of my teammates. And I was embarrassed.

Glenn wasn't offering me feedback about my motor behavior; he was offering me insightful feedback about my social, learning, and champion behaviors—or lack thereof. And in that moment of epiphany, I became a better athlete. In that moment, I saw myself not only for who I was but, more important, for who I suddenly wanted to become. I didn't want to be that person anymore: the emotionally-out-of-control athlete. I vowed to never again lose control. And I never did. I went the entire summer without losing my temper or shouting an inappropriate word. As a consequence, I discovered the diving consistency I had previously lacked, and I accomplished lifelong athletic goals.

Near the end of that summer of personal and athletic growth, I performed a dive badly in practice; Glenn looked at me and said with a smile, "Well, that dive was so bad you can lose your temper." I responded with a smile, "No, that's okay. I'll just hit it the next time." Besides becoming more likable to my teammates, more coachable to Glenn, and more accomplished as a diver, somewhere along the way I had also become more mature and more confident as an athlete and human being.

As the preceding story highlights, *what* coaches say is important, but *when* they say it, *where* they say it, *how* they say it, and *how often* they say it are equally important for reaching the ultimate communication goals: message sent and message received. The following two sections provide recommendations for coaches for sending external feedback and for divers for receiving and processing that feedback. Before considering these recommendations, however, let's first define external feedback.

External feedback (EF) is sensory information provided to a learner by an outside source, such as a coach's comments, a video replay, or a judge's score. For the purpose of this chapter, external feedback refers to a coach's comments. External feedback is information about the outcome of a movement and is in addition to internal feedback. There are two types of external feedback: knowledge of results (KR) and knowledge of performance (KP).

Knowledge of results (KR) is external, usually verbal or at least verbalizable information that informs athletes about the success of their actions with regard to the intended goal. For example, a coach might tell a golfer, "You hooked that last shot with your five iron." In many cases, but not all, KR is redundant because often it is information identical to internal information. The golfer who hooks a five iron probably can see the shot hook. Similarly, the diver who goes way past vertical on a reverse 2 1/2 somersault probably (but not always) knows it via internal feedback and might say: "Coach, I know I went way past vertical. I could feel the water hit the front of my legs."

Some types of KR, however, are not redundant with internal feedback. Divers, for example, must wait until the conclusion of their dives to receive their scores and know precisely how their performances were evaluated by the judges. In this case, KR is feedback about the overall execution and value of the dive, something the diver might not be able to determine using only internal feedback.

Another case in which KR is valuable is when the athlete is sensing incorrect diminished internal feedback. At the World Cup Championship in Athens, Greece, for example, U.S. Olympian and national champion Mark Ruiz was practicing double-bouncing reverse 2 1/2s on a 3-meter springboard and kept reporting that his entries were going over, when in fact, they were right on target and lining up vertically.

Knowledge of performance (KP) is feedback that provides the performer with information about the quality of the movement. KP also is sometimes referred to as kinematic feedback because it provides feedback about the displacement, velocity, acceleration, and other aspects of the movement. Consider, for example, the diver who is trying to speed up her arm swing on a backward press. Her coach might provide KP by saying: "Your arm swing is a little slow. Speed it up by 10 percent, turn your palms at the top of the press, and let them swing slightly behind your hips." This is an example of KP because it is information about the kinematics (in this case, the velocity and movement pattern) of the movement. KP informs athletes about the quality of their movements, whereas KR informs them about the level of goal achievement.

So what is the best way to send external feedback?

Sending External Feedback

Use external feedback to reinforce movement. Reinforcement increases the probability that the person will repeat the reinforced response; so, if you are a coach and you like what you see, reinforce it with positive external feedback. Consider, for example, the diving coach who has been stressing the importance of staying tight during an entry for a back 1 1/2 somersault in the tuck position. The coach finally sees what she wants to see from one of her divers and immediately reinforces the behavior with praise and positive feedback: "Great job, Jimmy! That's the way to stay tight on that entry! Keep doing it!" A less effective coach might miss that opportunity to reinforce the behavior, perhaps focusing on another deficient aspect of the dive.

Use continual reinforcement for early learning. Research indicates that in the early stage of learning, particularly for very young children, continual reinforcement is most effective (Lee & Belfiore, 1997). Continual reinforcement in the form of praise and KR encourages error-free learning and maintains motivation. KR given for each attempt helps performance by temporarily guiding, motivating, and energizing the learner (Schmidt & Lee, 2011). After the early stage of motor learning, however, it is better to reduce the frequency of KR (external feedback) as athletes become more proficient; otherwise, they can become dependent on this information and fail to process feedback information in a way that helps them permanently learn the task. In other words, they use KR as a crutch (Schmidt & Lee, 2011).

Use external reinforcing feedback intermittently after the early learning stage. **Intermittent reinforcement** refers to external feedback that is given only occasionally. Results of studies examining the effects of various schedules of reinforcement indicate that after reinforcing feedback has been withdrawn those who received intermittent reinforcement performed better than those who received continual reinforcement (Schmidt & Wrisberg, 2008). With less frequent KR after the very early learning stage, athletes must use other processes to detect their own errors, be more consistent, make between-task comparisons, and identify common motor-movement patterns (Schmidt & Lee, 2011; Wulf, Lee, & Schmidt, 1994).

Use motivating external feedback. **Motivating feedback** is feedback about a person's progress toward goal achievement that energizes and directs behavior. Because motivating feedback can cause athletes to increase their efforts, coaches should provide it fairly immediately. Without this type of feedback, athletes can become discouraged and ineffectual in practice. If you are a coach and you forget to comment on a noticeable improvement, however, do not despair. You can always remind athletes about their improvements before the next practice. For example, if you forget to compliment a diver on doing some great twister dives, at the next practice you could say: "David, I didn't get a chance to compliment you on your last practice set. I can't tell you how much better your twisting action looked. All your hard work is really paying off!"

Sometimes, athletes are doing the right things in practice but fail to see their improvements in the overall result. For example, at a competition a diver has an outstanding hurdle and perfect takeoff and then overrotates when entering the water and receives low scores. All she can focus on at the moment are the judges' scores, and she overlooks the fact that she has finally mastered her hurdle and takeoff. Athletes need to be reminded that they are getting closer to their goals, even when the results seem to suggest otherwise. In a sense, using motivating feedback is like playing the game of hot-and-cold. As divers progress closer to their movement goals, external feedback lets them know that they are getting warmer—that is, closer to their goals.

Research tells us that people who are given motivating feedback during practice report that they enjoy practice more, try harder, and practice longer (Schmidt & Lee, 2014). A pleasurable experience paired with practice classically conditions athletes to associate a positive physiological response with their sport. In a study conducted by the United States Olympic Committee (USOC), one of the top 10 factors U.S. Olympians cited for their success was a love of their sport, which was instilled in them by their youth coaches and the enjoyment they experienced early in their careers (Gibbons et al., 2003). Consequently, coaches, particularly coaches who work with youth, should provide motivating feedback during practice.

Use precise, detailed, and relevant informational external feedback. **Informational feedback** is feedback that provides performers with error correction information, either descriptive or prescriptive. For any given movement, there is often a large amount of information that can be supplied. The excellent coach, however, can rapidly select the most pertinent information, distill it into a succinct and detailed form, and expeditiously provide it to athletes. Athletes, particularly at the elite level, find informational feedback highly motivating. They want to know the errors in their performance and how they can fix them.

One factor separating the elite coach from the novice coach is the ability to provide precise, detailed, and relevant informational external feedback. Consider, for example, two coaches trying to help a diver perform a better forward 2 1/2 somersault in the pike position from the 3-meter springboard. The novice coach might say, "Well, the dive was a little slow and too far away from the board." In contrast, the elite coach would say, "The dive is slow because your arms are about 20 degrees short of vertical at the bottom of your press, and the dive needs to move 2 feet (60 cm) closer to the board." In this example, the novice coach talks in vague terms and simply provides redundant feedback, leaving the diver thinking, "Coach, I could tell the dive was slow, but why, and how far out was it?" In contrast, the elite coach provides a reason for why the dive was slow, a solution for how to fix the problem, and the exact distance the dive needs to move closer to the springboard.

Provide external feedback when requested. In a study by Janelle and colleagues (1997), subjects were asked to learn the task of throwing a tennis ball with the nondominant hand. One group of subjects received no feedback, one group received feedback after each group of five throws, and one group received feedback only when they requested it. The results of the study indicated that the two groups receiving feedback were more accurate and had better form than the group that received no feedback. Moreover, the group that received feedback only when requested performed better than the group that received feedback after each group of five throws. What this means is that the best time to provide feedback is when the learner requests it. Of course, coaches provide external feedback when they deem it necessary, but it is worth noting that sometimes providing feedback less often can be more effective.

Allow athletes several attempts before providing external feedback. Allowing athletes to make a number of attempts before providing feedback in summary form regarding those attempts, referred to as **summary feedback**, can be superior to providing immediate feedback. Lavery (1962) conducted a series of experiments that indicated the benefits of summary feedback. Lavery found that compared with giving feedback after every practice attempt, summary feedback produced poorer performances during practice but better performance later on, when the external feedback was withdrawn. The optimal number of attempts before providing summary feedback is generally five (Schmidt, Lange, & Young, 1990).

Why would less feedback contribute to increased learning and better performance later on? One plausible answer is that subjects who received instruction less often were less dependent on external feedback and relied more on internal feedback and information-processing activities. This is exactly what coaches hope to see: athletes thinking on their own and taking responsibility for their learning. It is difficult to learn how to think like an athlete if the coach is doing all the thinking. Under constant-feedback conditions, athletes ultimately become dependent on their coaches to do their thinking for them.

It is interesting to note that the group in Lavery's study that received both immediate feedback and summary feedback during practice performed as poorly when feedback was withdrawn as the group that received immediate feedback only. Presumably, this group ignored the summary feedback and simply relied on the immediate dependency-producing feedback. Results from Lavery's study suggest that when given a choice, athletes often will take the cognitively easy dependency-producing route instead of using their full cognitive abilities and taking ownership of their learning and performances. Athletes become more autonomous and responsible when they receive feedback after making several attempts.

Delay feedback when possible. **Instantaneous feedback** is feedback provided immediately after performance. In contrast, **delayed feedback** is feedback provided several seconds or more after the performance. Laboratory research suggests that external feedback given immediately after the performance, rather than after a few seconds, diminishes learning (Swinnen, 1990). In other words, external feedback is more effective after a delay, even of only a few seconds. Why? One plausible answer is that the short delay allows athletes to shift their goal state (from dive performance to dive analysis) and their attentional focus from internal (dive performance) to external (coach's feedback).

Remember that how *the message is delivered is as important as* what *the message is.* Recall the story of Glenn McCormick when I was a diver. If Glenn had shouted in an angry tone in front of my teammates that I looked like a fool, I am sure I would not have received his feedback. I would have immediately shut down, and his words would have fallen on deaf ears. Instead, his quietly delivered feedback exploded on my self-awareness like a bombshell.

Remember that how *the message is delivered sometimes* is *the message.* Consider a competition scenario in which victory comes down to the last dive. If the diver hits her dive, she wins the meet. The coach wants the athlete to remain calm, confident, resolute, alert, and focused. So, the coach calmly walks over to her and, with a smile on her face and her eyes bright and wide open, says: "Okay, we're going to get this done. You've done this dive a thousand times and know exactly what to do. Trust your training, let everything else go, and focus on the two things we talked about." Everything the coach wants the diver to do, feel, and think is embodied in the *delivery* of her message. The coach is calm, confident, resolute, alert, and focused—the same traits she wants to see in her athlete during that critical moment in the last round of dives.

Back in the day, I loved watching the interaction between NFL quarterback Joe Montana and his coach Bill Walsh. When Coach Walsh talked with Montana, it always looked to me as though they could have been standing on a street corner having a pleasant conversation, even though they were in the midst of a fierce football game with thousands of people watching from the stands and millions more watching on television. Coach Walsh was unlike most NFL coaches. By his own admission, he was not a firebrand coach who liked to do the ritual pregame psych-up with his team. He was often referred to as The Genius for his cerebral approach to the game. He was a calming presence on the sideline, and it is no coincidence that Montana was much the same as a player. When the game was on the line, Montana was calm and cerebral. If you are a coach, let the delivery of your message be the message.

Receiving External Feedback

So, the message has been sent. Good. Step 1 is complete. Now for step 2. The message must be received. Just as it takes two to tango, it takes two to communicate. Even if the message is effectively sent, it dies for lack of reception unless effectively received and processed. How do divers participate in this communication dance? In other words, what are the *hows* for divers for effectively receiving and processing external feedback?

Perceive external feedback as helpful hints for improvement, not as personal criticism. Some athletes, for whatever reason, perceive external feedback as personal attacks or jabs at their self-esteem. For the message to be effective, the receiver has to be receptive. Consequently, divers need to perceive external feedback for what it is intended to be—information for improving their dive performance and reaching their goals. Sometimes this information may be painful to accept. Divers need to remind themselves that the coach is simply the messenger, so don't shoot the messenger! The more they embrace the message, the more they will improve and be prepared and battle-ready to perform in competition.

Define learning as change. Learning may be defined in one word—change. Divers wishing to improve, to learn, must change. Accepting external feedback is the engine driving this change process. Consequently, divers should ready themselves before practice so that they are eager to receive external feedback and to translate the feedback into meaningful and lasting changes in their diving performances. If they receive feedback but don't make any changes, have they really received the feedback?

Arrive at practice cognitively alert, attentive, and ready to receive the message. The joke goes like this: Two antennas got married. The wedding wasn't much, but the reception was phenomenal. To process external feedback, athletes should arrive at practice ready for phenomenal reception. Reception can be promoted by things such as getting adequate rest, eating a nutritious prepractice snack, mentally reviewing previous practices, setting specific goals, and getting motivated. Athletes should see themselves as empty vessels waiting to be filled with external feedback that will be translated into significant and lasting changes.

Practice basic memory strategies. Research suggests that much newly presented information is soon forgotten unless it is acted on by the person receiving it. The words *acted on* mean cognitively doing something with the information. There are three basic strategies—rehearsal, elaboration, and organization— for remembering external feedback between dives and between practices. **Rehearsal** involves verbally repeating the information and physically repeating the motor movement. **Elaboration** entails making the feedback more meaningful or distinctive. **Organization** means putting the feedback information into some type of mental order. An example of organization is placing (organizing) backward and reverse dives into the same category because they have similar takeoff actions.

Be prepared for RIPS in practice. No, this is not the kind of rip in which you enter the water without making a splash. In this case, RIPS is an acronym for a simple learning strategy.

- **R**: *Review* quickly your coach's prior comments, and make the corrections on your next dive or drill.
- **I**: *Immediately* look at and listen to the coach after you perform your dive or drill.
- **P**: *Pose* questions if you are unsure of the coach's meaning.
- **S**: *Strategize*—Rehearse, elaborate, and organize the comments, and return to the first step.

Be prepared to MURDER *in practice.* And, no, certainly not that kind of murder! Classroom learning strategies can be adapted and applied in an athletic practice setting. For example, Dansereau (1985) created a wonderful strategy that uses the acronym MURDER, which can be modified for athletes. Following is this complex strategy modified for divers:

- **M**: Set your *mood* before practice.
- **U**: *Understand* what you want to accomplish during practice.
- **R**: *Recall* what you learned from your last performance or practice.
- **D**: *Digest* your coach's comments.
- **E**: *Expand the* information.
- **R**: *Review* your mistakes.

Interpreting Internal Feedback

Internal feedback (IF) is sensory information the athlete senses both within and outside of the body. Like external feedback, internal feedback can be highly informative and reinforcing. It can also be misleading. Consider, for example, the diver who continues to perform an incorrect movement but reports that it feels (IF) correct. In this case, the diver is misinterpreting internal feedback.

How can we explain this phenomenon and use this explanation to guide *how* coaches teach and *how* athletes learn? To better understand the role of internal feedback in diving performance, let's consider Adams' simple but useful closed-loop theory of motor learning.

Adams' Closed-Loop Theory of Motor Learning

A closed-loop system essentially means that feedback is coming from within the system, not outside of it. According to Adams' (1971) theory, movements are made by comparing the ongoing feedback from the limbs during the motion to an internal within-the-system **perceptual trace** that is learned through practice. When someone makes a positioning movement, internal feedback stimuli are produced that represent the particular locations of the limbs in space. Through practice, these stimuli leave a perceptual trace in the central nervous system and memory.

The perceptual trace acts as a **reference of correctness** that includes the feedback associated with the correct movement. When the person must learn to place the limbs in a certain position in space, the feedback qualities (muscle, movement, and environmental sensations) are compared with the reference of correctness. By minimizing the difference between the feedback received and the reference of correctness, the person brings the limbs to the correct position using a closed-loop process. For a quick demonstration of the perceptual trace in action, ask a friend to close his eyes and slowly touch the tips of both index fingers together in front of his face. Notice the slight adjustments (minimizing the difference between the feedback and the reference of correctness) of the positioning of the fingers as they slowly come together.

Internal feedback can be a powerful source of reinforcement, which is sometimes good and sometimes bad. Consider confident, self-assured, and talented athletes. They trust themselves and their internal feedback, which is good, unless they have established an imperfect perceptual trace, which is bad. In this case, their bodies tell them that their movements are correct, even though their coaches tell them otherwise. Consequently, these athletes continue to repeat the incorrect movements because of internal feedback reinforcement. This explanation helps us comprehend in part why athletes at any level can repeatedly make the same mistake.

Consider divers who honestly feel that their arms are in the correct 12 o'clock position in their hurdle even though their arms are, say, too low. Now, there could be a technical cause (e.g., leaning back in the last hurdle step) or physiological cause (e.g., lack of shoulder flexibility) for their low arms. However, when these divers stand on the pool deck and their arms are guided to the correct position, they often report that their arms are too far back. It is interesting to note that even when these divers watch their hurdles on video and can visually confirm their incorrect arm position, they sometimes make comments such as "There must be something wrong with the angle of the camera." Internal feedback is a powerful reinforcer.

Implications for Coaches

So what does this discussion on internal feedback and Adams' theory mean for coaches? Well, there are several rather significant implications for guiding *how* coaches teach.

Make early learning as error free as possible. According to Adams, the perceptual trace is the most important part of motor learning, and the accuracy of any response depends on the quality of the trace. The structure of practice, therefore, becomes extremely important because it affects the shaping and eventual accuracy of all perceptual traces. Adams believed that feedback in the form of knowledge of results (KR) is not just a positive reinforcement; it provides information about errors, which the person uses to solve the motor problem. Contrary to some theorists, Adams believed that any errors produced during practice are harmful to learning because they degrade the perceptual trace. Consequently, in the early stages of learning, Adams believed that errors should be avoided when at all possible and that KR should be maintained until the trace is well established.

Establish a prepractice reference of correctness. Error-free learning can be enhanced by establishing a **prepractice reference of correctness**—a perceptual trace ingrained before performing the actual movements. The prepractice reference of correctness can be established by providing athletes with specific feedback in the form of demonstrations, detailed verbal reports, instant video replay, and delayed video replay. Research suggests that replay feedback is perhaps most effective when coaches guide athletes in examining salient aspects of the performance (Kernodle & Carlton, 1992; Rothstein & Arnold, 1976).

Explain the concept of Adams' theory to athletes. Athletes are thinking and feeling human beings who are highly responsive when they understand why they are doing something, such as mastering a technique before moving to a subsequent technique. Providing a simple understanding of a perceptual trace motivates athletes to be patient, thorough, error free (as much as humanly possible), and mastery oriented when learning a new skill (establishing a perceptual trace).

Retrace the motor learning process when athletes must relearn. Not many athletes, particularly experienced athletes, like to start from scratch as if they were beginners. Unfortunately, that is the message they need to receive if they have established an incorrect perceptual trace. If they didn't get it right the first time, then they must return to the drawing board and relearn the skills. An explanation of Adams' theory can go a long way in motivating divers to form new perceptual traces.

Implications for Divers

What does the discussion on internal feedback and Adams' theory mean for divers? As there are for coaches, there are specific implications for guiding how divers learn.

Don't always trust what you feel. Sure, internal feedback is accurate much of the time; however, at times it isn't. At these critical times, divers must trust and rely on external coach feedback. If athletes could feel everything they do, they wouldn't need coaches, and they certainly wouldn't need all of the replay systems many coaches and divers use.

Be willing to relearn. Athletes need to be willing to tweak things. Relearning (establishing a new perceptual trace) won't occur without change, without tweaking. Just because an athlete has done it one way for a long time doesn't mean that it is correct. And just because it feels comfortable certainly doesn't mean that the athlete should continue doing it that way. An understanding of Adams' theory should motivate athletes to journey outside their comfort zones and relearn skills. So let the tweaking begin!

Learn it right the first time. Of course, tweaking (relearning) is unnecessary to a great extent when athletes take the time, trouble, and toil to learn skills correctly initially. It is far easier and less time-consuming to learn it right in the beginning than it is to go through the more difficult and time-intensive process of discarding bad habits and donning new ones. Remembering the importance of establishing initial accurate perceptual traces should motivate athletes to patiently master the fundamentals of diving.

Managing Practice

Providing feedback and receiving feedback should consume the majority of practice time. Unfortunately, some coaches, especially beginning coaches, do a poor job of managing practice and therefore spend much of their time attempting to gain control of their athletes rather than dispensing feedback. When this happens, very little teaching and learning occurs. In part, then, managing *how* coaches teach and *how* athletes learn involves establishing an environment that promotes effective teaching and substantive learning. This environment is established through practice management.

Practice management is the arrangement of practice activities to facilitate coach teaching and athlete learning. The best and easiest approach to managing practice is to employ preventive strategies. Following are surprisingly simple but proven strategies for developing organized and smooth-running practices in which coaches spend most of their time teaching and athletes spend most of their time learning.

Preventive Practice Management Strategies

Set rules. People are generally more apt to behave properly when they know what's expected of them. Consequently, divers should know from day 1 the team rules, policies, expectations, penalties, and punishments that clearly spell out what is expected of them and the consequences if they do not conform. The sidebar Team Rules provides a sample of rules for coaches to consider when establishing team rules.

Team Rules

- Divers must arrive on time for practice.
- Divers arriving late for practice will not be permitted on the trampoline.
- Divers must follow all policies for using the trampoline and other diving equipment.
- Divers must attend all team meetings and team functions.
- Divers must jump in the water after balking.
- Divers must look at the coach when being coached.
- Divers not looking at the coach, whining, or pouting will be asked to leave practice.
- Divers must attend all practices to participate in competition.
- Divers missing practice must call the coach before practice and explain why he or she cannot attend.
- Divers must have a valid reason and be excused by the coach for missing practice.
- Divers missing practice must make up those practices to participate in competition.
- Divers must be polite, supportive, and cooperative with coaching staff, teammates, and pool staff.
- Divers must wear team apparel at all competitions.
- Divers may receive three warnings per season. A fourth incident results in dismissal from the team.
- First incident: The diver meets with the coach to discuss the infraction and penalty.
- Second incident: The diver and parents meet with the coach to discuss the infraction and penalty.
- Third incident: The diver and parents meet with the coach to discuss the infraction and penalty.
- Fourth incident: The diver is dismissed from the team.

Care for athletes. Genuinely caring for divers goes a long way in maintaining good behavior, developing close coach–diver relationships, and generating an effective teaching and learning environment.

Use humor. Humor is perhaps the most important factor in keeping things fun, defusing confrontation, and creating a positive practice teaching and learning environment. Teams that work hard, have fun, and use humor are more productive and more successful than teams that simply work hard.

Personalize the practice environment. Putting up posters, recognizing individual athletes on a bulletin board, playing music selected by the divers, hanging team banners, and displaying motivational quotes are all examples of personalizing the practice environment. But the environment encompasses more than just the physical environment. It also includes a warm, friendly, positive, accepting, and encouraging climate in which cooperation, self-management, and personal growth are highly valued.

Use with-it-ness. **With-it-ness** is the coach's ability to know what is going on at every minute of practice with each diver. The best coaches possess with-it-ness, and unsuccessful coaches don't. Coaches possessing this quality make sure that every diver is on track and engaged. Those who aren't are quickly redirected by the coach. How do coaches cultivate with-it-ness? They do so by bringing their A game for the duration of every practice and by being fully engaged mentally, emotionally, and physically. With-it-ness requires sustained high effort.

Use overlapping. **Overlapping** is the ability to deal with two or more things simultaneously so that practice runs smoothly. Coaches using overlapping can, for example, administer a **desist** (a verbal command to an athlete to stop engaging in an off-task behavior), then quickly coach a diver, and then instruct another diver to move on to another dive—all in one graceful performance ("Johnny, stop snapping your chamois. Suzy, nice dive but a little over. Greg, move on to the back dive."). Voila! Overlapping also requires sustained high effort.

Maintain smoothness and momentum. Coaches maintain smoothness and momentum by making quick and smooth transitions and avoiding interruptions. Maintaining momentum eliminates moments when divers are standing around waiting for something to do or when something occurs and practice grinds to a halt. Developing individualized practice plans promotes smoothness and momentum.

Lay a solid foundation. Grossnickle and Sesko (1990) offer 10 guidelines for establishing classroom management that can be translated into relevant guidelines for practice management. Some of these guidelines have already been discussed but are worth repeating: establish clear behavior guidelines; adopt a teamwork approach; design a discipline ladder (i.e., spell out specific consequences for various severity levels of athlete infractions); teach self-management and self-discipline; invite good behavior; focus on athlete successes and self-esteem; use fair, firm, and calm enforcement; plan and implement specific practice activities; continually monitor the practice environment; and manage problems early.

Use legitimate praise. The best way to manage behavior is to invite appropriate behavior often. The best way to invite appropriate behavior is to arrange situations in which legitimate praise can be given. This scenario falls under the category of catching them being good. According to Marland (1975), praise is one of the most powerful teacher tools. When athletes exhibit good behavior, coaches should positively reinforce them by offering legitimate praise. They should remember to praise publically and criticize privately and to link praise and criticism to specific behaviors.

Maintain focus. Keeping everyone cognitively focused and engaged is perhaps the most effective technique for managing practice and promoting teaching and learning. Cognitive focus and engagement, as well as many of the other strategies identified in this section, can be achieved by developing an individualized practice plan (IPP) which is discussed in the following section.

Developing an Individualized Practice Plan

An **individualized practice plan** is an outline for each phase of a practice for each diver. It lets divers know what they will be doing, when they will be doing it, and how they will be doing it for that specific practice. This IPP first depends on an annual individualized training plan (AITP), which is an overview of the entire season that outlines what divers will be doing during the different phases of the season to peak for the championship. Completing an AITP will be discussed in detail in chapter 9. Included in this annual plan is periodization. **Periodization** is an organized approach to training that involves the progressive cycling of aspects of training (e.g., strength and conditioning, skill work, simple dives, optional dives) during periods of time throughout the season.

An IPP takes into account many factors for each diver. For example, one diver might have a personal goal of peaking for the conference meet, whereas another might have a goal of peaking for the state or national championship. Each diver, therefore, will have a unique IPP. Figure 1.1 provides an example of an IPP worksheet.

Mastery Learning

When developing an IPP, coaches must keep in mind the concept of **mastery learning**, a teaching approach that presumes every learner can learn if provided the appropriate time and instruction (Carroll, 1963), as well as appropriate evaluation and corrective procedures, such as individualized coaching, additional practice, reteaching, peer tutoring, and alternative instructional materials (Bloom, 1987). With mastery learning, learners advance to the next learning objective only after they have demonstrated proficiency on the current one. For example, using a mastery approach, a young diver would not progress to a forward somersault with one twist until mastering a forward somersault in a straight position. Some divers progress faster than others; however, given more time, instruction, corrections, and, alternative drills, all divers can master specific skills. Mastery learning is a highly effective learning concept for establishing correct perceptual traces.

Task Analysis and Skill Progression

Developing an IPP and a mastery climate requires task analysis and skill progression. **Task analysis** is the process of determining the key skills that comprise a motor performance. **Skill progression** refers to the order for learning these key skills. It is easy to forget the many subskills that comprise even the most basic dive such as the forward dive in the tuck position. For this dive, the subskills are the forward approach, hurdle, takeoff, tuck position, pike-out, line-up, and entry (which is composed of a hand grab, swim, and pike save.) Task analysis and skill progression allow coaches to select the appropriate skill for each athlete and progress the athlete to the subsequent appropriate skill once

INDIVIDUALIZED PRACTICE PLAN

Coach: Karen Coach						Date: July 2nd, AM Practice				
Diver: Danny Diver						**Level: Intermediate**				
Dives	**Springboard**	**Platform**	**Dives**	**Springboard**	**Platform**	**Dives**	**Dryboard**	**Trampoline**	**Dives**	**Floor**
100			5223			100	3 C&B	3 C&B	100	3
101			5225			102	3 C&B	3 C&B	102	3 C&B
102			5227			104			200	
103			5231			200	3 C&B	3 C&B	202	3 C
104			5233			202	3 C&B	3 C, B, A	300	
105			5235			204			302	3 w/spot
106			5237			300		3 C&B hurdle	400	
107			5251			302	3 C&B	3 A, B, C	402	3 w/spot
200			5243			304			611	3 A to back
201			5253			400			621	3 stomach
202			5311			402	3 C	3 C&B	631	
203			5321			5221			6111	3 A stomach
204			5323			5223		3 in belt	6112	
205			5325			5321			6211	3 A to back
206			5327			5323		3 in belt	6213	
207			5331							
300			5333			**Entries**	**Level/No.**			
301			5335			001C/B				
302			5337			101	3mx5			
303			5351			103	1mx5			
304			5343			105				
305			5353			002C/B				
306			5355			201	3mx5			
307			600			203	1mx5			
400			611		1m/3A	205				
401			612			301	1mx3B			
402			614			303				
403			621		1m/3A	305				
404			622			401	1mx3C			
405			623			403	3mx3C			
407			624			405				
5111			631			612				
5121			632			622				
5122			6111		1m/3A	632				
5124			6112							
5126			6122			**Coach Comments:**				
5132			6132							
5134			6124							
5136			6142							
5142			6211		1m/3A					
5144			6213							
5152			6221							
5154			6231							
5156			6233							
5211			6241							
5221			6243							

Figure 1.1   Individualized practice plan.

mastery has been attained. The best coaches are masters at task analysis, skill progression, and mastery learning. They avoid asking divers to attempt drills, skills, and dives that they are ill prepared to perform safely and successfully. Skill progression is outlined in the diver checklists in chapter 7.

Transfer of Learning

Mastering skills and progressing to new skills can be enhanced through **transfer of learning,** which means gaining proficiency on one task as a result of practicing another. There are a number of methods for promoting transfer of learning. One method is **part practice,** in which parts of a skill are rehearsed independently (Christina & Corcos, 1988). Wightman and Lintern (1985) outlined three types of part practice: fractionalization, segmentation, and simplification. **Fractionalization** is a type of part practice in which one or more parts of a complex skill are practiced separately. **Segmentation**, also referred to as **progressive-part practice**, is a type of part practice in which successive parts of a skill are gradually added together. In other words, one skill is practiced for a time, then a second part is added to the first part and the two are practiced together, and so on until the entire skill is practiced. **Simplification** is a type of part practice in which the complexity or difficulty of the serial skill is reduced. For example, in learning a back dive, young divers can be placed on a mat or board with their arms over their heads and manually slid into the water.

Other methods for transfer of learning include guidance, rehearsal, mental practice, and simulation. **Guidance** is the process of manually helping divers move through the motions of the skill. **Rehearsal** involves divers going through the exact motions of a particular skill on the ground. They start with slow-motion rehearsal until they can model the skill correctly and then increase the speed to eventually match the actual speed of performance. Rehearsal is critical for learning because divers who can't model the skill correctly certainly won't perform it correctly on the board or in the air.

Mental practice involves thinking about and mentally imagining aspects of the skill being learned. *Take your diving home with you* has new meaning when you consider that in some instances mental practice has been shown to produce results similar to those from physical practice (Feltz & Landers, 1983). And, when mental practice is combined with physical practice, the result is improved performance (Etnier & Landers, 1996). **Simulation** involves performing the skill or dive in a similar but not identical or real situation. Examples of simulation include putting divers in a spotting belt over a trampoline, dryboard, or water board. Another example is strapping divers into a somersaulting chair to practice somersaulting forward and backward, as well as spotting.

Individual Differences

Individual differences are the dissimilarities among divers in terms of learning and performing. No two divers are the same. They differ on factors such as cognitive development, physiological and emotional maturity, motivation, learning style, emotional personality, handling fear, time required to achieve mastery, body type, physical abilities and limitations, heartiness, speed of recovery, personality, level of goal attainment, self-esteem, patience, and learning style. Coaches need to account for athlete differences when developing IPPs. For example, although all of similar chronological age, divers in a 10-year-old group will vary widely in physical, psychological, and emotional development.

This variance affects what they are physically capable of performing, psychologically capable of understanding (e.g., concrete versus abstract concepts), and emotionally capable of managing at least at this point in their athletic careers.

In addition to temporary maturational differences, permanent individual differences among athletes exist as well. In talking about his development as an MLB (Major League Baseball in the United States) hitter, Shawn Green (Green & McAlpine, 2011) shared the following.

> My former teammate Paul Molitor had no stride. He just picked up his front heel and put it back down. This made his swing extremely efficient and contributed to his amassing more than three thousand hits in a Hall of Fame career, but he didn't hit many home runs. On the other hand, Reggie Jackson had a big stride and big swing, striking out often but hitting more than five hundred homers in his Hall of Fame career. Only the very best all-around best hitters in each generation, guys like Barry Bonds and Albert Pujols, have the ability to take short, quick strides and still have home run power. I could never do that. The goal for me was to find a happy medium. (p. 26)

Teaching and learning well requires finding a happy medium. In other words, it requires accommodating individual differences as Shawn Green did. For example, some divers, no matter how much they engage in weight training, will always be finesse divers rather than brute strength divers. Consequently, these divers and their coaches must accommodate this quality (e.g., use adaptive techniques). Unfortunately, some coaches futilely attempt to forcefully shape divers into molds with which they lack compatibility.

Athlete Readiness

At this point in the chapter, *how* coaches teach and *how* athletes learn can now be restated as how coaches *ready* athletes for learning and how *readied* athletes learn. Teaching and learning depend on athlete readiness. Learning success is guaranteed when coaches lay a solid foundation of athlete readiness. As outlined in this chapter, promoting athlete readiness, on the part of both coach and athlete, involves accounting for individual differences, performing task analyses, following sequential skill progressions, incorporating transfer of learning, adhering to mastery learning, developing IPPs, managing practice, providing effective feedback, and interpreting internal feedback.

Unfortunately, learning failure is guaranteed when coaches, whether through lack of effort or lack of understanding, do not lay a solid foundation. In this case, athletes are asked to perform drills, skills, and dives for which they are ill-prepared. They may not have mastered the subskills necessary for safely and successfully performing the more advanced task they are being asked to perform. Or, they may possess the mastery but not the necessary emotional stability. In this case, the diver is standing on the springboard sobbing and so nervous that he can't think clearly or relax enough to perform the task.

Failure is an unavoidable part of any sport. Even elite divers occasionally smack on a dive. At an international meet in Vienna, Austria, U.S. national champion and Olympic silver medalist Bruce Kimball missed his spots on a routine 304C lead-up on 5-meter platform and landed flat on his back. A smack, however, should be the exception, not the rule. Divers repeatedly smacking have not been readied by their coaches. Following are four questions to ask when considering athlete readiness.

Can the diver perform the subskills necessary for safely learning the new task? For example, in learning a 303C, the diver should be able to perform an adequate hurdle, a reverse dive tuck a safe distance from the board, and a reverse somersault that has adequate speed of rotation and goes past vertical on entry. O'Brien (1992, 2003) does a nice job of outlining skill progressions.

Is the diver physically prepared to safely perform the new task? Components to assess when determining athlete readiness include strength, power (the combination of strength and quickness), flexibility, muscular endurance, cardiorespiratory endurance, body composition (the ratio of lean body mass to nonessential fat body mass), and skill (O'Brien, 1999). Unfortunately, many coaches and divers overlook the importance of physical preparation. They believe that nothing important occurs until the diver is on the springboard or platform; that the arena for becoming a good diver is limited to the diving well. Dryland training and physical conditioning are necessary for ensuring diver readiness.

Is the diver emotionally prepared and personally motivated to learn the task? Does the diver have a reasonable expectation of success in performing the dive? If not, she should regress to more lead-ups and skill work until her confidence increases. Does the diver want to learn the dive? If not, he should move to another dive and wait until he is motivated to learn the dive. Does the diver possess the emotional equilibrium to remain calm and execute the dive, or is she an emotional wreck, standing on the springboard sobbing, shaking, and scared? Again, such a diver should regress to simpler drills, skills, and dives in which she can gain confidence, find success, and recapture her emotional balance.

It is worth remembering the following when it comes to learning new dives: It isn't a matter of *if*; it's only a matter of *when*. Coaches should remain patient, continue developing diver readiness, and ask the diver to perform the new dive only when skill level, confidence, and motivation have increased to the point of readiness.

Does the diver know the key points for safely performing the new task? Using the 303C as an example again, does the diver know to land on the tip of the board, keep the head down, tilt the dive out, and wait for the coach's call? Rehearsing is often helpful. Coach and diver can review key points to remember before attempting the drill, skill, or dive. When learning, say, a 305C on a 3 meter, the diver can perform a 303C on a 1 meter and have the coach remind him of certain key points needed for the 305C. The coach could then call the diver out of the 303C so the diver rehearses waiting for the call on the 3 meter for the 305C.

Deliberate Practice

In 1973, Simon and Chase famously proposed their 10-year or 10,000-hour rule for attaining expertise. In further research, Ericsson, Krampe, and Tesch-Romer (1993) suggested that what separates experts from nonexperts—and elite athletes from nonelite athletes—is not just the *amount* of practice time invested but also the *type* of practice. Experts engage in a specific type of practice they call **deliberate practice**. Ericsson (1996) extended this discussion by suggesting that engagement in deliberate practice, not talent, is the determining factor in attaining expertise. So, before moving to subsequent chapters and the Xs and Os of diving, let's briefly consider 13 characteristics of deliberate practice that inform us about how coaches can teach like elite coaches and how divers can practice and learn like elite athletes.

1. *Motivation and desire.* Passionate athletes can accomplish amazing feats. Divers should fuel their passion outside the pool (e.g., post goals and inspirational quotes, read motivating books and magazine stories) so that they arrive at practice motivated to give their full effort in everything they do. Elite athletes come to practice every day, not some days, with motivation and desire.

2. *Preexisting knowledge.* Knowledge is power, especially for passionate athletes. The more athletes know, the more they understand and accomplish with their diving. This knowledge should be broad based and include areas such as diving fundamentals, laws of physics, stretching techniques, physiology, mental training, relaxation, energy management, and nutrition. U.S. Olympic gold medalist Mark Lenzi applied his knowledge of physics to his dive performance. The best divers are also the most knowledgeable. So are the best coaches.

3. *Explicit goals.* Elite divers have goals for everything they do in practice, even simple daily drills such as dryland somersaults that many nonexpert divers consider boring. In contrast, elite divers find these drills fascinating and squeeze every drop out of each repetition. During her career, U.S. Olympic gold medalist Laura Wilkinson eagerly practiced thousands of inward dryland somersaults. What was once her worst dive category she transformed into her best category. At the end of her career, she could finish an inward 3 1/2 somersault tuck almost 7 meters above the water!

4. *High relevance.* Everything elite athletes do in practice has relevance. *Relevance* is defined by elite divers as improvement. In other words, everything they do in practice is meant to accomplish one overriding goal—improve their dive performance, or to be more specific, their competition dive performance. Before every drill, skill, and dive, elite divers ask this question: What can I do right now to improve my performance?

5. *High level of effort.* It is easy to just be at practice—to be physically present but not truly physically, mentally, and emotionally engaged. During practice, elite divers exert and sustain high levels of physical, mental, and emotional effort. Every diver can work hard occasionally. Elite divers work hard in every practice, every day. This sustained day-to-day effort is perhaps the ultimate challenge for divers—and coaches—seeking to reach their greatest potential.

6. *High level of concentration.* Elite divers are mentally dialed-in. They leave distractions and concerns in the locker room and intently focus on each practice segment, each drill, each repetition, and each coaching comment. Concentration is like a muscle; the more it is used, the stronger it becomes. A high level of concentration is necessary for achieving elite-level performance, and the more it is demanded and used in practice, the more it becomes a habit during dive performance, especially during critical competition situations. Coaches need to be equally dialed-in.

7. *Not inherently enjoyable.* Elite divers define enjoyable differently from nonelite divers. Elites derive a sense of fulfillment and intrinsic satisfaction

from working hard, engaging in practice tasks, and making improvements. They know their efforts will culminate in goal attainment. Elites find enjoyment in these activities because they produce a sense of flow (Jackson, 1996). According to Csikszentmihalyi (1990) flow occurs

> when a person has not only met some prior expectation or satisfied a need or a desire but also gone beyond what he or she has been programmed to do and achieved something unexpected, perhaps something even unimagined before. (p. 46)

Elites also find enjoyment in social interactions with teammates (Csikszentmihalyi, Rathunde, & Whalen, 1993; Scanlon, Stein, & Ravizza, 1989). Enjoyment, fun, social interaction, and activities facilitating flow should be incorporated into the training program for every level of diver.

8. *High structure.* Elite divers want, crave, and demand structure. They want well-defined practice phases with smooth, coherent, and rapid transitions to other phases so that precious practice time is never wasted. Every practice detail is scripted, and they follow this script. A coach-developed IPP creates this structure.

9. *Careful monitoring.* Elite divers and elite coaches monitor every practice phase to ensure that they are on task and accomplishing their goals for every practice task, whether it is stretching, line-ups, simple drills, dryland exercises, or dives.

10. *Working closely with authority.* Elite divers develop a close working relationship with their coaches. This relationship is typified by a sense of trust, devotion, faith, and often love. This relationship also includes mutual cooperation, open communication, and the effective transmission and reception of feedback. The elite diver needs the elite coach. Consequently, the elite coach must demonstrate the 13 characteristics of deliberate practice. Ultimately, the most important role model on any team is always the coach.

11. *Immediate information feedback.* Elite divers don't want to wait to receive valuable informative and motivational external feedback. They train with a sense of urgency, with a sense of *now*. They know that day 1 of practice is when champions are developed. They do the work at the beginning of the season rather than waiting until the end of the season, as many nonelites do.

12. *Using different methods and refining methods in response to feedback.* Elite athletes and elite coaches are not wedded to one training method. They are open to new ideas and new approaches. If, through careful monitoring, they determine that something isn't working, they quickly jettison it and adopt a new method. Remember, the overall goal is improvement. If a drill is ineffective, it is discarded and a new drill is substituted. For example, a double-bouncing 105B on a 3-meter springboard wasn't helping two-time U.S. Olympian and NCAA champion Christina Loukas improve her starts and come-outs for her 107B, so she switched to a standing 105B drill.

13. *Time and energy.* Of course, there is no substitute for time and energy. Elite athletes and elite coaches never give less time and energy than is necessary for reaching elite-level performance. They put in the training hours and the physical and—perhaps more important—mental and emotional energy. Even away from the pool, they devote time and energy to their diving by engaging in activities such as journal writing, goal setting, mental imagery, video analysis,

mental review, critical thinking, problem solving, self-talk, and motivational experiences.

Developmental Model of Sport Participation

The developmental model of sport participation (DMSP) suggests that athletes progress through three stages. During the **sampling years**, athletes participate in a variety of sports and engage in a low amount of deliberate practice and a high amount of deliberate play. **Deliberate play** is characterized as games with flexible rules, little or no adult supervision, and a pretend quality. Young athletes engage in deliberate play for simple enjoyment and in various settings, such as backyard American football and street basketball. During the **specializing years**, athletes participate in fewer sports, and deliberate play and deliberate practice are balanced. During the **investment years**, athletes focus on one sport and engage in a high amount of deliberate practice and a low amount of deliberate play.

Allowing very young athletes to engage in a variety of sports during the sampling years and incorporating varying amounts of deliberate play throughout the levels of a diver's career is necessary and beneficial. For a more in-depth look at aspects that positively affect coaching effectiveness and athlete learning, see Huber (2013).

Forward Approaches

Chapter 1 considered *how* coaches teach and *how* athletes learn. Chapter 2 now considers *what* coaches teach and *what* athletes learn. Although it is important to know how to teach and how to learn, it is equally important to know precisely what to teach and what is to be learned. No matter how effective coaches are as teachers, they will ultimately fail if they do not understand the Xs and Os of the sport of diving. Remember from chapter 1, by Xs and Os I mean the basic elements, mechanics, and fundamentals of the sport of diving.

This chapter highlights the principles of perhaps the most important and most challenging aspect of our sport: the forward approach.

But first, a short story . . .

Some years ago, I participated in a clinic with the Dutch national diving team in the city of Amersfoort in the Netherlands. We were discussing the springboard forward approach, and former Dutch springboard diver Edwin Jongejans said something I have never forgotten: "The forward approach is the first thing we are taught but the last thing we master." Edwin's words are even more memorable and poignant when you know a little bit of his background. He was a fairly accomplished but erratic diver early in his career. A prodigious leaper, he could never quite harness his leaping ability and hurdle throughout an entire contest. However, around his mid-20s, he mastered his forward approach and found the consistency he was lacking. At the age of 25 at the World Championships in Perth, Australia, he became world champion on the 1-meter springboard. He beat out some highly touted divers and a late charge from U.S. diver Mark Lenzi, who the following year would go on to win the Olympic gold medal on the 3-meter springboard.

Springboard Forward Approach

Asmentioned in the preface, former Indiana University and International Hall of Fame diving coach Hobie Billingsley liked to say that the forward approach is the most difficult part of diving. Few coaches and divers would dispute Hobie's claim. As many elite divers will attest, once the forward approach is mastered, the rest of the dive is relatively simple compared to the hurdle. After 37 years of teaching the springboard forward approach, I have discovered that it isn't quite the wicked or wild beast we make it out to be. In fact, once we get to know the critter, it is a fairly easy beast to tame.

The first section of this chapter deconstructs the forward springboard approach by identifying the critical Xs and Os—the five essential positions for *what* to teach and *what* to learn. Once they have mastered these positions, divers can perform proficient forward approaches in no time at all. Gaining consistency in the approach, of course, takes more time and more practice, but these five essential positions outlined in the following section will have divers quickly on their way to having an accomplished forward approach.

Before considering the first essential position, let's briefly review two movements that occur before the hurdle: the stance and walk.

Stance and Walk

The **stance** is the position the diver assumes before taking the first step in the hurdle. It is important for several reasons. First, because it is the initial impression the diver gives the judges, it needs to be a good one. Second, the stance is also important because the diver needs to be in the body alignment that will be used during the walk in the approach. The diver should stand with head neutral, shoulders square but relaxed, feet together, abdomen in, front of torso slightly concave, hips rolled under, arms at the side of the body, and fingers straight. Figure 2.1 depicts the proper stance.

The **walk** constitutes the steps taken toward the end of the board. Diving rules state that a diver must take a minimum of three steps in a forward approach. Although there is no hard-and-fast rule about the maximum number of steps, I have always taught divers to take at least four steps. A walk with four or five steps allows the diver to make a grander impression with the judges and to more easily get in rhythm with the board—and rhythm is important for the forward approach, as we will see. During the walk, the diver's shoulders should be forward over the plane of the toes, angling from the ankles and not the hips. Figure 2.2 shows this position in the walk.

The **arm swing,** as you might guess, involves moving the arms in synchronization with each step in the walk. The arm swing is easy to syncopate with the steps. If the diver takes five steps, the arms move backward as the first step is taken. If diver takes four steps, the arms move forward as the first step is taken. Many divers and diving coaches overlook the importance of the arm swing, focusing more on what happens at the end of the approach than on what happens at the beginning. Of course, both are important; however, even though the arm swing may seem like a simple and unassuming element of the forward approach, it is more critical than divers and coaches might first think.

The diving board is like a stringed musical instrument with its own vibration and rhythm, and the diver must be in rhythm with the board. The board won't

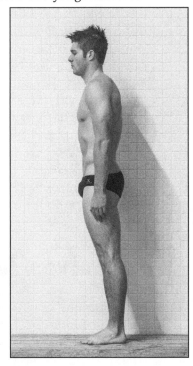

Figure 2.1 The stance for the springboard forward approach.

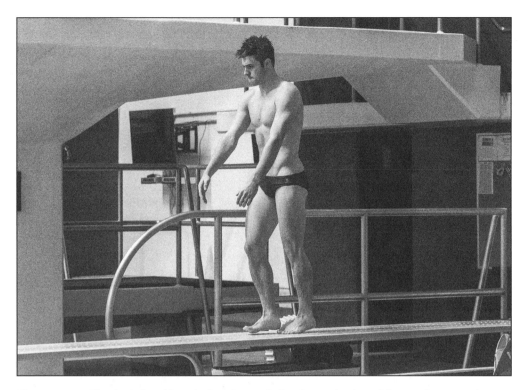

Figure 2.2 The body position during the walk for the springboard forward approach.

accommodate the diver; the diver must accommodate the board. In other words, the diver's rhythm must match the board's rhythm. At a U.S. national championship, one of my divers had a disastrous event on the 1-meter spring-board, pounding the board with every hurdle and finishing in last place. In a late-evening practice, I asked him to focus on swinging his arms and finding more rhythm in his approach. That did the trick. In the next day's event, the 3-meter springboard, he caught the board at its apex with every hurdle and made finals.

When swinging the arms in the approach, the diver must remember to dis-engage the trapezius muscles so that the arms swing freely. *A big part of diving is learning which muscles to engage and which to disengage during motor perfor-mance.* Figure 2.3 provides pictures of the first three steps with an arm swing in a four-step approach.

The **last step** is when the diver plants the foot (i.e., the drive leg that propels the diver up into the hurdle) in preparation to hurdle to the end of the board. There are two critical components of the last step to pay attention to because they directly influence the quality of the subsequent hurdle. The first is to swing the arms back early enough in the last step so that they pause before swinging forward (figure 2.4). The arms then swing forward as the last step is taken.

Many divers swing their arms back much too late, waiting until they plant their last step to begin swinging the arms forward. Even great divers make this mistake. World champion Russian diver Aleksandr Dobroskok, for example, during his up-and-down (no pun intended) career, occasionally found himself over the tip of the board in some competitions because his arm swing was much too late on his last step. In some competitions, in fact, he was so far over the end of the board that he failed the dive.

Figure 2.3 The arm swing for the four-step springboard forward approach.

Figure 2.4 The early backswing before the last step for the springboard forward approach.

Unless the diver has good shoulder flexibility, it is easier to bring the arms back wide so the shoulders aren't pulled back causing the diver to lean backward. For the other steps in the approach, the arm swing should be much shorter.

The first essential position for the springboard forward approach is that all or nearly all of the body weight should be over the front foot immediately on contact with the board in the last step (figure 2.5). This placement allows the diver to depress the board maximally. Many divers make the mistake of leaning backward as they place their last step (often because they get their arms back too late in the last step and then are afraid of jumping over the end of the board in their hurdle, like Dobroskok) and then transferring their weight to the front leg. This approach might guarantee that they won't be over the end of the board in their hurdle, but it also guarantees that they won't maximally load (i.e., depress) the board to create a good hurdle.

Because they depress the board so deeply, many elite male divers stay over their last step but then sit back slightly in the last step. Notice that in the last step the arms are near the hips when the foot contacts the board.

Now, let's consider the question of where to place the front plant foot in the last step. A rule of thumb used to be to place the last step where the rivets on the board stop but that is too far back from the end of the board. The modern springboard is more tapered and hence more flexible closer to the tip, so placing the foot more toward the end of the board allows for greater depression of the board, especially if the diver's weight is over the last step on contact. Approximately 8 inches (20 cm) from the end of the springboard is appropriate for most divers. This distance will vary slightly among divers.

Hurdle consistency is achieved by doing the same things every time. So, placing the last step the same distance from the board each time will greatly increase hurdle consistency. To make this exact

Figure 2.5 The first essential position for the springboard forward approach: the body position on contact for the last step.

placement, divers must train their eyes to watch the placement of their last step. Training the eyes is especially helpful so that in competition divers' eyes don't wander to some external irrelevant cue such as the crowd. Many coaches mistakenly teach their divers to look straight ahead or out at the water during the approach. Elite divers watch where they place their first step; then they watch where they place their last step before shifting their focus and looking at the tip of the board during the hurdle decent until about 3 or 4 inches (7 to 10 cm) from contact. This focal point makes sense because getting to the tip of the board is critical. A dive is easy when the diver lands on the end of the springboard. Conversely, a dive is more difficult when the diver lands far back or far over the tip of the springboard.

To foster consistency in foot placement for the last step, the coach or diver can wrap athletic tape around the springboard approximately 8 inches (20 cm) from the tip of the board. This gives the diver a specific target to aim at for foot placement in the last step. For even greater precision, a piece of athletic tape about the length of the diver's foot can be taped to the board exactly where the foot will be planted in the last step. On each forward approach, the diver should try to place the foot directly over the tape.

Hurdle

The **hurdle** involves jumping off one leg after the last step while raising the knee of the opposite leg. The five key elements of the hurdle are early arm swing, high knee, step-down position, contact position, and magic position. The following sections describe these elements.

The second essential position for the springboard forward approach is to swing the arms to approximately 12 o'clock in the last step when the board is fully or nearly fully depressed. This is one of the most critical positions for performing a consistent hurdle: arms up when the board is down in the last step. Unfortunately, it is one of the biggest mistakes many divers make in the hurdle. They make this mistake because many diving coaches don't teach this technique and because it seems intuitively natural to swing the arms up as the board comes up. Figure 2.6 depicts this all-important early arm swing position into the hurdle.

Swinging the arms up when the board is down in the last step helps establish a vertical jump into the hurdle rather than a horizontal jump, which causes the diver to land over the end of the board. Generally, two movements produce a vertical hurdle: the early arm swing in the last step and a high knee in the hurdle.

The **hurdle knee** is the knee that is raised and bent during the jump (hurdle) to the end of the board. The diver must lift the knee high enough to achieve approximately a 90-degree angle between the thigh and the upper body. Many divers step down too early and therefore never achieve the correct angle with the hurdle knee. The correct position of the hurdle knee is shown in figure 2.7.

The 90-degree hurdle position is less critical and arguably not quite as essential to the forward approach. Video analysis indicates that a number of elite springboard divers do not lift the knee quite high enough to achieve a 90-degree angle. This is particularly true for some elite female divers, perhaps because they do not depress the board as far as some male divers. However, two divers who possessed quintessential hurdles—U.S. female diver Christina Loukas and Russian male diver Dmitri Sautin—achieve 90-degree angles in their hurdles.

Figure 2.6 The second essential position for the springboard forward approach: the 12 o'clock arm position on the last step.

Figure 2.7 The 90-degree thigh–upper body hurdle position in the springboard forward approach.

Figure 2.8   The third essential position for the springboard forward approach: the position of the hurdle foot.

When it comes to the position of the hurdle foot, however, there is no debate. All elite springboard divers keep the hurdle foot back when lifting and lowering it during the hurdle. The third essential position, then, is keeping the hurdle foot back so that it slides along the opposite leg when raised and lowered. Figure 2.8 indicates the correct position of the hurdle foot while being raised and lowered.

Some coaches mistakenly teach their divers to kick the foot out so that the thigh and lower leg form a 90-degree angle. Although this 90-degree hurdle leg angle was commonly used for decades when teaching the hurdle, analysis of elite-level divers reveals that they keep the foot considerably farther back in the hurdle, as pictured in figure 2.8, thus eliminating the 90-degree leg angle. Figure 2.9 depicts the outdated, incorrect hurdle leg position.

At first glance, the hurdle foot position may seem insignificant in the grand scope of performing a hurdle. However, it is critical for several reasons. The most important reason is that keeping the foot back forces divers to keep their body weight over the front foot on contact in the last step and thereby achieve the first essential position. Many divers kick the hurdle foot out to compensate for sitting back on contact in the last step with the board. Often, simply asking divers to keep the hurdle foot back automatically forces them to get over the last step on contact.

The other reason for keeping the foot back in the hurdle is to eliminate unnecessary movements. *One definition of beauty in diving is simplicity of movement.* Kicking the foot out requires

Figure 2.9   The outdated and incorrect 90-degree hurdle leg position.

the diver to then kick the foot back before stepping down in the hurdle; otherwise, the diver has to do an awkward scissor kick (which some divers do) to get the feet together. Keeping the foot back, as depicted previously in figure 2.8, eliminates these two irrelevant movements.

As mentioned earlier, one challenge of diving is recognizing which muscles to engage during motor performance and which muscles to disengage. *Another challenge we can now consider is recognizing when to try hard and when to hold back.* Driving up into the hurdle, many elite divers report exerting anywhere from 40 to 60 percent effort. For example, one day Marc Carlton, future U.S. national team member, was dipping the dryland springboard onto the floor. His face looked so calm that I asked him how hard he was trying in his hurdle, suggesting 90 percent effort. He said, "Oh, no. I feel like I am giving only 50 percent effort." I pointed out that when he performed his forward 2 1/2 somersaults with two twists on the 3-meter springboard, the grimace on his face suggested that he was giving 110 percent in his hurdle, yet he didn't jump nearly as high off the 3-meter board as he did giving 50 percent on the dryland board. The lightbulb went on in his head. He learned to give less effort on his 5154B, and it became his best dive. Sometimes, less is more.

The next position is the **step-down position,** in which the hurdle leg straightens out and the diver assumes a straight body line. *Forming a straight line is another way to define beauty in diving.* The step-down position should be achieved while the body is still ascending. After the step-down, the diver's body should still be moving upward approximately 2 or 3 inches (5 to 7 cm). Figure 2.10 shows the step-down position. Remember, when stepping down, the hurdle foot should move downward along the opposite leg or slightly behind the opposite leg.

A common mistake young divers make is slightly dropping the arms during the step-down and then swinging the arms in the hurdle. To load the board more effectively and gain height off the board, divers should shrug the shoulders and arms up during the step-down before taking an arm swing.

After the step-down position is the **contact position,** in which the feet initially contact the board from the descent in the hurdle. As the body descends, the diver begins bending the knees and swinging the arms. Notice in figure 2.11 that the arms are slightly past the hips on contact with the board. This is the fourth essential position: the arms are slightly past the hips on contact with the board after dropping down from the hurdle.

Many coaches mistakenly teach divers to wait until contacting the board to swing their

Figure 2.10 The step-down for the springboard forward approach.

arms, perhaps because that's what they were taught or that's what they felt they were doing when they were divers. However, a cursory video analysis quickly reveals that holding the arms until contact is clearly not what elite divers do, or for that matter, what any divers do. Remember, athletes can't always feel what they do. Their internal feedback isn't always correct. Olympic gold and bronze medalist Mark Lenzi, for example, used to feel his arms getting up before his knee in the hurdle, even though he knew that wasn't what was really happening.

As mentioned earlier, during the descent to the end of the board, the diver looks at the tip of the board until about 3 or 4 inches (7 to 10 cm) from contact, at which point he lifts the chin and looks straight ahead, as depicted in figure 2.12.

The final position in the forward approach is what I call the **magic position.** For this position, the knees are bent, the board is fully depressed, and the arms are overhead, as highlighted in figure 2.13.

The magic position, then, is the fifth essential position of the springboard forward approach. It is called the magic position because once this position is achieved, the rest of the dive goes like magic, as if automatic and effortless. Ninety percent of performing

Figure 2.11 The fourth essential position for the springboard forward approach: the contact position.

Figure 2.12 Eyes and head positioning on the contact position.

a good dive involves attaining a good hurdle (although 90 percent of achieving a good score, as we will see later in the book, requires getting a good entry). Often, divers get a sixth sense that they are going to nail the dive before they even leave the board. They sense this because they have achieved the magic position and intuitively know that the dive they are about to perform will be a good one.

The magic position is achieved by holding the knees bent while swinging the arms overhead as the board goes down. Unfortunately, many coaches to this day teach their divers to swing their arms down when the board goes down and swing their arms up as the board goes up.

The incorrect arm swing and ensuing body position seems intuitively right because it is a more natural movement. When performing a vertical jump on the ground, for example, athletes swing their arms down when they squat and up when they jump. But performing a jump on the end of the springboard is another animal altogether. Taming the beast means holding the knees bent as the arms swing through. During this movement phase, the diver should lift the head up and back as if squatting with a barbell in the weight room. Yes, the diver should look down with the eyes until 3 or 4 inches (7 to 10 cm) from contact, but on contact the head moves up and back to keep the chest from dropping forward.

Figure 2.13 The fifth essential position for the springboard forward approach: the magic position.

Setting the Fulcrum

Where should a diver set the fulcrum? The answer is simple: as far back as possible. Most elite divers—but not all—set the fulcrum all the way back on 9. Some outstanding divers set the fulcrum slightly forward on number 7 or 8. In general, though, the farther back a diver sets the fulcrum, the better—for both the forward approach and the backward press.

Some novice divers set the fulcrum forward (e.g., number 4 or 5) because they believe that they can better maintain their balance during the hurdle. A tighter board is helpful for introductory and beginning divers. However, divers should move the fulcrum back as soon as possible as they progress and master the hurdle. It doesn't take divers long to adjust to a looser board. Obviously, moving the fulcrum back makes the springboard more flexible. Isn't that what a *spring*board is supposed to be—springy? Consequently, divers shouldn't be afraid to learn—that is, to change (remember, we defined learning as change) their fulcrum setting and make the board more flexible.

Jump Hurdle

In the 1960s and early 1970s, divers performed a bunny hop (jumping off two feet instead of one foot in the hurdle) before it was outlawed (the rule now states that the diver must jump off one foot from the hurdle). Many coaches now teach a variety of hop hurdles. In truth, some of these coaches don't fully understand what a hop hurdle is or how to control it. Although there are many variations of the **hop hurdle**, it basically involves leaping high off one foot and landing on the other foot on the last step into the hurdle.

There are several problems with the hop hurdle. One is that it is extremely difficult to control, especially when performing more difficult optional dives or in critical competitive situations. In the finals of the national and international championships, many elite divers using a hop hurdle have lost control of the hurdle. Another problem is that the hop hurdle isn't always aesthetically pleasing to the judges because, in part, it lacks the simplicity of the conventional hurdle. Another problem is that it is often no more effective than a conventional hurdle, particularly for male divers.

There is, however, an effective hurdle for most female divers and some male divers (most male divers don't need a hop-type hurdle) that eliminates the problems associated with the hop hurdle. I call it the **jump hurdle** because it involves jumping off two feet, rather than one, in the second-to-last step and landing on one foot to initiate the hurdle. The jump, rather than hop, makes this a much more controllable and, therefore, preferable hurdle, as evidenced by the fact that all women finalists on the 3-meter springboard at the 2014 FINA World Cup performed the jump hurdle.

The jump hurdle is easy to teach and relatively quick to learn. There are two versions: one with a slight skip into the second-to-last step, as pictured in figure 2.14, and one without a skip.

For some divers, the skip into the last step seems to be the missing piece of the puzzle. It helps them acquire better rhythm with the board. For other divers, however, the skip doesn't help, perhaps because they make the skip too long or they are already in rhythm with the board. The skip should be anywhere from 8 to 12 inches (20 to 30 cm) long and as low as possible so that the feet remain as close to the board as possible (figure 2.14*a* and *b*). On contact after the skip, the back foot should be approximately 3 or 4 inches (7 to 10 cm) behind the front foot (figure 2.14*c*). During the two-legged jump phase in the second-to-last step, the diver's weight should be evenly distributed between the front and back feet (figure 2.14*d*). During the jump, the legs come quickly together and straighten out (figure 2.14*e*) and then split with the back foot staying low to the board (figure 2.14*f*).

Some divers have a tendency to kick the back foot high in the air, as indicated in figure 2.15. Keeping the back foot low to the board, however, provides greater stability in the hurdle because it eliminates unnecessary movement and keeps the center of gravity low and over the contact foot. The jump hurdle, like the conventional hurdle outlined earlier in the chapter, has the same five essential positions. Divers should master the conventional hurdle before progressing to the jump hurdle.

Recap of the Five Essential Positions for the Springboard Forward Approach

Before moving on to the platform forward approach, let's do a quick recap of the five essential positions to achieve in chronological order during the springboard forward approach.

1. Body weight over the front foot on contact in the last step.
2. Arms at 12 o'clock when the board is fully depressed in the last step.

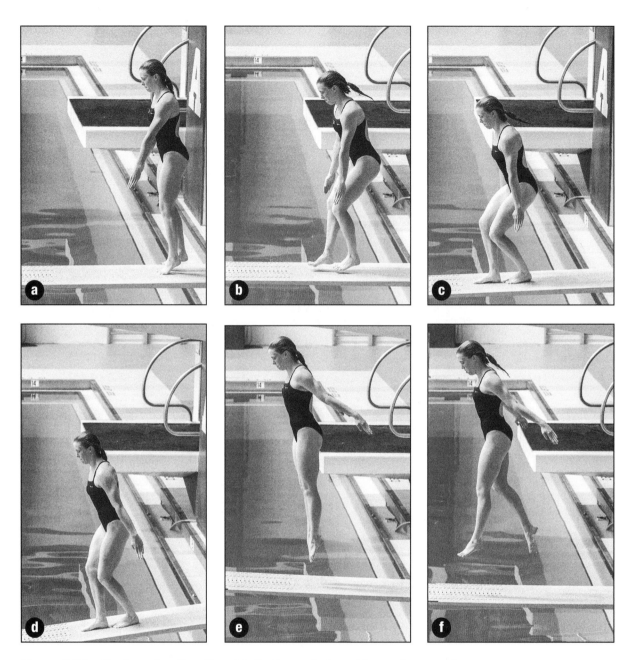

Figure 2.14 The jump hurdle with a skip for the springboard forward approach.

3. Foot back in the hurdle.
4. Contact position: Knees bent and arms past hips.
5. Magic position: Knees bent, arms at 12 o'clock, board fully depressed.

So, the unwieldy beast, the springboard forward approach, can be reduced to a pussycat by focusing on five basic and easily comprehended and achievable positions. From my experience working with literally hundreds of divers, a proficient hurdle is easily attained by mastering these five essential positions. It really is that simple. Of course, other considerations, such as strength training, are important for developing a good hurdle. Also, there are subtle nuances to the forward approach, such as turning the palms outward at the top of the hurdle just prior to the arm swing so that the arms move more freely in the shoulders. For an extensive and detailed listing of more of these nuances, consult O'Brien (2003).

Keep in mind that the essential positions outlined throughout this chapter and other chapters may vary from diver to diver as a result of individual differences in characteristics such as leg strength, flexibility, and leg proportions. The essential positions, however, are fairly standard among elite-level divers and variation is slight.

The sidebar Springboard Forward Approach Drills offers some surefire drills for quickly gaining proficiency with the forward approach.

How to Teach the Springboard Forward Approach

Many coaches forget how much time and energy it took for them to learn the springboard forward approach when they were young divers. Because it is so critical to diver

Figure 2.15 Incorrect back foot in the jump hurdle.

success, it is especially important to follow the Guidelines for Using the How to Teach Sections (in the preface) when teaching the springboard forward approach.

Begin by having divers become accustomed to the rhythm of the springboard by simply standing on the end of the board and repeatedly bending their knees to gently move the board. No jumping is necessary for this drill. Next, introduce a standing jump with arms overhead and then a jump with an arm swing. Next, have divers perform a double-bouncing jump into the water, first with no arm swing and then with an arm swing. Next, introduce the successive ankle jumps drill. Young divers may need a fair amount of time to become accustomed to the movement of the board.

Next, divers should progress to double- and then triple-bouncing knee lift drills. Encourage them to keep their bounces low. To make it easier, consider moving the fulcrum forward to make the springboard less springy. Remind divers to keep the hurdle foot next to the opposite leg, as highlighted in figure 2.8, during the knee lift drill.

While performing these water drills, divers should simultaneously be working on simple dryland drills such as body position for the stance, slow-motion forward approaches, and step-up to low box. These drills prepare them for the next drill, the one-step hurdle with a jump into the water. Remind divers to start with their arms back so that they can swing them during the last step and hurdle. Next, introduce the two-step hurdle with a jump into the water. The last phase of teaching the forward approach and hurdle is introducing all four steps. During this phase, emphasize body position and arm swing for each step. An effective drill for making a nice transition to the takeoff is the standing jump from a squat position with arm swing (beginning with the arms overhead) from the end of the springboard.

Springboard Forward Approach Drills

1. *Slow-motion rehearsal.* Divers can't perform a correct springboard approach if they can't perform it perfectly on the ground in slow motion. Slow-motion rehearsal helps establish a prepractice reference of correctness. It can be done looking into a mirror for immediate feedback. Supervision is necessary in the early stages of learning to ensure correct motion.

2. *Step-up to low box.* The diver does a one-step hurdle and lands with both feet on top of a box. Beginning with a low box allows the diver to easily perform the step-up. Once the step-up has been mastered, box height should be increased. The diver must have both legs straight and arms in the 12 o'clock position before contact.

3. *Step-up over padded block.* This drill is just like the step-up to low box drill except the diver jumps over a low padded block on the one step. It teaches a small jump in the hurdle because the diver starts with feet apart and jumps over the padded block to the power/drive leg.

4. *Step-up to hanging bar.* The diver takes a one-step hurdle, grabs a bar, and hangs from it. This is good for feeling the step-down stretch position.

5. *Drop-down from a low box.* The diver drops down from a box and lands with knees bent and arms slightly past hips, swings the arms overhead, and then jumps. This is a good drill for practicing the contact and magic positions as well as holding the knee bend while swinging the arms to 12 o'clock.

6. *One-step hurdle.* The diver starts with the arms already back and then begins swinging the arms and takes a step. This is a good drill for practicing the early arm swing and having the body over the front foot on contact in the last step. It can be done on a springboard, dryboard, trampoline, or floor mat.

7. *Double-bouncing knee lifts.* The diver stands on the end of a springboard and, keeping jumps low, raises the hurdle knee with the foot next to the opposite leg. This is a good drill for practicing bringing the hurdle foot up and down correctly.

8. *Double-bouncing front jumps with arm swing.* This is a good drill for practicing looking at the end of the springboard and then lifting the head and eyes when loading the board.

9. *Double-bouncing forward dive open pike.* This drill helps divers practice keeping the chest up and achieving the magic position. Most divers have a tendency to anticipate the pike in the forward dive and to drop the head and chest.

10. *Successive ankle jumps.* The diver jumps using only the ankles—no knee bend. This is a good drill for practicing catching the board and landing toe-heel.

11. *Hold hands during step-down.* The diver holds the hands in the 12 o'clock position until the step-down has been completed. This is a favorite drill of mine for teaching divers to shrug on the step-down before taking a full arm swing.

12. *Four-hop forward approach.* In this drill, each step in the approach is taken as a small hop. It is a fun and effective drill for learning about the rhythm of the board and getting in sync with it.

Platform Forward Approach

Like the springboard forward approach, the platform forward approach is composed of easily comprehended and attainable components. This section describes five simple essential positions to focus on when teaching and performing this approach. Like the springboard approach, the platform approach requires practice, but the five essential positions will help divers very quickly look like seasoned platform divers.

The three basic phases of the platform forward approach are the run, the skip, and the landing. The following sections examine these phases and their corresponding essential positions.

Run

The **run** includes the steps taken toward the end of the platform for the approach. It begins with the stance, which is the same as the stance for the springboard forward approach. The approximate starting position is determined by having the diver go to the end of the platform over the water and then taking an approach toward the back of the platform, marking where the diver lands, and then adding 3 to 5 inches (7 to 12 cm).

The forward body position and run is shown in figure 2.16. According to the rules, the run must contain a minimum of three steps. As with the springboard approach, my preference is a four- or five-step approach. The diver initiates the run by keeping the upper body slightly forward (shoulders over toes, angling from the ankles, not the waist) and accelerating toward the end of the platform.

Figure 2.16 The forward body position and run for the platform forward approach.

Accelerating toward the end of a concrete slab, especially a 10-meter slab, can be intimidating, and it is only human nature to want to proceed with caution. A certain amount of speed, however, is necessary for a correct landing position, as we will see in a subsequent section.

During the run, the hands should touch or slightly cross in front of the body and move down by the hips in the second-to-last step. The arms then lift laterally along the plane of the body in the last step and are at 12 o'clock before initiating the skip. This, then, is the first essential position for the platform approach: arms up before initiating the skip (figure 2.17).

Skip

The **skip** is the distance from the last step in the approach to the end of the platform. The length of the skip is approximately the length of the diver's body. To determine the length of the skip, the diver should lie on her back with her heels on the end of the platform. The skip should begin about where the top of the diver's head is on the platform. Its path follows a parabolic curve as depicted in figure 2.18.

At the beginning of the skip (beginning of the parabolic curve), the legs should be completely straight and the arms should be straight and next to the ears. This is the second essential position of the forward platform approach: legs straight during the ascent in the skip. The diver should straighten the legs as quickly as possible during this phase of the skip, as shown in figure 2.19.

Some elite divers bend their knees during the ascent and then straighten their legs and then bend them again before landing. Although there may be some benefit to this additional knee bend, such as a quicker reaction time during the push on contact with the platform (Sands, McNeal, & Schultz, 1999), it is best, especially during initial learning, to maintain straight legs during the ascent because it shows a straight body line and eliminates the unnecessary movement of bending, straightening, and then bending the legs again before

Figure 2.17 The first essential position for the platform forward approach: the 12 o'clock arm position before the skip.

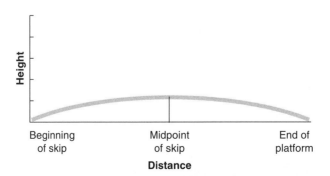

Figure 2.18 The parabolic curve trajectory of the body during the skip in the platform forward approach.

landing. Again, forming a straight line and simplicity of movement are two aspects of beauty in diving.

The third essential position is to have the knees bent during the descent in the skip. As the body descends toward the end of the platform, the knees bend and stay bent until contact with the end of the platform, as shown in figure 2.20.

Landing

The **landing** occurs the moment the diver's feet make contact with the end of the platform. As with the forward springboard approach, divers should look at the end of the platform until approximately 3 or 4 inches (7 to 10 cm) before contact. The fourth essential position, which occurs just before landing, is to have the center of gravity behind the heels, the feet flat and slightly in front of the body, and the arms bent at 90 degrees with the elbows at 12 o'clock. This position is outlined in figure 2.21.

On landing, the toes contact the end of the platform, followed by the heels. The knees should be bent, hips rolled down and under, and back flat as the arms begin straightening out (now bent only approximately 45 degrees); the head is neutral; and the eyes look straight ahead. The horizontal movement developed in the run carries the body forward so that before takeoff the center

Figure 2.19 The second essential position of the platform forward approach: legs straight on the ascent in the skip.

Figure 2.20 The third essential position of the platform forward approach: knees bent in the descent in the skip.

Figure 2.21 The fourth essential position for the platform forward approach: the position of the center of gravity, feet, and arms before landing.

of gravity is directly over the ankles as shown in figure 2.22. This is the fifth essential position: the knees are bent, the arms extend 45 degrees overhead, and the center of gravity is directly over the ankles on landing. Immediately on contact, the legs begin to extend and the feet push forward into the platform.

Many divers make the mistake of landing with the head and shoulders over the ankles but the center of gravity behind the heels, as depicted in figure 2.23. Although there is some comfort in this incorrect position because they are safely back from the end and won't slip off, they have unintentionally ensured a poor takeoff, an unsatisfactory dive, and possibly an injury.

Many platform divers land back on the end of the platform not only because they are apprehensive about slipping off but also because they don't look down long enough to ensure that they land on the end. Landing with the center of gravity behind the heels makes it difficult to generate a forward somersault rotation and causes divers to cut in dangerously close to the platform.

Recap of the Five Essential Positions for the Platform Forward Approach

Let's recap the five essential positions for the platform forward approach.

1. Arms straight and at the 12 o'clock position prior to initiation of the skip.
2. Legs straight during the ascent in the skip.
3. Legs bent during the descent in the skip.
4. Center of gravity behind the heels, feet flat, arms at 90 degrees, elbows at 12 o'clock.
5. Landing position: Center of gravity over the ankles, knees bent, arms at approximately 45 degrees.

The sidebar Platform Forward Approach Drills offers some time-tested drills for quickly learning a proficient platform forward approach.

Figure 2.22 The fifth essential position for the platform forward approach: the landing position.

Figure 2.23 Incorrect body position on landing for the platform forward approach.

Platform Forward Approach Drills

1. *Three- or four-hop takeoff.* The diver starts with arms overhead, takes hops, and lands on the end of the platform, skill mat, or spring floor. This is a good drill for practicing shifting the eyes down and then up, staying tall in the skip, getting to the end of the platform, and landing with bent knees and then immediately pushing up off the platform. If done on a mat or spring floor, a strip of athletic tape can be used to mark an end point. Divers who slip off the platform often do so because they don't look down long enough and land over the end.

2. *One-step skip takeoff.* In this drill the forward approach is reduced to a single step and skip to the end of the platform, mat, or spring floor. The diver starts with the arms already at 12 o'clock to become accustomed to having the arms up before initiating the skip.

3. *Arms up on run.* The diver places the arms straight and at 12 o'clock before and during the approach. This is a good drill for learning to get the arms up early in the approach.

4. *Two-jump front somersault.* The diver starts with the arms straight and at 12 o'clock, keeping the core tight so there is no give in the midsection during both jumps. This drill helps divers practice essential positions 4 and 5.

5. *Running forward jump.* The diver contacts the end of the platform and jumps up and slightly away from the platform. This drill is good for converting horizontal movement into vertical movement off the platform. The diver must contact the end of the platform with the feet slightly in front and then push forward forcefully into the platform through the legs. The legs should be straight immediately off the platform. Deceptively difficult drill but once mastered divers can progress to a running forward dive tuck and forward somersault.

CHAPTER 3

Backward Presses

The springboard backward press isn't typically thought of as quite the wild beast that the forward approach is sometimes considered to be, probably because the backward press seems less complex: stand, swing the arms, and jump. However, the backward press is no less important. Every diver is required to do backward and inward dives in competition. And divers who opt to perform a backward twister or double up on a backward or inward category will perform an additional backward press. So, backward presses can comprise up to half a diver's list. Learning a good backward press, then, is critical for successful diving. Let's begin by looking at the essential elements of the springboard backward press.

But first, a short story . . .

At an NCAA championship, a very talented and strong diver is having the meet of his life. It is the finals of the 1-meter springboard, and he is about to perform an inward 2 1/2 somersault. If he hits the dive, he likely wins the contest and reaches his dream of becoming NCAA champion. Shockingly, as he oscillates the board, he loses his balance. He tries to recover during the press, but it is too late. Because it is the finals, he goes for the dive and barely misses hitting his head on the board but only because he jumps to the side. The dive wasn't nearly the disaster it could have been, but it was bad enough to knock him out of contention for the title. He finishes last in finals. Learning a solid backward press is as important as learning a solid forward approach.

Springboard Backward Press

In many ways, the springboard backward press is similar to the springboard forward approach. At first glance, this might seem untrue, but many of the essential positions embedded in the forward approach are also embedded in the backward press. This chapter deconstructs the backward press, identifying five essential positions for quickly learning to perform a proficient press. The backward press consists of seven phases: the stance position, oscillation, arm swing, step-down position, knee draw position, contact position, and magic position.

Stance Position

The stance for the backward press is important for the same reasons that the stance for the forward approach is important: a correct stance makes a positive impression on the judges and creates a balanced body position by holding the center of gravity over the ankles. Because that level thing a diver stands on very quickly changes to a drastically downward-sloping thing, establishing a balanced position before the press is critical; otherwise, it is easy to lose balance like the diver in the story at the outset of this chapter.

As in the forward approach stance, the head should be neutral, shoulders square but relaxed, abdomen pulled in, hips rolled down and under, front of torso slightly concaved, back flat, arms at sides, and fingers straight and together. Divers should breathe through the chest and not the abdomen to maintain core tightness and balance and to avoid looking as though they are inflating and deflating a balloon in the abdomen. Rather than starting with their arms at their sides, some divers stand with their arms in a T position, which makes performing the press slightly easier, particularly in stressful competitive situations.

One difference from the forward approach stance is that the feet are in a V position with the heels anchored together and at board level or slightly above the board. This foot position helps divers maintain their balance during board oscillation. Standing with the heels very high is not recommended because it is difficult to maintain that position for any length of time, especially in competition. Figure 3.1 depicts the first essential position, the stance, for the backward press.

Figure 3.1 The first essential position for the springboard backward press: the stance.

Oscillation

Oscillation is the act of moving the heels up and down to move the springboard up and down before initiating the backward press. This **priming** of the board makes it easier to more fully depress the board. To maintain consistency and to know precisely when to begin the arm swing, divers should use the same number of oscillations for each press. During a meet his freshman year, a diver lost track of his oscillations and rocked the board 35 times! By establishing a specific number of oscillations and the exact time to begin his arm swing during the oscillations, he developed a consistent backward press and went on to win several U.S. national titles.

During the oscillation, the heels rock approximately 3 to 4 inches (7 to 10 cm) upward and then downward to board level. The heels should never rock below board level. The core remains tight so center of gravity remains over the ankles. Elite divers typically use one, two, or three oscillations; note, however, that whatever number they select, they use that number of oscillations for all of their backward presses. More than three oscillations makes it difficult to stay relaxed and maintain balance, especially during competition. The oscillations should begin by moving the heels upward.

Arm Swing

For a three oscillation press, the arms begin moving laterally upward as the heels and board descend after the second oscillation. When the arms are at 12 o'clock, they pause and wait for the heels and board to rise all the way up on the third oscillation, as depicted in the series of pictures in figure 3.2. As in the forward approach, the arms should not drift slightly downward but remain at 12 o'clock until the arm swing begins. At this point, the diver is now in the step-down position described in chapter 2 for the springboard forward approach.

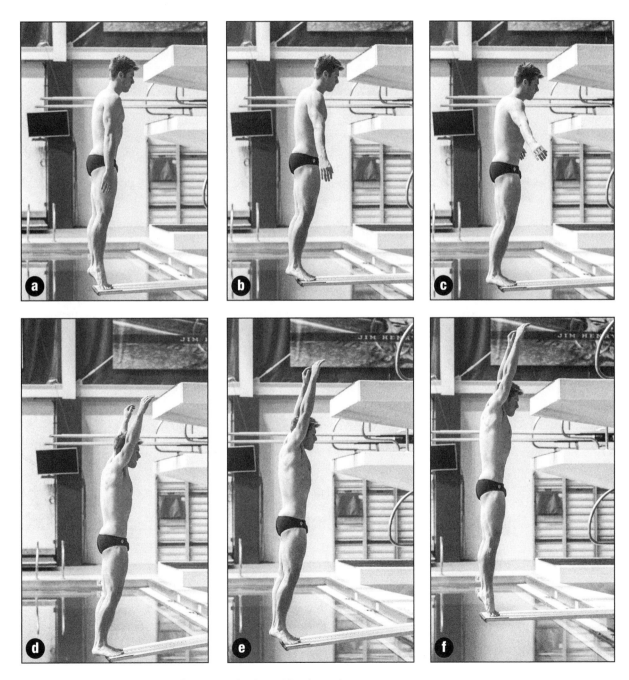

Figure 3.2 The arm swing for the springboard backward press.

Step-Down Position

The second essential position for the springboard backward press is the step-down position. Recall that in the step-down position, the arms are at 12 o'clock, the body is in a straight line, and the feet are pointed. As we will see subsequently in discussing the unloading of the board, even the feet-pointed position in the step-down for the forward approach can be attained in the backward press. During the step-down, the body elongates as much as possible, as shown in figure 3.3. This elongation keeps the center of gravity over the ankles and positions nearly all of the body weight directly over a focal point on the tip of the board, allowing for greater depression.

Knee Draw Position

The third essential position is the knee draw position, which involves holding the arms in the step-down position while slightly drawing (bending) the knees to approximately 150 degrees, as shown in figure 3.4. As the knees draw, the board continues to rise. As this happens, the arms shrug up rather than drift slightly downward in anticipation of the ensuing arm swing.

Contact Position

The fourth essential position is the contact position, which is similar to the contact position in the springboard forward approach. After the knee draw position is established, the knees continue bending and the arms begin swinging downward. During this phase, the board remains level, even though many coaches and divers mistakenly think the board moves downward. At the contact position, the board is level, the knees are bent between 90 and 100 degrees, and the arms are next to the hips, as depicted in figure 3.5. As the board is depressed, the diver holds the knee bend position while continuing to swing the arms upward.

Some elite male divers tend to achieve a 90-degree knee bend, whereas female elite divers tend to achieve less of a knee bend. The difference in the degree of knee bend in the fourth essential position has to do with overall leg strength.

Magic Position

The fifth essential position for the backward press is the magic position, which is identical to the magic position in the springboard forward approach. When

Figure 3.3 The second essential position for the springboard backward press: the step-down position.

Figure 3.4 The third essential position for the springboard backward press: the knee draw position.

the board is fully depressed, the knees are bent, heels are at or above board level (my preference is above), arms are straight or nearly straight and at approximately 12 o'clock, back is flat, and head is up, as shown in figure 3.6.

During the arm swing phase, the arms relax and the elbows bend to approximately 90 degrees between 10 and 12 o'clock and then straighten out as the board begins to rise. Relaxing and bending the arms makes it easier to get the arms through to the magic position. Some divers can bend their elbows quite a bit and still get them straight at the magic position. Those who have trouble doing this should try to keep their arms straight throughout the swing. In this way, they generally get a slight elbow bend and are able to have straight arms at the magic position.

Springboard Inward Press

The five essential positions for the springboard inward press are the same as those for the springboard backward press with minor exceptions. One exception is that some elite divers move their feet slightly forward during the unloading phase and press the board with their feet flat on the board for the backward press. For their inward press, however, they keep their feet in the same spot and their heels above the board.

Another exception is that elite divers tend to get their arms up to 12 o'clock slightly earlier and with more knee bend for inward somersaulting dives than they do for backward somersaulting dives. Because of the similarities between the backward and inward presses, the term *backward press* is used for both.

Unloading

Unloading is the process of removing most of the body weight from the board during the backward press. To achieve unloading, divers oscillate through their ankle and feet joints (referred to as **articulation**) and on the last oscillation rise up on their toes so there is only slight contact with the board, as indicated in figure 3.7. If this is performed correctly, the board will continue rising upward past horizontal essentially giving divers the benefit of a double bouncing effect. If it is performed incorrectly, the board will rise up only to its original horizontal position before initiating the backward press, thereby negating any double bouncing effect.

World champion and Olympic silver medalist Alexandre Despatie demonstrated some of the best fundamentals (Xs and Os) of any diver in the history of our sport.

Figure 3.5 The fourth essential position for the springboard backward press: the contact position.

Figure 3.6 The fifth essential position for the springboard backward press: the magic position.

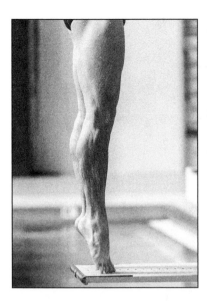

Figure 3.7 Unloading on the backward press.

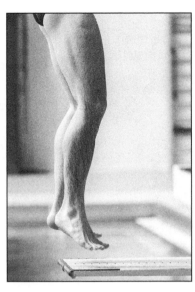

Figure 3.8 Incorrect technique includes flat feet and a crow hop during unloading on the backward press.

Careful analysis of Alexandre's springboard backward press reveals a perfect execution of the unloading action. Note that flattening the feet during unloading results in a crow hop, as shown in figure 3.8. A crow hop can result in a 1/2- to 2-point deduction from each judge and the potential for slipping off the springboard.

During unloading, the feet must not slide away from the board; otherwise, the diver might slip off. Divers must avoid this backward movement, and coaches must vigilantly monitor it. Divers who move their feet backward should undertake remedial skill work. The sidebar Springboard Backward Press Drills offers some simple but effective drills for helping divers learn a proficient backward press.

Recap of the Five Essential Positions for the Springboard Backward Press

1. Stance position: Tight core and slightly concaved body position.
2. Step-down: Straight body line while the board is still ascending.
3. Knee draw: Arms up while slightly drawing the knees upward.
4. Contact: Board level, knees bent, arms by hips.
5. Magic position: Board fully depressed, knees bent, arms at 12 o'clock.

How to Teach the Springboard Backward Press

The first goal for teaching the springboard backward press is acclimating divers to standing backward on the end of the board. Begin by having divers perform the correct stance on dryland on a mat and then on a bench or box. Then have them hold that position on the end of the 1-meter springboard. Next, have them slightly oscillate the board so that they learn to keep the heels from dropping below the board and to maintain core and body position for balance. Next, introduce the backward jump with hands on hips and no arm swing, and then the backward jump with arm swing (start with the arms overhead). Once these drills have been mastered, introduce low ankle oscillations with a backward jump, no arm swing, and then low ankle oscillations with a backward jump and arm swing. Once divers have demonstrated mastery of these skills, they can be permitted to perform a backward press and jump back onto the board. As with the forward approach, divers can perform the backward jump from a squat position with arm swing (start with arms overhead) as a transition to learning the takeoff.

Springboard Backward Press Drills

1. *Backward press and jump back onto board.* This simple but extremely effective drill forces divers to keep the center of gravity over the ankles and load the board during the press. Otherwise, they will fall off the board. When performing this drill, divers should jump forward far enough to safely land back on the board.

2. *Slow-motion modeling.* Divers must be able to perform the skill correctly in slow motion before performing it on the board. Modeling can be practiced on the pool deck, at the end of the board, or in front of a mirror. Supervision is necessary for error-free early learning.

3. *Oscillation.* The diver stands on the end of the board in the starting position and oscillates the board by moving the heels up and down—no knee bend or arm swing. This is a good drill for practicing priming the board while simultaneously maintaining body position.

4. *Squat press with arms overhead.* The diver starts with knees bent and arms straight overhead and then jumps either off the board or back onto the board. This is a good drill for practicing keeping the chest up and the core tight, and jumping from the magic position.

5. *Magic position hold.* The diver assumes the magic position on the end of the board and holds for 5 to 10 seconds. This can be done on a slant board for a more realistic feel, just make sure the diver has good traction and doesn't slip off slant board. Sometimes using shoes can help provide traction.

6. *Wall sit.* This drill helps divers feel the correct muscles to load in the backward press (figure 3.9).

7. *Successive ankle jumps.* Standing backward near the end but not on the end of the board, the diver jumps using only the ankles—no knee bend. This drill helps divers practice maintaining balance in the backward position.

8. *Hands on hips and no arm swing.* The diver puts hands on hips and jumps either off the board or back onto the board. This is a good drill for beginning divers.

9. *Double-bouncing backward jump.* The diver double bounces and then jumps back onto the board or into the water. Once this is mastered, the diver can perform inward and backward dives into the water. This is a good drill for practicing maintaining core position and balance in the backward position.

10. *Knee draw jump.* The diver starts with the arms overhead and a slight knee bend and then swings the arms and jumps. This drill can be performed on a springboard, platform, mat, or trampoline. It is good for practicing attaining the magic position.

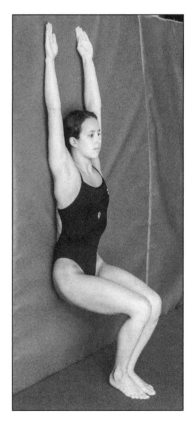

Figure 3.9 Wall sit drill.

Platform Backward Press

The platform backward press is similar to the springboard backward press in many ways and is just as important. A considerably different platform press is used for inward takeoffs, which is addressed in a later section.

Stance Position

The same body position, heel position, and T arm position used for the springboard backward press are used for the platform backward press. Unlike with the springboard backward press, however, there is no priming (oscillation) of the platform. The first essential position, the stance, is depicted in figure 3.10.

Heel Raise

To initiate the press, the arms move laterally downward from their T position and pause momentarily on the front of the thighs until the heels rise upward approximately 3 or 4 inches (7 to 10 cm), as depicted in figure 3.11. This is the second essential position—the heel raise.

Figure 3.10 The first essential position for the platform backward press: the stance.

Figure 3.11 The second essential position for the platform backward press: the heel raise.

Lift and Drop

The third essential position, the lift and drop, is initiated by lifting the arms while simultaneously dropping the body down into the platform (i.e., bending the knees). Elite divers vary in the exact movements of their arms. For example, some lift their arms in front of their bodies, and some lift them more laterally. All elite platform divers, however, lift their arms during the drop.

The lift and drop for many beginning divers seems intuitively wrong when they are first introduced to the action. Recall the springboard approach in which the arms move upward as the body and board move downward. Similarly, during the lift and drop, the body moves in the opposite direction of the arms. This action continues until the lift and drop position is fully achieved: the knees are bent and the arms are above the shoulders or at shoulder height (figure 3.12).

Stall

From the lift and drop position there is a stall (pause) in the squat as the arms continue swinging through, as depicted in the series of photos in figure 3.13. This stall is the fourth essential position for the platform backward press. Elite platform divers differ in squat depth during the stall based on leg strength and individual preference. For example, Hu Jia, Chinese 2004 Olympic gold medalist, squatted so deep that his glutes appeared to hit his heels. In contrast, Australian

Figure 3.12 The third essential position for the platform backward press: the lift and drop.

Figure 3.13 The fourth essential position for the platform backward press: the stall.

2008 Olympic gold medalist Matthew Mitcham squatted significantly shallower during his stall. However, both divers stalled during the squat to allow their arms to swing through to approximately 12 o'clock.

Magic Position

After the stall comes the fifth essential position, the magic position, the position from which all good things happen for divers! In the magic position, shown in figure 3.14, the knees are bent, arms are overhead, and feet remain level with the platform. Although elite divers may differ slightly in the degree of knee bend when the arms swing overhead, all have some knee bend when the arms are overhead. The knee bend tends to be less on the platform than it is on the springboard.

The platform reverse press is essentially the same as the platform backward press. The diver stands on the end of the platform in the same stance and achieves the same five essential positions for all dives in the reverse category.

The only difference is that the center of gravity tilts slightly forward during the jump off the platform. No tilting should occur until after the magic position has been established.

The sidebar Platform Backward Press Drills provides some excellent exercises for learning the platform backward and reverse presses.

Recap of the Five Essential Positions for the Platform Backward Press

Figure 3.14 The fifth essential position for the platform backward press: the magic position.

1. Stance: Similar to the springboard stance; it is important to keep the hips rolled down and under and to breathe through the chest.

2. Heel raise: Drop the arms laterally and pause while keeping the body shape as the heels rise.

3. Lift and drop: Begin squatting while simultaneously lifting the arms in front of the body or laterally.

4. Stall: Briefly hold the squat position while the arms swing through to 12 o'clock.

5. Magic position: Arms are up and knees are bent. The degree of knee bend varies among divers.

Platform Backward Press Drills

1. *Drop arms and lift heels.* From T position stance, diver drops arms to thighs and then raises heels. Good drill for segmenting first initial move in backward press.

2. *Slow-motion lift and drop squat.* The diver bends the knees while simultaneously lifting the arms. This is a good drill for overcoming the natural tendency of dropping the arms into the squat. All slow-motion drills can be done in front of a mirror. Supervision is necessary for error-free early learning.

3. *Slow-motion arm swing from squat position.* The diver swings the arms while keeping the legs bent. This is a good drill for learning the magic position.

4. *Jump squat to bench with arms overhead.* The diver jumps to a bench from the magic position—no arm swing. This is a good drill for learning to jump with the arms overhead.

5. *Knee bend with arm swing jump.* The diver starts in a squat position, swings the arms, and then jumps up to mat, box, or bench. This drill helps divers achieve the stall position and arm swing. Diver must swing arms overhead before attempting to jump. It can be done on a mat or on a 1-meter or 3-meter platform. Once this is mastered, the diver can perform a backward dive tuck and pike on a 1- or 3-meter platform.

Platform Inward Press

The platform inward press has its own section because, although it is a simple press with only five essential positions, it is quite different from the platform backward press. The first noticeable difference is that there is no arm swing. The second difference is the stance position.

Stance Position

Like both the springboard and platform backward presses, the platform inward press begins with the first essential position: the stance. Unlike the backward presses we have examined thus far, however, the platform inward press stance begins with the arms straight overhead, as depicted in figure 3.15. Similar to all the stances, though, the head is neutral, the heels are level or above the platform, and most important, the hips are rolled down and under to maintain the center of gravity over the ankles.

The balls of the feet should be on the platform to ensure that all toes are firmly on the platform. Some divers feel more comfortable with the small toes off the platform; however, this position must be avoided because even a small amount of movement backward with the feet during the press can cause the diver to slip off the platform.

Many beginning and intermediate divers incorrectly assume the inward stance with the hips slightly pushed back from the platform and arms slightly forward. There is an understandable urge to nudge the center of gravity away from the concrete platform before initiating an inward press. However, as will be explained in chapter 4, shifting center of gravity away from the platform in the stance can cause dives to move too close to the platform during dive execution. Therefore, the hips should remain rolled down and under. Both squeezing the gluteus maximus muscles and keeping the arms pulled back to 12 o'clock rather than in front of the body plane force the hips under (otherwise, the diver is likely to fall backward) and ensure a straight body line.

Figure 3.15 The first essential position for the platform inward press: the stance.

Oscillation

Although the platform doesn't move the way the springboard does, an ankle rock similar to the oscillation for the springboard backward press is useful for priming the jump. During this second essential position, the oscillation, the heels move up and down one to three times (the diver should have a set number) and lift as high as possible on the last oscillation. The heels do not drop below the platform. The series of oscillations is depicted in figure 3.16. Some elite divers place almost their entire feet on the platform in the stance position because during the oscillation they move their feet slightly back away from the platform. This action is not recommended.

Step-Down Position

On the last oscillation, an unloading occurs in which nearly all of the body weight is off the platform and the toes barely contact the platform, much like

Figure 3.16 The second essential position for the platform inward press: the oscillation.

in the springboard press. This unloading is achieved by pushing (articulating) through the ankles and feet in the last oscillation and elevating the body. At this point the body is in the by now familiar step-down position, the third essential position (figure 3.17), in which the body is in a straight line and the feet are pointed or nearly pointed.

Knee Lift Position

During this unloading phase, the fourth essential position occurs: the knee lift. The knee lift involves lifting the knees slightly upward (figure 3.18) and forward over the toes as the body descends from the step-down position. The core must remain tight and the hips rolled down and under to maintain the center of gravity position. The knee lift is similar to the contact position on the springboard except that there is no arm swing.

Many elite divers employ an unloading on the platform similar to unloading on the springboard. Unloading is highly effective but somewhat difficult to master. For this reason, only experienced elite divers should consider using it. Even at the elite level, some elite divers are hesitant to unload for fear of moving their feet backward and slipping off the platform. Some elite divers actually slide their feet slightly forward during unloading so their feet don't move backwards. Divers interested in using the unloading

Figure 3.17 The third essential position for the platform inward press: the step-down.

technique should practice many repetitions under coach supervision on a safe dryland training mat until they demonstrate mastery of the technique on an inward jump and inward somersault.

Magic Position

The magic position is the fifth essential position for the platform inward press. Characteristics of the magic position, shown in figure 3.19, include feet firmly on the platform, knees bent approximately 150 degrees and slightly over the toes, heels up or level with the platform, back flat or slightly arched, hips rolled down and under, center of gravity over the ankles, and arms bent between 45 and 90 degrees behind the head with elbows at 12 o'clock. The magic position is immediately followed by a ballistic (rapid) punch on the platform. The arms are straight and overhead just prior to throwing into the somersault.

Figure 3.18 The fourth essential position for the platform inward press: the knee lift position.

Figure 3.19 Fifth essential position for the platform inward press: the magic position.

Some divers bend the knees too much in the inward press. Analysis of some of the world's most powerful platform divers indicates that even these elite athletes maintain a shallow knee bend, at least compared to the knee bend in the springboard inward press. Power for the platform inward press is generated from a quick, shallow knee draw and a powerful ankle snap. Bending the knees too deeply in the magic position slows down the pop off the platform and allows the diver time to shift the center of gravity away from the platform, which results in an effect best described as "getting the carpet pulled out from under you." In other words, the diver slides off the platform rather than jumps up.

Recap of the Five Essential Positions for the Platform Inward Press

1. Stance: The hips are rolled down and under, the heels are level or slightly above the platform, and the arms are at 12 o'clock. Good alignment ensures good balance during the press.

2. Oscillation: The diver performs a set number of oscillations with the hips over the ankles.

3. Step-down: The body is elongated, and the feet are pointed or nearly pointed.

4. Knee lift: Body drops and the knees draw upward and stay over the toes.

5. Magic position: Knee bend is shallow compared to that in the platform backward press, elbows are at 12 o'clock, and arms bent between 45 and 90 degrees.

Platform Inward Press Drills

1. *Heel kicks into mat.* The diver assumes an inward stance position and then quickly pops off the floor and rapidly kicks a mat with the heels.

2. *Hips pop.* The diver puts both hands on the railing of a ladder used to get out of the pool and rapidly pops the hips up. This is a good drill for learning to snap the hips up and back from the platform.

3. *Ankle pops with no knee bend.* The diver puts the arms overhead and does successive ankle pops down a panel mat without bending the knees. This teaches the diver to use the calves and articulate through the ankles and feet for the inward press.

4. *Hands-on-hips pop.* The diver places hands on hips and pops down a panel mat with a slight knee bend. This helps divers learn to keep the core tight and the hips rolled down and under, and to react quickly with an ankle pop.

5. *Inward ball throw.* The diver stands on a mat, assumes an inward stance while holding a ball about the size of a volleyball, and then throws the ball up in the air at 11 o'clock while performing an inward jump.

6. *Inward to stomach drop.* The diver does a stomach drop to a landing mat from an inward stance position.

7. *Hand spotted inward jump.* The coach places a hand on the diver's center of gravity (approximately slightly above the waistline) and shifts the diver away at the appropriate time. This is an excellent drill for teaching divers to wait to shift. It can be done on a mat, at poolside, or on a 1-meter platform for inward jumps and somersaults.

Platform Armstand

The armstand might seem to be a misplaced category in the sport of diving. Coaches and divers spend an inordinate amount of time practicing takeoffs from the feet and then suddenly are confronted with a dive category in which every takeoff is initiated from the hands. Nonetheless, this upside-down category is a cool one (who doesn't like impressing friends and family by demonstrating an armstand?) and also a required category that can't be ignored. Many divers have ruined terrific lists of platform dives in competition by faltering on an armstand that they never practiced.

The armstand isn't such a difficult thing to master if the coach and diver work on it as much as any other dive category. The following sections provide some simple guidelines and suggestions for learning and performing a solid armstand for backward, reverse, and forward armstand dives.

Kick-Up

There are two types of armstands—forward (the reverse armstand is performed using the forward armstand) and backward—and two methods for kicking up into an armstand. The **split-leg kick-up** involves first placing the hands on the end of the platform and then kicking the top leg past 12 o'clock in a straight position, while keeping the bottom leg down as depicted in figure 3.20.

Some divers with extensive gymnastics backgrounds find using a **cartwheel kick-up** effective for kicking up into an armstand, as depicted in figure 3.21. Notice that the diver bends over, stops, and first places the hands approximately 8 to 10 inches (20 to 25 cm) from the platform before throwing into the armstand. Especially in competition, a throw initiated from a greater distance can result in a kick-up with too much force, causing the diver to move past vertical and lose balance. Notice that the arms are straight. Also notice that there are two positions during the cartwheel kick-up. When the diver first cartwheels into a split-leg position, the legs are approximately in line with the end of the platform. The diver then swivels to the second position, in which the top leg is over the platform and the bottom leg is over the water. Some divers falter in the armstand, especially in competition, because they impatiently cartwheel directly into the second position. The core must remain tight to maintain the center of gravity, and solid balance must be attained in the second split-leg position *before* bringing the legs together.

The second method for kicking up into an armstand is the **press kick-up,** which involves first placing the hands on the end of the platform and pressing up with legs bent (tuck position), straight and together (pike position), or apart (straddle position), as depicted in figure 3.22. The press

Figure 3.20 The armstand split-leg kick-up.

kick-up is more difficult to master because it demands more strength, balance, and flexibility. Once mastered, however, it is easier to control, especially in competition. For all types of kick-ups, balance must be attained in the press kick-up position before fully extending up into the armstand.

Balance Position

Divers vary in their balance positions, but as a rule of thumb, the hands should be placed shoulder-width apart on the end of the platform. The fingers should be on the end of the platform for the forward armstand, although some elite divers place their fingertips slightly over the end of the platform. For the backward armstand, the heels of the hands should be on the end of the platform, although some elite divers place them approximately 1 inch (2.5 cm) from the end of the platform. Pressure should be maintained on the fingertips, and the fingers should be spread slightly apart.

Once the diver is fully extended in the armstand, the hips should be rolled down and under and the legs and arms fully locked out to form a straight body

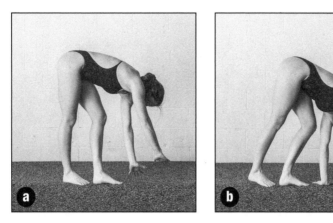

Figure 3.21   The armstand cartwheel kick-up.

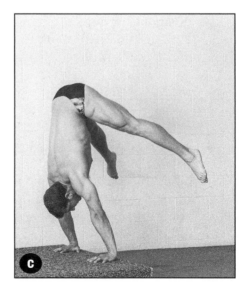

Figure 3.22   The armstand press kick-up in *(a)* tuck, *(b)* pike, and *(c)* straddle positions.

line (feet, hip joint, shoulders, and hands form the points of the straight line). The head should be slightly up. Immediately before takeoff, the head lowers to a neutral position, the body weight shifts slightly in the opposite direction (so that when the head is lowered, the diver doesn't fall), and the shoulders shrug to elevate the body and accentuate the straight line, as shown in figure 3.23.

Learning an Armstand

Learning an armstand is simple, but it takes practice. A simple but effective practice plan is to incorporate armstands into daily practice warm-ups and cool-downs. I never coached a diver who couldn't hold an armstand after a semester of consistently following this plan. Doing six to eight armstands before and after each practice distributes the number of repetitions, which helps divers avoid developing sore wrists.

 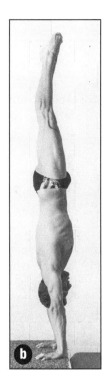 

Figure 3.23 The armstand straight line balance position.

The primary goal in the beginning is learning to find a balance position before bringing the legs together into the final armstand position. The sidebar Platform Armstand Drills outlines some simple but proven drills for learning a consistent armstand.

Five Focus Points for the Platform Armstand

1. If using the cartwheel kick-up, place the hands approximately 8 to 10 inches (20 to 25 cm) from the platform before initiating the cartwheel.
2. Keep the elbows locked out during all phases of the armstand, core tight, hands approximately shoulder-width apart, and pressure on fingertips.
3. Establish balance in the split-leg or press-up position before lifting the feet to 12 o'clock and bringing the feet together.
4. Establish a straight body line with the hips rolled down and under, back flat, legs straight, and toes pointed.
5. Practice armstands before and after every practice.

Platform Armstand Drills

1. *Balance with split legs.* The diver balances in the armstand with split legs. The diver should not try to come up to the armstand position. The top leg should be at approximately 2 o'clock; and the bottom leg, at approximately 8 or 9 o'clock. This drill can be done on a mat, dryland platform, or low platform.

(continued)

Platform Armstand Drills *(continued)*

2. *Balance with press-up.* The diver starts with the hands on a mat and presses up into a pike or tuck and holds that position. The diver should not attempt to lift the legs into the armstand position. This drill can be done on a mat, dryland platform, or low platform.

3. *Balance armstand with foot on wall.* The diver stays close enough to a wall and uses the top foot and wall to maintain balance in a split-leg armstand (figure 3.24). The wall should be touched only to avoid falling over.

4. *Balance with arms against bench.* The diver places the arms against a bench and kicks up into an armstand using split leg, or presses up. Balance is maintained by pressing the arms into the bench (figure 3.25).

5. *Hand spotting.* The diver kicks up to a split-leg position or pike-up position, and the coach hand spots the diver to help maintain balance (figure 3.26).

6. *Manipulation of armstand position.* The diver kicks up to an armstand, and the coach holds the diver and manipulates the diver's body position so that the hips are rolled down and under, the shoulders are shrugged, and the body is in a straight line.

7. *Cartwheel kick-up.* The diver places the hands on a piece of athletic tape on a mat and performs a cartwheel kick-up. The cartwheel begins on the platform side of the tape.

8. *Shoulder shrug.* The diver holds an armstand against a wall and elongates the body by shrugging the shoulders (figure 3.27). This is a good drill for acquiring shoulder strength, learning to maintain a straight body line, and practicing the shoulder shrug.

Figure 3.24 Balance armstand with foot on wall drill.

Figure 3.25 Balance armstand with arms against bench drill.

Figure 3.26 Hand spotting drill.

Figure 3.27 Shoulder shrug drill.

CHAPTER 4

Takeoffs and Connections

So you have the forward approach and backward press down pat. You are on the tip of the board and ready to rock and roll because you are in the magic position. Now what? What follows are two phases—the takeoff and the connection. Just like the approach and press, the takeoff and connection are composed of some essential elements. The following sections deconstruct these two phases, highlighting some easily comprehended, teachable, and learnable essential positions. Let's briefly review our old friend the magic position.

But first, a short story . . .

My sophomore year in college, I observed a teammate perform a forward 3 1/2 somersaults on the 3-meter springboard, and I was frustrated and baffled. Granted, he was a talented athlete, and I admired his diving very much. But by my estimation he didn't jump any higher or spin any faster than I did. So why, I asked myself, did he finish the dive higher above the water than I did? After observing him perform the dive multiple times, I realized that the difference lay in his deft ability to get his arms through sooner on takeoff and connect sooner into his tuck position. The difference between his takeoff and connection and mine made it possible for him to finish his dive much sooner and much higher above the water. Takeoff and connection matter.

Okay, let's revisit the magic position now. Recall that it is called the magic position because, once achieved, the dive goes like magic—as if somehow the dive is being done mysteriously without any assistance from the diver. That really isn't the case, but the dive is indeed much easier to perform from the magic position. The magic position is achieved when the board is fully depressed, knees are bent, upper body is vertical, and arms are overhead, as depicted in figure 4.1.

Figure 4.1 The magic position.

Takeoffs

The reason for revisiting the magic position is that the following essential positions for the takeoff are impossible to attain to any degree of proficiency without first establishing the magic position. From the magic position, there are five basic takeoff positions for springboard and platform takeoffs. They are described in the following sections.

90-90-90 Position

The first essential position for the takeoff is the **90-90-90 position,** which comprises three 90-degree angles and is used for all forward and inward somersaulting dives. Many divers and coaches mistakenly believe that the diver should wait until off the board to throw for a somersault. This is not the case. The throw should occur while still on the board. As in the game Where's Waldo (in which you must find the character Waldo embedded in a picture), can you find the three 90-degree angles in figure 4.2? The first is the diving board and the diver's legs. The second is the diver's legs and upper body. And the third is the diver's upper body and arms.

The easier the dive is, the less the 90-90-90 position is required. A diver performing a forward single somersault, for example, doesn't need to achieve this position because the dive will rotate faster than necessary. For other dives, however, such as a forward 2 1/2 or 3 1/2 somersault, this position is critical for success. The more difficult the dive is, the more necessary the 90-90-90 position becomes. The diver should begin throwing when the board is fully depressed to attain the position.

Take note in figure 4.2 that the legs are straight and the diver has extended through the ankles. The push through the ankles finishes the leg push and further drives the hips upward to form the 90-90-90 position while the diver is still on the board. As we will see in the takeoff position for reverse and backward somersaulting dives, the push through the feet plays an equally important role in those dives as well.

Figure 4.2   The first essential position for *(a)* forward and *(b)* inward takeoffs: the 90-90-90 position.

Head Pop Position

Also notice in figure 4.2 that the diver is looking forward rather than down at the water. The diver does not have the chin down into the chest, as many beginning and intermediate divers make the mistake of doing. In achieving the 90-90-90 position, the diver establishes the second essential position, the **head pop position**, by popping the head up as the arms and chest move down to form the third 90-degree angle. Although there is a slight lifting of the head, the head pop is primarily achieved by keeping the head in a neutral position and fixating on a point of reference during the throw. Many divers, however, feel as if they are popping the head.

Figure 4.3 Newton's third law and the second essential position for forward and inward takeoffs during the 90-90-90 position: the head pop position.

The reason for this head pop is fourfold. The first has to do with Sir Isaac Newton and his famous third law: For every action there is an equal and opposite reaction. In response to the force of the head moving backward, the hips (i.e., center of gravity) move forward in the direction of the rotation. This reaction is better understood by examining figure 4.3.

The second reason for the head pop is spatial orientation. The vestibular system, located within the ears, helps divers determine up and down. By keeping the head up, divers maintain better spatial orientation during dive rotation. The third reason for the head pop is that keeping the head up in the dive makes it easier for divers to pick up their visual cues during dive rotation (i.e., spotting). If the chin is buried on the chest, divers are unlikely to see much during dive rotation.

Finally, the fourth reason for the head pop has to do with the entry. It is a rule of thumb in diving that if the diver's head is down getting into the dive, it will tend to be down getting out of the dive. This down head down position often causes divers to miss seeing the water or to reach under (i.e., past their water entry point) and rotate past vertical on forward and inward entries into the water.

Many divers make the mistake of popping the head too early: they pop the head and then throw instead of throw and then pop the head. By initiating the head pop too early, they don't achieve the action–reaction effect and the head usually drops down in the 90-90-90 position. In analyzing figure 4.3, notice that the head pop occurs when the legs and torso form a 90-degree angle.

C Position

The third essential position is the **C position,** which occurs when the diver forms a C shape with the body on takeoff for backward (figure 4.4a) and reverse (figure 4.4b) somersaulting dives. The C shape begins at the toes and follows through the body to the tips of the fingers, as depicted in figure 4.4. Notice that the fingertips point approximately at 2 or 3 o'clock. The more rotation the diver performs, the farther back the diver should reach. For a reverse 1 1/2, for example, a diver may reach to 1 or 2 o'clock, but for a reverse 2 1/2 or 3 1/2, the diver may reach to approximately 2 or 3 o'clock.

Some divers mistakenly conceptualize the C as beginning from the waist, instead of the toes, and extending through the arms. The C position, however,

Figure 4.4 The third essential position for *(a)* backward and *(b)* reverse takeoffs for somersaulting dives: the C position.

is formed using the entire body. It is established by pushing the hips forward rather than pulling the shoulders backward. Pulling the shoulders causes the diver to pull into the board for reverse somersaulting dives and to pull too far away from the board on backward somersaulting dives.

Notice in figure 4.4 that the chin is touching or almost touching the chest. In achieving the C position, the head remains neutral and the chest opens up to touch the chin. Many divers feel as if they are pushing the chin down, but they are actually holding it still. If the chin isn't down and touching or nearly touching the chest, the diver is pulling the head upward and backward.

During the arm swing, the arms bend approximately 90 degrees between 11 and 12 o'clock and then, most important, straighten back out to complete the fully formed C position. Finally, notice that the extension through the ankles pushes the hips forward and upward and significantly contributes to forming the C position.

Tip Position

Tipping occurs when the upward force of the springboard or force of the platform moves through the diver's center of gravity and essentially tips the diver's hips into the somersault. The fourth essential position, the **tip position**, is depicted in figure 4.5. This tipping effect occurs for somersaulting dives in all directions and acts much like the tipping that occurs when divers are in a somersaulting belt and being tipped at each somersault by the spotter (i.e., the spotter pulls on the rope at each somersault to tip the hips up to increase the speed of rotation) or when a coach hand spots a diver on a dryland somersault.

The diver must keep the center of gravity over the end of the springboard or platform long enough for the tipping effect to occur. Notice in figure 4.5 for the forward *(a)* and inward *(b)* takeoffs and in figure 4.6 for the backward *(a)* and reverse *(b)* takeoffs that the diver's hips are over the end of the springboard as the board begins to move upward.

As mentioned earlier in this chapter, many diving coaches and divers mistakenly believe that divers should wait until after leaving the springboard or platform to throw for a somersaulting dive. They believe that throwing any sooner will cut off the height of the dive. As the preceding figures make clear, this belief is incorrect. By waiting until after leaving the springboard or platform, the diver will fail to achieve the C position, the 90-90-90 position, and the tipping action. *It is the diver's center of gravity that needs to elevate, not the diver's upper body.*

Figure 4.5 The fourth essential position for *(a)* forward and *(b)* inward takeoffs: the tip position.

Figure 4.6 The fourth essential position for *(a)* backward and *(b)* reverse takeoffs: the tip position.

Because the platform doesn't move upward like the springboard, how does it tip the diver's center of gravity into the somersault? As the legs extend and push into the platform, the platform pushes back with an equal and opposite reaction. The force of this reaction extends through the center of gravity, thereby creating a tipping effect. The direction of the push of the legs matches the direction of the somersault. For forward somersaulting dives *(a)*, the feet push forward into the board or platform. For backward somersaulting dives *(b)*, the feet push backward. For reverses *(c)*, the feet push backward (i.e., reverse direction), and for inwards *(d)*, the feet push inward into the board. This concept is shown in figure 4.7.

Figure 4.7 The direction of the push of the legs and somersault: *(a)* forward, *(b)* backward, *(c)* reverse, *(d)* inward.

Tilt Position

Timing is everything. This expression is certainly true in the sport of diving. For example, divers must be in time with the rhythm of the board during the forward approach. Timing is no less important in the takeoff and achieving the fifth essential position, called the tilt position. **Tilting** is the act of shifting the center of gravity slightly away from the springboard or platform during takeoff so the dive moves safely away from the board (figure 4.8).

Figure 4.8 The fifth essential position for takeoffs: *(a-b)* reverse tilt and *(c-d)* inward tilt positions.

Timing is important during tilting because if tilting is done too early, the dive goes out and not up, and if done too late, the dive is too close to the board. The degree of tilting also is critical. Tilting too much causes the dive to move too far away from the board. And tilting too little causes the dive to be too close to the board. To better understand the concept of tilting, recall that two points determine a line. In the case of tilting, our two points are approximately the ankles and the hips (i.e., near the center of gravity). Now draw an imaginary line from the ankles to the hips using the positioning depicted in figure 4.8, which depicts the fifth essential position for the takeoff, the **tilt position**, specifically the reverse tilt (a-b) and the inward tilt (c-d). This line is the vector (direction of movement) in which the dive moves away from the board.

The keys to performing a perfect tilt are practice, patience, and, honestly, more patience. In the preceding section, we talked about tipping and how the center of gravity needs to be over the tip of the board during takeoff. Only at the last millisecond should the center of gravity tilt. *This may be one of the greatest challenges in diving: waiting to perform the tilt position at the correct moment.* Tilting is the last thing to do on takeoff, but for many divers it is often the first thing they do. Consider, for example, inward somersaulting dives. For many divers, as soon as they begin oscillating or moving their arms in the backward press, the first thing they do is slightly shift (tilt) their hips backward. They do this to feel more comfortable, safe, or assured that the dive won't be too close to the board. Unfortunately, they also can be assured that they won't perform a good dive because titling too early causes divers to scoot straight back, as though someone had pulled the rug out from under them.

Ironically, tilting too early to move away from the springboard or platform often has the opposite effect and causes divers to be too close. How is this possible? Consider the inward somersaulting dive again. The correct sequence for performing an inward somersaulting dive is press-throw-tip-tilt. The last action in this sequence is the tilt. For divers who tilt too early, the sequence is press-tilt-throw-tip. In this incorrect sequence, the tip is the last action to occur. Because the tilt is out of sequence, the loading of the board and the tipping effect are minimized, causing dive rotation to be slower than needed. To compensate for the early tilt and slow rotation, these divers often lean into the springboard or platform at the precise moment when they should tilt away. Patience is a virtue, especially when establishing the tilt position.

The push through the ankles and feet is extremely important for the tilt position because the ankle snap helps shift the center of gravity up and away immediately before takeoff from the springboard or platform (Miller, 2001). The sidebar Takeoff Drills offers some excellent drills for learning the five essential springboard and platform takeoff positions.

Armstand Takeoffs

The five essential takeoff positions apply to armstand somersaulting dives; however, the sequence of the positions is different: the tilt comes before the tip. For armstand backward and reverse somersaulting dives, the diver establishes an armstand position (figure 4.9a), places the head in a neutral position and shrugs up with the shoulders (figure 4.9b), tilts the center of gravity slightly away from the platform while the keeping the shoulders over the hands (figure 4.9c), opens to a C position while opening the shoulders (figure 4.9d), and then pushes through the shoulders and arms for the tip (figure 4.9e).

For armstand forward somersaulting dives, the sequence is similar to backward and reverse armstands except instead of a C position the diver performs a pike position (figure 4.10a) and after the tip (figure 4.10b) performs the 90-90-90 and head pop positions (figure 4.10c).

The sidebar Takeoff Drills outlines some exceptionally simple but highly effective drills for helping divers learn the five essential springboard and platform takeoff positions.

Figure 4.9 The takeoff sequence for backward and reverse armstand somersaulting dives.

Figure 4.10 The takeoff sequence for forward armstand somersaulting dives.

Takeoff Drills

1. *Slow-motion modeling.* The diver models the 90-90-90, head pop, and C positions with coach supervision. Incorrect modeling leads to incorrect dive performance. Consequently, both coach and diver must pay attention to details. For example, when modeling the 90-90-90 position, the heels should be up, all 90-degree angles should be clearly demonstrated, and the head should be up with the eyes looking straight ahead. Most divers tend to drop their heads when first modeling this drill.

2. *C position into wall.* The diver stands facing a wall approximately 5 or 6 inches (13 to 15 cm) back (figure 4.11). The diver establishes the C position by reaching back with the arms and then lifting the heels up and pushing the hips forward into the wall. This is an excellent drill for teaching the proper way to form the C and tilt positions.

3. *Somersaults on mat.* This drill helps divers practice takeoff positions in all directions while teaching them how and when to tip and tilt the center of gravity. Use a folded panel mat for takeoffs and a landing mat for landings. Do not use a solid surface such as a wood platform for takeoffs. Use elevated mat for takeoffs for beginners.

4. *Hand-spotted somersaults.* This drill, in which the diver is spotted by the coach, is good for learning all five essential positions for all directions of somersaulting, especially reverse and inward. The diver keeps the abdomen firmly pressed into the coach's spotting hand during the knee bend for inward somersaults so that the center of gravity does not tilt early. For more information on hand spotting, see Gabriel (2007).

Figure 4.11 C position into wall drill.

5. *Standing dive and somersault.* The diver does open pike dives and somersaults on 1-meter springboard in all directions. This is a good drill for learning the five essential takeoff positions.

Connections

Connection is the term diving coaches use to refer to the process of collapsing into a tuck or pike position. For example, a diving coach might say, "I want you to connect sooner into your backward 2 1/2 somersault tuck." In this case, the coach wants the diver to get into the tuck sooner. There are essential connections for somersaulting dives and for twisting dives. Let's begin by considering the three essential connections for somersaulting dives. The first is the quick connect.

Somersault Connections

The **quick connect** is the process of getting into a dive as quickly as possible after leaving the springboard or platform. Recall my story at the beginning of this chapter and my epiphany regarding my teammate's quick connect into his forward 3 ½ somersaulting dive. The advantage of the quick connect is that it allows divers to perform more of the dive during the ascent. Many divers and diving coaches hold the misconception that the dive should be performed on the descent (i.e., they should jump as high as possible in the air and then begin the dive). However, doing so makes performance more difficult. A diver has only so much air time: the time going up (ascent) and the time going down (the descent). Waiting to reach the apex of the jump to initiate the dive wastes valuable air time.

Elite divers are extremely efficient at using ascent time. For example, analysis of a male elite diver's forward 3 1/2 somersault in the pike position indicates that 2 1/2 somersaults are completed before beginning the descent! So when does the diver begin the quick connect? The answer: as soon as possible. The first essential position for connections, the quick connect (figure 4.12), should begin as soon as the diver has extended through the legs and ankles and the

Figure 4.12   The first essential position for the springboard and platform connection: the quick connect.

diver's feet are off the board. The quick connect is applicable to somersaulting dives in all directions on both springboard and platform.

The quick connect involves both timing and speed—it needs to be performed soon (timing) and quickly (speed). A diver, for example, might connect rapidly but begin performing the connection too late after leaving the board. Or, a diver might initiate the connection at the correct time but perform the connection too slowly. Connection speed is affected by two factors: physical conditioning and Newton's third law of motion. A diver, for example, who can't perform a single hanging pike-up or who is inflexible will be slow connecting into a somersaulting dive, particularly in the pike position, because of a lack of physical readiness. And as we will subsequently see, a diver using incorrect mechanics will be slow connecting because of a failure to take advantage of Newton's third law of motion regarding action–reaction.

10 O'Clock Throw Connect

The second essential position for connection is the 10 o'clock throw for forward and inward somersaulting dives as well as twisting dives that require multiple somersaults, such as a forward 2 1/2 somersault with a full twist out (i.e., the twist is done at the second somersault, as opposed to in, when the twist is done getting into the dive). The **10 o'clock throw** involves throwing past the legs all the way to 10 o'clock, as depicted in figure 4.13. To conceptualize this throw, imagine the hands of a clock. The diver starts with the arms straight at 12 o'clock and throws past the legs (i.e., past 1, 2, 3, 4, 5, 6, 7, 8, and 9 o'clock) until the hands of the clock point to 10 o'clock, at which point the diver connects into the dive by either grabbing the legs for a tuck or wrapping the arms underneath the legs for a pike. Many divers make the mistake of throwing well short of 10 o'clock, typically to only 5 or 6 o'clock.

Figure 4.13 The second essential position for the springboard and platform connection for forward and inward somersaulting dives: the 10 o'clock throw.

The 10 o'clock throw makes it easier for divers to gain faster rotation and establish a quick connect. How rapidly the quick connect occurs is influenced by Newton's third law, the speed of the arm throw, and physical conditioning. The action of throwing to 10 o'clock with the arms and upper body is countered by an equal and opposite reaction of the legs moving into the upper body. The faster the throw is, the faster the legs connect into the upper body. Divers, however, with poor flexibility and weak core strength will squander valuable air time struggling to connect into a tight pike. By now it should be obvious that physical readiness is a necessary prerequisite for performing the essentials elements of diving.

To emphasize the importance of physical readiness, consider the story of one of my divers who struggled with a 107B. Her hurdle and takeoff positions were exceptional, but she nevertheless struggled to make her dive. So she set a goal to work on her 10 o'clock throw and flexibility. She learned to perceive stretching as an important part of her practice rather than a frivolous social activity done before and after practice. She worked so hard on her stretching that her T-shirt would be soaking wet. Her efforts paid off. Instead of taking almost two somersaults connecting into a pike, she was able to effortlessly and quickly collapse into a deep pike and perform more of the dive on the ascent. She transformed her 107B from her worst optional dive into her best.

C-Circle-Slam Connect

The 10 o'clock throw is the connection for forward and inward somersaulting dives. For backward and reverse somersaulting dives, the connection occurs through the third essential position for the connection: the C-circle-slam. The **C-circle-slam** involves first establishing the C position outlined earlier in this chapter and then circling the arms either behind the body or along the plane of the body and slamming the upper body downward.

Why slam the upper body downward in the opposite direction of a backward rotating dive? The answer, again, is Newton's third law: For every action there is an equal and opposite reaction. By slamming the upper body downward, the equal and opposite reaction is for the legs to rapidly move upward into the torso to form the tuck or pike position, as shown in figure 4.14. The speed of

Figure 4.14 The third essential position for the springboard and platform connection for backward and reverse somersaulting dives: the C-circle-slam.

the connection is affected by the force of the slam and the diver's flexibility and core strength.

The slam is really a downward action rather than the forward action many divers mistakenly conceptualize. The diver should feel as though the upper body is being thrown down to 3 o'clock, much like throwing for a forward somersaulting dive. The slam is ballistic; hence, the word *slam*. If asked to slam a door, you wouldn't slowly and gently push the door shut. You would forcefully and rapidly throw it shut. The same is true with the C-circle-slam connect. The entire action is forceful and rapid.

This ballistic action, however, can't occur without first establishing the C position. Trying to slam without the C position is like trying to throw a baseball without first bringing the arm back behind the body. To create the C position, the arms should swing rapidly and close together along the midpoint of the body in the press, as shown in figure 4.15. This rapid and narrow arm swing opens up the hips to create the C position. The arms should also rapidly circle into the tuck or pike position to complete the connection.

The sidebar Somersault and Twist Connection Drills offers some effective drills for helping divers learn not only the correct action for a C-circle-slam, but also the intensity and force associated with this type of connection. When rehearsing the C-circle-slam on dryland, divers should be forceful, extend

Figure 4.15 A view of the arm swing in the press for creating the C position.

Figure 4.16 Three different arm movements for connecting into backward and reverse somersaulting dives: *(a)* behind the body; *(b)* along the body; *(c)* forward.

through the ankles, lift the heels off the ground, keep the chin neutral (i.e., on the chest), reach to 2 or 3 o'clock with straight arms, and extend the hips forward.

Elite divers vary in how much circle occurs in this type of connect. Some divers circle behind their bodies (figure 4.16a), some circle along the plane of their body (figure 4.16b), and some don't circle at all but, rather, throw their arms and hands forward for their legs as if throwing for a forward somersault (figure 4.16c).

So, what is the correct circle action? It depends on the diver and what works best for that particular athlete. Some athletes effectively connect with a circle action, whereas others find more success with no circle action but rather a forward throw. The best plan of action is to experiment and see which action is most effective for the athlete.

Twist Connections

Many divers and coaches erroneously believe that twisting is difficult, perhaps because they never learned how to correctly connect into twisting dives. The truth is that twisting is easy. In fact, if divers can perform a good full twisting jump, they have accomplished about 90 percent of what is required to twist. There are four essential positions for connecting into backward and reverse twists. The best way to conceptualize backward and reverse twisting is to think of the connection as a smooth flowing sequence of these four essential positions. The four positions are reach (figure 4.17a), drop (figure 4.17b), turn (figure 4.17c), and close (figure 4.17d).

The most effective way to learn this twist sequence is to practice dryland slow-motion rehearsal. As the positions are mastered, divers can gradually increase the speed of rehearsal until it matches the actual speed of performance on the springboard and platform.

▪ Movement 1: Reach to 12 o'clock with straight arms (figure 4.17a).

- Movement 2: Drop the lead twist arm to the side and keep it straight (figure 4.17*b*).
- Movement 3: Do a half twist to a T arm position (figure 4.17*c*).
- Movement 4: Pull the arms into a twist position (figure 4.17*d*).

If the diver twists to the left, the lead hand is the left hand. If the diver twists to the right, the lead hand is the right hand. Beginning divers who don't know

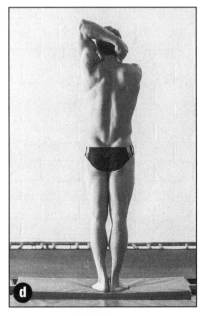

Figure 4.17 The four essential positions for the springboard and platform connection into backward and reverse twisting dives: *(a)* reach; *(b)* drop; *(c)* turn; *(d)* close.

which way they twist should stand on a mat with their arms in a T position, jump in the air, and, without thinking, do a full twisting jump. Most divers instinctively twist in the direction they find most comfortable and natural.

Focus points for a slow-motion rehearsal and actual performance are *patience*, *neutral head*, and *tight core*. Many divers rush into initiating the twist by skipping positions 1, 2, and 3 and going directly to position 4. Patience is a virtue in diving, especially when initiating all four movements. One of the best twisting divers I ever observed said that when he twisted, he looked at his lead hand into the twist and focused on keeping his core tight. When connecting into a twist, the diver is turning not just the shoulders but, more important, the hips. Many divers connect into a twist with a loose core and the head thrown back. Keeping the core tight and following the hand with the eyes keeps the head neutral and allows the entire body to twist as one solid unit around the center of gravity. In this case, everyone is on the same bus. In other words, the head, shoulders, and hips are all moving in the same direction.

The forward twist connect is similar to the backward twist connection. In fact, ten meter platform Olympic silver medalist Scott Donie used to conceptualize the start of a backward 1 1/2 somersault with 3 1/2 twists as a backward half twist and then performing a forward 1 1/2 with three twists. For forward twisting dives, the diver starts with arms overhead (figure 4.18*a*), then snaps from a slight pike (figure 4.18*b*), to a straight body position with arms in a T position (figure 4.18*c*), and then pulls the arms into the twist position (figure 4.18*d*).

The most important drill to learn for the forward twist is the forward somersault in straight position in which the body is straight immediately off the board. Because a diver can't twist very well until the body is straight, learning this drill is critical for learning a forward twisting dive. Chapter 5 discusses in greater detail forming the straight position.

Figure 4.18 The twist connect for a forward somersault with twist.

Connecting into a twist coming *out* of a forward somersaulting dive such as a full twisting 2 1/2 somersault in the pike position is similar to the forward twist action in figure 4.18. The diver typically spots the water just prior to the 1 1/2 somersault and then snaps to a straight body position with arms in a T position while connecting into the twist. The diver uses the snap action to help generate the twist rather than waiting to establish the straight body position and then twist. In other words, the diver begins the twist during the snap.

All dive categories are important, but perhaps none more so than the twist category because, when performing six optional dives, many divers elect to double up on twisters. When you add in the voluntary dive, many divers actually perform three twisting dives. Because twisting figures prominently in most divers' lists, it is important to learn the twisting action correctly. The How to Teach section highlights a simple but incredibly effective progression for teaching divers to perform a backward somersault with 1 1/2 twists in the twisting belt.

How to Teach Twisting With A Twisting Belt

In teaching a backward somersault with 1 1/2 twists, many coaches mistakenly begin by having the diver do a backward somersault straight. The problem with this approach is that from the outset the diver associates twisting with somersaulting. Consequently, a common problem for many divers when they attempt to add more twists is that they also add more (i.e., too much) somersault. Too much somersault causes the diver to finish the twist too late to effectively square out and stop the twist. In teaching twisting, then, never use the S word—somersault. The twist should be completed so the feet point to approximately 5 o'clock or earlier so the diver has time to initiate the square-out.

During the progression, the arms are overhead and no arm swing is used during the jump to ensure that the diver initiates each step from the magic position. Each step in the progression is preceded by three jumps. Divers should progress to the next step only once they have mastered the preceding step. They can use a twisting belt or a somersault belt with the ropes wrapped around the waist. Following is the progression.

- Perform three jumps with the arms overhead and no arm swing.
- Perform three jumps and then drop lead twist arm and perform a full twisting jump.
- Perform three jumps and then finish to a backdrop in a straight position. The spotter keeps the diver from landing on the trampoline bed in the twisting belt. The diver should NOT progress to step 4 until the straight backdrop has been mastered.
- Perform three jumps and then throw a full twisting backdrop using the four-movement twisting sequence in figure 4.17. The diver must follow the lead hand with the eyes, keep the core tight, and turn the hips. The spotter keeps the diver from actually landing on the trampoline bed in the twisting belt.

I used this progression to teach hundreds of beginning divers how to twist, most of whom learned to twist within 5 to 10 minutes. I call it down-and-in twisting because on the third bounce, the diver lifts the feet, throws the lead arm laterally and then *down* towards the center of the trampoline bed, and then brings the hands *in* to the body to twist. I thought I was teaching something revolutionary until I discovered an archived video on twisting by Charlie Pond, developer of the famous Pond twisting belt. The name of the video was *Look-In Twisting*. It wasn't titled *Down-and-In Twisting*, but close enough!

At no time during the progression is the diver asked to perform a backward somersault, and in fact, somersaulting is never mentioned. However, very often when divers attempt the full twisting backdrop, their feet magically pop up and they flip into a somersault (which is why this progression needs to be done in a twisting belt), even though they weren't trying to somersault. This, of course, is what the coach hopes will ultimately happen. The diver is then asked to stay in the twist longer to complete 1 1/2 twists. If he doesn't flip over, have him lift his feet higher on the backdrop, throw the lead arm down harder, or do both. If he gets too much somersault, regress to the full twisting backdrop.

Down-and-in twisting is much different from the up-and-back twisting that many diving coaches teach, in which divers reach *up* (to initiate the back somersault) and pull *back* with the throw arm and shoulders to twist. If more twisting is required, these divers simply pull back more with their shoulders, creating additional and unnecessary rotation and little twisting. This up-and-back twisting action explains why many divers, for example, can perform a 5253B on a 10-meter platform, but not a 5237D.

In teaching the forward somersault with one twist, the diver needs to learn a forward somersault in the straight position with the arms in a T position. Once this position has been established, it is easy for divers to learn the forward twist connect. The following chapter will discuss the straight position in greater detail.

Because using a trampoline and belt is the best means for teaching twisting, consider purchasing a trampoline, spotting rig, and belt if you don't own one or more of these apparatuses. Coaches who go this route should make sure to get certified through their country's national governing body (e.g., USA Diving in the U.S.) so that they learn to spot safely and efficiently. Many divers and coaches, however, fight the good fight with limited facilities, and this book is written with these persevering people in mind. So, what if you have only a 1-meter springboard and water but no trampoline and no spotting belt? No problem. You can still teach twisting.

Many simple and effective drills exist for teaching twisting. They are so simple, in fact, that at first glance they might seem ineffective. Don't be fooled. And don't overlook what is available to you. The side of the pool, the end of the 1-meter springboard, and a basic landing mat may be all you have and all you need. Make the most of what you have. Where there is a will, there is a way. Champions find ways to succeed. The following sidebar outlines some effective drills for learning how to twist without using a trampoline and spotting belt.

How to Teach Twisting Without A Twisting Belt

Using a Landing Mat

- Half twist jump with the arms in a T position the entire time
- Full twist jump with the arms in a T position the entire time
- Full twist jump pulling the arms into the twist position after a half twist (finish with a T arm position)
- Half twist jump to a seat drop with the arms in a T position (use hands on landing)

- Full twist jump to seat drop pulling the arms into a twist position after a half twist (use hands on landing)
- Half twist jump to the back with the arms in a T position
- Half twist jump to the stomach with the arms in a T position
- Full twist jump to the back pulling the arms into a twist position after a half twist (land with the arms in a T position)
- Full twist jump to the abdomen pulling the arms into a twist position after a half twist (land with the arms in a T position)

Using the Poolside

- Divers must jump safely away from the poolside and use a solid nonslick surface to safely perform these drills. Coach can spot if necessary.
- Forward and backward half twist jump with the arms in a T position the entire time
- Forward and backward full twist jump with the arms in a T position the entire time
- Forward and backward full twist jump pulling the arms into a twist position after a half twist (finish with a T arm position)
- Forward full twist dive—Start with the arms in a T position and no arm swing.
- Back dive with a half twist—Start with the arms directly overhead, use no arm swing, and use a down-and-in action to move arms to a T position.
- Back dive with 1 1/2 twist—Perform like a back dive with a half twist, and pull the arms in after a half twist.

Using the 1-Meter Springboard

- Half and full twist jumps with the arms in a T position the entire time
- Double twist jump, standing with the arms in a T position (pull the arms into a twist at a half or full twist)
- Backward and reverse half and full twist jump with the arms in a T position the entire time
- Backward and reverse 1 1/2 twist jump (pull the arms into a twist at the half twist)
- Backward and reverse dive with a half twist—Start with the arms directly overhead, use no arm swing, and use a down-and-in action to move arms to a T position (close arms for entry). Reverse can be done standing.
- Backward and reverse dive with a half twist and arm swing press
- Front dive with half twist, standing without and then with a press
- Front dive with full twist, standing without and then with a press
- Backward somersault straight with a press
- Reverse somersault straight with a press (standing and then with an approach)
- Forward somersault straight with a press (standing and then with an approach)

Other connection drills are provided in the following sidebar Somersault and Twist Connection Drills. Connection drills also can be viewed in educational DVDs (Huber, 2001, 2007).

Somersault and Twist Connection Drills

1. *Standing forward somersault open tuck and pike.* The diver performs a 10 o'clock throw connect on a trampoline or 1-meter springboard and does not grab the legs. The arms are straight on the throw and throw past the legs.

2. *Open pike somersault quick connect.* The diver tries to put the chest on the legs before the feet leave the trampoline bed. This is a highly effective drill.

3. *Backward and reverse somersaults in open tuck and open pike positions.* The diver C-circle-slams on a trampoline or 1-meter springboard but does not grab. This is a good drill for learning the action–reaction principle and attaining tuck and pike (figure 4.19) positions without using the arms to pull into a tuck or pike.

4. *Pike and snap somersault.* The diver initiates a somersault, slightly pikes, and snaps to a straight position with the feet at 12 o'clock (figure 4.20). This can be done standing and then with a double bounce on a trampoline or an approach on a 1-meter springboard.

5. *Chamois throw.* The diver stands on a mat with the hands at 12 o'clock and holding a chamois. The diver rapidly bends over, throws past the legs, and tries to throw the chamois to 10 o'clock.

Figure 4.19 Backward and reverse somersaults in open tuck and open pike drill.

(continued)

Somersault and Twist Connection Drills *(continued)*

Figure 4.20 Pike and snap somersault drill.

6. *Ball throw.* The diver holds a ball with both hands down by the thighs and forcefully throws it overhead and back into a wall (approximately 2 or 3 o'clock) while pushing through the ankles, elevating the heels, and extending the hips forward. This is a great drill for learning to use the arms, hips, and ankles for achieving the C position.

7. *Hit and slam.* The diver throws the hands rapidly backward forcefully hitting a mat held approximately 12 inches (30 cm) behind the head by the coach and then quickly throws the torso downward while quickly raising one leg into a tuck. This simulates a ballistic arm swing and C-slam.

8. *Hanging C snap.* The diver hangs from a bar, arches the back, and snaps the legs upward. This is a good drill for feeling the C slam action. Drill is best done on a hanging bar rather than mounted wall rack.

9. *Forward and backward twisting jumps.* This drill is cited in the sidebar How to Teach Twisting Without a Twisting Belt but is an excellent twist connection drill for beginning divers. The focus should be on a tight core, a straight body line, and the twist position.

10. *Full twisting backdrop.* The diver does a full twist to the back on a trampoline or landing mat. This move must first be learned in a spotting belt and then spotted by a coach. This is an easy and effective drill for learning how to twist without generating a somersault. However, an inexperienced diver can easily generate too much somersault and land unsafely. The diver should perform this first without an arm swing (figure 4.21) and then with an arm swing after demonstrating proficiency.

Figure 4.21   Full twisting backdrop drill.

Armstand Connections

Connections for armstand somersaulting dives are similar to the connections already mentioned. The only difference is that for backward and reverse armstand somersaulting dives, there is no circle in the C-circle-slam connect. Instead of a circle, the arms move forward in front of the body. The connection into armstand twisting dives is the same as it is for springboard twisting dives. See the sidebar Armstand Connection Drills for additional information and photos.

Armstand Connection Drills

1. *Armstand backward fall to stomach onto a landing mat.* Diver kips up and keeps arms and body straight coming off platform.
2. *Armstand backward half twist to back onto a landing mat* (figure 4.22). Diver keeps arms into ears and straight off platform and during twist, and watches the end of platform during kip.

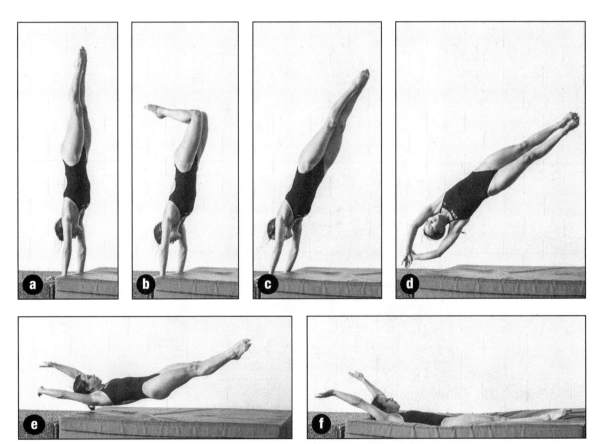

Figure 4.22 Armstand backward half twist to back drill.

3. *Armstand backward half twist to a seat drop onto a landing mat.* Keep arms into ears and straight off platform and during twist. Finish to seat drop with arms in T position after completing a half twist.

4. *Armstand backward fall to the feet on a 1-meter platform* (figure 4.23). Establish straight body position prior to leaving platform. Keep arms straight and into ears. Watch end of platform to keep head neutral.

Figure 4.23 Armstand backward fall to feet drill.

(continued)

Armstand Connection Drills *(continued)*

5. *Armstand backward half twist to the feet on a 1-meter platform* (figure 4.24). Keep arms into ears and straight off platform and during twist. Lift arms up and watch end of platform during kip and initiation of twist.

Figure 4.24 Armstand backward half twist to feet on 1-meter platform drill.

6. *Armstand backward 1 1/2 somersaults with half twist and 1 1/2 twists* (figure 4.25) *to the feet in a spotting belt on a trampoline*. Fantastic dryland preparatory drill and not as difficult as it looks for diver or spotter. Important for the diver to forcefully lift the arms up before initiating the twist.

Figure 4.25 Armstand backward 1 1/2 twist in spotting belt drill.

(continued)

Armstand Connection Drills *(continued)*

7. *Armstand backward half twist somersault on a 3-meter* (figure 4.26) *or 5-meter platform.* Effective drill for learning to separate the kip action from the twist. Diver kips while looking at end of platform, lifts arms up and then twists with straight body position. This action is similar to a swivel hips on trampoline where the diver must first bring the arms up, straighten the body, and then twist.

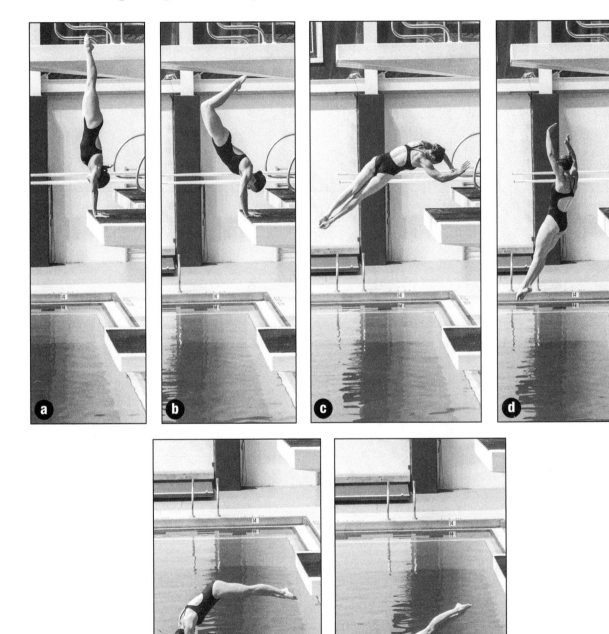

Figure 4.26 Armstand backward half twist somersault on 3-meter platform drill.

8. *Armstand backward snap to feet onto landing mat.* Good drill for practicing the kip into a backward somersaulting dive such as backward armstand with 2 somersaults.

9. *Armstand forward pike snap to the back onto a landing mat* (figure 4.27). Good drill for learning to pike snap early while on the platform.

Figure 4.27 Armstand forward pike snap to back drill.

(continued)

Armstand Connection Drills *(continued)*

10. *Armstand forward pike snap to the feet from an elevated mat.* Both this and preceding drill are good for learning the kip into a forward somersaulting dive such as an armstand forward somersault with 2 somersaults.

11. *Armstand forward pike snap to the feet on a 1-meter platform* (figure 4.28). Notice that the diver shrugs through the shoulders during the snap and keeps the head neutral.

Figure 4.28 Armstand forward pike snap to feet on 1-meter platform drill.

CHAPTER 5

Positions, Spotting, and Come-Outs

Chapters 2, 3, and 4 considered mainly everything that occurs *on* the board. The topic of connections in chapter 4 makes for a smooth transition to three additional aspects of diving that occur *off* the board: positions, spotting, and come-outs. Although attaining a good hurdle is important for performing a good dive, what occurs in the air can negatively or positively affect the dive, even when the hurdle and takeoff are less than perfect. Let's take a look.

But first, a brief story . . .

In an extremely close final of the men's 10 meter at the U.S. Olympic Trials, a well-known diver got a rather poor start on a reverse 3 1/2 somersaults in the tuck position. As he came off the platform, I am sure many spectators thought, "Oh, he isn't going to make the dive. He isn't going to make the Olympic team." The only thing he had going for him on the dive was an incredibly small tuck. He squeezed his tuck, waited until the last minute (he must have waited to smell chlorine), kicked vertically above the water, smoldered the entry, scored straight 9s on his dive—and punched his ticket to the Olympic Games.

Positions

A tight position, whether it is tuck, pike, or straight, can be very forgiving. In other words, a good position can make up for a mediocre takeoff, as it did for the diver in the Olympic trials. Let's look at how to achieve great tuck, pike, straight, and twist positions.

Tuck Position

For a **tuck position**, the feet are together but the knees are shoulder-width apart (but not outside the shoulders) so that the lower legs form a V as depicted in figure 5.1a. Separating the knees allows the diver to round the back and gain a more compact tuck. Notice in figure 5.1 that both the lower and upper back are rounded (figure 5.1*b*). This compact tuck draws the body closer to the horizontal axis resulting in a faster rotation speed. Separating the knees also provides a window that allows the diver to both spot and track visual cues during the dive rotation. The concepts of spotting and tracking are discussed later in this chapter.

Even though the knees are apart in the tuck, they are initially together so that the diver throws with narrow arms. As the knees draw into the upper body, the diver then separates them. If the knees are apart at the beginning of the arm throw, the diver will throw incorrectly with wide arms toward the legs.

Figure 5.1   Correct tuck position.

Notice in figure 5.1 that the hand grab is approximately 2 to 4 inches (5 to 10 cm) above the ankles. This low grab allows the diver to pull the heels into the tuck. Notice also that the elbows are into the body rather than sticking out in the incorrect tuck position depicted in figure 5.2. Other mistakes noticeable in figure 5.2 are the knees outside the shoulders, the hands too high on the legs, the feet apart and flat, the lower and upper back flat instead of rounded, the heels sticking out, and the eyes looking down, not out.

Before grabbing the legs in the tuck, the diver should be fairly compact so that little effort is required to squeeze into a small tuck. This is accomplished by rounding the lower and upper back before connecting, using good mechanics (e.g., a 10 o'clock throw and a C-circle-slam), and developing good flexibility and core strength. An analysis of the 407C on 10-meter platform, for example, reveals that elite divers are approximately 80 to 90 percent into the tuck position before grabbing their legs.

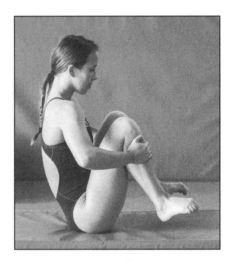

Figure 5.2   Incorrect tuck position.

Pike Position

A compact pike position is equally as important as a compact tuck in contributing to an outstanding dive and making up for a poor takeoff. A tight **pike position** should have the abdomen on the legs, the arms wrapped under the legs, and the head neutral (i.e., the chin not buried on the chest), as depicted in figure 5.3. Notice that the back is flat, the legs are into the elbows and straight, and the

Figure 5.3   Correct pike position.

feet are pointed. A good pike position should be flat with little or no rounding of the back. Achieving this position requires diligent work on acquiring good flexibility.

Some common mistakes divers make in the pike position are hands grabbing legs, elbows sticking out, feet flat, (figure 5.4a), back humped, and chin on chest (figure 5.4b).

The diver should be 80 to 90 percent into the pike before wrapping the arms under the legs and pulling into the pike. Like the tuck position, this is achieved by using good mechanics (e.g., a 10 o'clock throw and a C-circle-slam) and developing good flexibility and core strength. Many elite divers slightly split their legs (figure 5.5a) or bow the knees out (figure 5.5b) to attain a slightly tighter pike and to more easily spot and track while somersaulting, as they do in the V tuck position.

Figure 5.4 Incorrect pike positions.

Figure 5.5 Pike position with *(a)* split legs and bowed *(b)* legs.

Straight Position

The **straight position** involves attaining a straight, tight body line from head to toes. To form this position, divers should focus on keeping the knees locked, the legs squeezed together, the gluteus maximus muscles engaged, the hips rolled down and under, the lower abdominal muscles tight, the head neutral, and the toes pointed, as shown in figure 5.6. The straight position is used for forward (101A), backward (201A), reverse (301A), inward (401A), and half twist (5111A) dives and all twisting dives.

Every diver needs to proficiently perform forward (101A), backward (201A), reverse (301A), and inward (401A) dives straight as well as forward (102A), backward (202A), and reverse (302A) somersaults straight. At national and international competitions, for example, elite divers routinely practice backward and reverse somersaults straight because these basic dives allow them to focus on and practice the essential elements in the more difficult optional dives. The reverse somersault straight, for example, requires, among other things, forming the magic, C, tip, and tilt positions as well as maintaining a tight core and spotting the water.

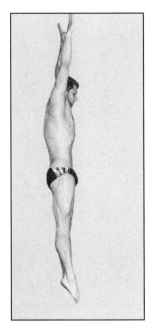

Figure 5.6 Correct straight position.

Many divers can perform a 202A (usually because their coaches have them learn it in preparation for a backward twister). These same divers, however, often have never attempted a 302A. Granted, the 302A is more difficult than the 202A, but after practicing the 302A for even a few days, most divers can perform it with a moderate level of proficiency. The 302A should be part of every diver's workout regimen. The 202A and 302A are often referred to as back and reverse **hollow somersaults** because, when performed as lead-ups, they are most effective for transfer of learning when done with a slight concave position as depicted figure 5.7.

On takeoff, the diver must extend through the knees and ankles, keep the lower abdominal muscles tight, lift the toes, spot the water, and keep the head neutral to form the hollow position. All of these actions are critical for success in more difficult reverse and backward somersaulting and twisting dives. By practicing the simple hollow somersault, divers can focus solely on these actions (i.e., not be distracted by a more difficult dive) until they become automatic and incorporated (transferred) within the performance of the more difficult dives.

Figure 5.7 Reverse hollow somersault position.

The 102A is an equally important preparatory skill for learning forward twist-ing optional dives such as the 5132, 5134, and 5136. To perform these dives correctly, the diver must learn to establish a straight body position immediately off the board. The 102A is a fun and interesting physics lesson because, when first performing it, divers must do what seems counterintuitive: lift the head and upper body. Again, Newton's third law of motion comes into play. The force of the head and upper body moving up is countered by the equal and opposite reaction of the lower body moving up, as shown in figure 5.8.

When first attempting a 102A, most divers throw the head and upper body down causing an equal and opposite reaction of the legs moving forward into a pike position, as shown in figure 5.9. Here again, Newton's third law comes into play, only in this case it causes a pike rather than a straight position. This pike position delays the initiation of the twist because the diver can't begin twisting until the body gets straight. Notice how much later the diver establishes a straight position in figure 5.9 compared to the diver in figure 5.8.

Figure 5.8   The sequence for performing a correct forward somersault in the straight position.

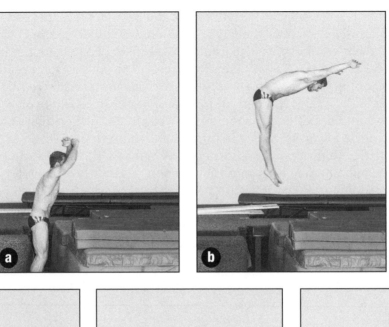

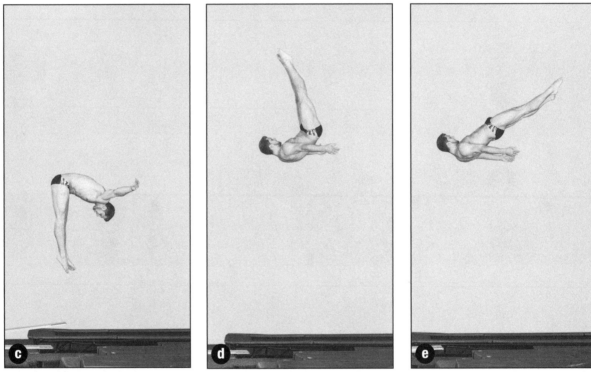

Figure 5.9 An incorrect sequence for performing a forward somersault in the straight position.

Twist Position

There are two equally effective twist positions. In figure 5.10, the throw hand into the twist is placed behind the neck and the opposite hand is placed under the chin and on the chest. In figure 5.11, both hands are placed under the chin and on the chest. The smaller the tuck position is (i.e., the closer to the horizontal axis), the faster the rotation will be. Similarly, the tighter the twist position is (i.e., the closer to the vertical axis), the faster the twist will be. Squeezing the legs and gluteus maximus muscles together and squeezing the arms and hands into the body forms a tighter twist position and increases twist speed.

Figure 5.10 The twist position with the top hand behind the head.

Figure 5.11 The twist position with both hands under the chin.

The sidebar Position Drills offers some excellent drills for learning the four dive positions.

Position Drills

1. *Tuck pick-up.* The diver sits in a tight tuck position on a mat, rolls back, and is picked up by the back of the heels (figure 5.12). The diver must maintain the tight tuck while being lifted.

2. *Hanging tuck hold.* The diver hangs from a bar, bends the knees, lifts the knees up into the shoulders, rounds the lower and upper back, and holds the tuck position (figure 5.13). During this drill the legs come up together and then split at the top to form a V position and the feet are tucked under.

3. *Hanging pike hold.* This is the same as the hanging tuck hold

Figure 5.12 The tuck pick-up drill.

Figure 5.13 The hanging tuck hold drill.

(continued)

Position Drills *(continued)*

except that it is done in the pike position.

4. *Somersault without grab.* The diver does a standing somersault off a 1-meter springboard without grabbing the legs to form good tuck (figure 5.14) and pike positions.

5. *Hollow rock.* The diver lies on the back with arms straight and overhead, lifts the feet and back slightly off the mat, and rocks back and forth (figure 5.15). This is a good drill for feeling the tight lower abdominal muscles in a hollow position.

6. *Hollow hold.* The diver lies on the back with the feet and shoulders propped on mats and holds the hollow position (figure 5.16).

7. *Tuck roll.* The diver does forward and backward rolls in a tight tuck position on a mat.

Figure 5.14 The somersault without grab drill.

8. *Somersault on mat.* The diver works on attaining good tuck and pike positions. An elevated mat and/or hand spotting can make this drill easier initially and ensure good mechanics. The diver may need to work up to a pike position. As with every drill, use appropriate landing mats

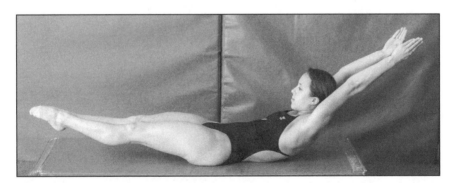

Figure 5.15 The hollow rock drill.

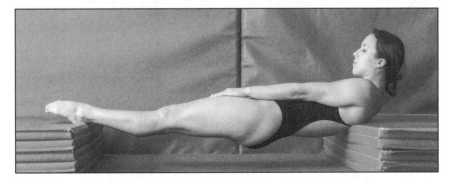

Figure 5.16 The hollow hold drill.

and follow spotting guidelines as recommended by your national governing body (e.g., USA Diving in the U.S.)

9. *Pike push-down.* The diver sits on a mat in the pike position and a coach pushes down on the hump part of the back to further flatten it and help the diver attain a flatter pike position (figure 5.17). The diver works on pushing the abdomen to the legs and the head towards the toes.

10. *Straight somersault.* The diver works on straight somersaults in all directions. Can be done on trampoline and a 1-meter springboard.

11. *Twist pick-up.* The diver lies on the floor in a tight twist position and the coach picks up the diver's feet (figure 5.18). The diver's body should rise off the floor in a straight, hollow position (i.e., the hips and back come off the floor). The coach then shakes the diver back and forth while the diver attempts to maintain a tight body alignment. The coach next releases one foot while the diver tries to keep the feet together, and then does same thing with the opposite foot.

12. *Pike snap full twist from backdrop.* Diver jumps up and lands on back on trampoline bed in L position with legs straight, feet pointing to 12 o 'clock and arms in T position. Diver then snaps to straight position, initiates twist, and lands on feet. It is best to start with a simple pike snap to straight position to feet, then pike snap to half twist to feet, and then pike snap to full twist to feet. Diver must wait until off mat to twist and coach should spot diver, as twisting too early will cause the diver to move laterally towards the side of the trampoline.

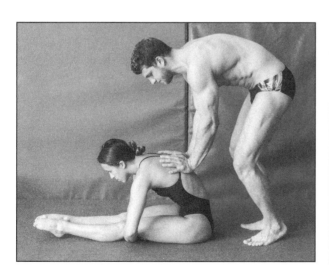

Figure 5.17 The pike push-down drill.

Figure 5.18 The twist pick-up drill.

Spotting

Consistency is crucial for diving success. Elite divers are elite in part because they consistently hit their dives. They derive their consistency from several factors, such as a consistent hurdle, but one monumental reason for their consistency is their ability to spot. Spotting isn't seeing a flash of something somewhere during a dive. **Spotting** is the process of clearly seeing specific visual cues at specific times during a dive rotation—in all directions. In other words, whether somersaulting forward, backward, reverse, or inward, divers should see specific cues, such as a small area on the water surface or the tip of the board, at each somersault during a dive rotation. Unfortunately, many diving coaches don't teach spotting, and many divers never learn spotting. Are there any motor skills that can be performed proficiently with closed eyes? Would you ride a bicycle, play tennis, or shoot a basketball with closed eyes? Hardly. Yet many divers dive blind. The following sections further describe spotting and how it can be taught by coaches and learned by divers.

Tracking

As mentioned earlier, one benefit of the V position in the tuck and the bowed- or split-leg position in the pike is the ability to track. **Tracking** is the process of fixating on a visual cue while somersaulting. To understand this process, consider riding in a car and passing a stand of trees. If you look straight out the window, a tree appears blurred. However, if you pick out a tree ahead of you, fixate on it, and move your head as you pass by it, the tree now looks clear and distinguishable. The same phenomenon occurs in spotting when divers track their visual cues. By making a V in the tuck and a split or bow in the pike, divers give themselves a bigger window in which to track their spots. If you observe elite divers carefully, you will see their heads bobbing (tracking) while somersaulting.

I have heard divers say, "Well, coach, I saw something. I'm not sure what it was or when I saw it, but I spotted!" Often, these divers see a flash of light or color after the come-out. Spotting is not seeing a flash of something somewhere during the dive. Spotting is tracking specific visual cues to clearly see them. So what are these cues?

Visual Cues

For most dives, elite divers see the water surface underneath them at each somersault. This is true for somersaulting dives in all directions, even forward and inward somersaults (some divers and diving coaches omit these two dive categories when it comes to spotting—but they shouldn't). Some elite divers spot the tip of the springboard for backward somersaulting dives, or both the water surface and the tip of the board. Some begin reacting (coming out) to the visual cue of the water surface and then anchor (point) their feet to a specific spot such as the end of the board for backward somersaulting dives, and a specific hour on an imaginary clock for reverse somersaulting dives.

In the past, 10-meter platform divers spotted the end of the 5-meter platform underneath the 10-meter platform when performing backward optional dives. In many new diving facilities, however, the 5 meter is not underneath the 10. Consequently, it is wise to spot the water surface directly underneath the dive (i.e., where the diver will be entering the water). There is some variation, however, among elite divers as to where on the water surface they spot. Some divers find it helpful to have a spot on the water surface 10 feet (3 m) from their entry, some like 15 feet (4.6 m) out in front of their entry, and so on. For a 207C on a 10 meter, some divers spot the end of the 10-meter platform at the first somersault and then the water at the second and third somersaults. Note, however, that all elite divers utilize spotting during dive rotation.

Divers and coaches should experiment until the diver finds the spot that works best for getting out of the dive at the right moment. In preparation for the Olympic trials, my diver kept kicking out late and going over on her reverse 305B. At one point, I asked her what her spot was, and she said it was the same as it was at home—the lane line out in front of her. This particular diving well, however, was about 12 feet (3.7 m) longer than the one in her home pool, and the lane line was also 12 feet farther out. So she moved her spot 12 feet in, nailed her 305B in competition, and made the U.S. Olympic team.

For forward and inward somersaulting dives, the diver should come out before seeing the water on the last somersault unless the dive is slow. If the diver waits until seeing the water directly underneath to come out, the kick-out will be too late and the dive will rotate past vertical. For forward and inward somersaulting dives, the best come-out is the pike-out, which is examined in the subsequent section on come-outs.

Learning to Spot

Learning to spot requires knowing what, where, when, and how to spot. *What* is the spot? The spot is the cue that divers use for orienting themselves at each somersault and for knowing when to come out of a dive. If the dive is fast, the diver sees the spot sooner and comes out sooner. If the dive is slow, the diver sees the spot later and comes out later. For backward and reverse somersaulting dives, a diver sees the spot and then comes out—not the other way around.

Where should a diver spot? For forward and inward somersaulting dives, the spot is the entry point at each somersault. For backward and reverse somersaulting dives, the first spot is approximately 45 degrees in front of the diver, and subsequent spots are either the entry point or the spot 45 degrees in front, or both. Spots vary among divers, but once determined, they should remain constant. Many divers are inconsistent because they don't see the same spots on each dive. In contrast, elite divers see the same spots each time. In fact, elite divers report seeing more than just their spots on the water surface. They see such things as the tip of the board, the gutter, and the entire water surface of the pool. Young Chinese divers, for example, are taught to see the entire trampoline and all the numbers on a banner that hangs down from the ceiling and drapes the trampoline bed.

When should a diver spot? The most effective and easiest way to spot during the dive is to *pick up the spot getting into the dive*. For a reverse 1 1/2 somersault, for example, the diver should see two spots. The first spot is the water when performing the C position and connecting into the dive, and the second spot is the water at the first somersault before the come-out. For a reverse 2 1/2 somersault, the diver should spot at three points: getting into the dive, at the first somersault, and at the second somersault. For forward and inward 1 1/2 somersaulting dives, the diver should see straight ahead at the

90-90-90 position, then see water, and pike out and see the water again. For the 2 1/2 somersaulting dives, the diver sees straight ahead, water, water, and then pikes out and sees water again.

How should a diver spot? As previously mentioned, spotting requires tracking. To track, the diver lifts the head slightly in the somersault to anticipate picking up the spot and then lowers the head to maintain visual contact with the spot, thus creating the head-bobbing tracking effect.

How to Teach Spotting

The first step in teaching spotting is to set a goal. Many divers never learn to spot simply because they never set a goal—nor do their coaches. Divers who do set a goal learn to spot fairly quickly. It really is that easy and is something every diver can learn and every coach should teach. It just takes practice. So how do divers practice spotting?

Introduce divers to the concept of spotting at the beginning of their careers so that they learn to associate spotting with all aspects of diving, such as watching their first hurdle step, looking at the end of the board in the hurdle descent, and spotting the water on forward jumps and the springboard on backward jumps. Emphasize and incorporate spotting into as many drills and skills as possible. As elite divers report, through repeated practice, spotting eventually becomes an automatic response. Next, divers should spot getting into and out of somersaults in all directions and in all positions. Once they have learned to spot somersaults, they can easily learn to spot 1 1/2 somersaults in all directions. The spotting drills provided in this section are simple, time-tested, and effective. Many of the drills require nothing more than a springboard, water, and diver!

Early in my coaching career, some divers fooled me into believing that they could spot. Only after watching these self-professed spotters consistently miss backward and reverse optional dives did I realize that I couldn't take them at their word—not because they were lying, but because they had a skewed concept of spotting. Spotting to them was simply seeing something at any point during the dive.

The most effective testing tool is a simple and inexpensive plastic placard (20 by 20 in., or 50 by 50 cm) with different colors on each side. A teammate wearing a life vest treads water and gives the diver a color at each somersault. The same can be done with the diver in a spotting belt on a trampoline. Often, divers who swear that they spot are lucky to identify the correct color one out of four times. With practice, however, these divers learn to spot consistently. For beginning divers, the placard is used for basic dives, such as a reverse dive where the divers spot the placard coming off the board and a reverse somersault where the divers see the spot coming off the board and then come out of the somersault early to track the spot as they rotate to their feet into the water. Elite divers can be challenged by placing a laptop screen underneath the trampoline that displays random numbers at each somersault and then asked to report the numbers spotted at each somersault. This task may sound impossible, but exceptional divers can pick out the numbers.

Testing communicates to divers that spotting involves seeing a specific spot, not just random indiscernible flashes of something. It also forces them to be honest with themselves about what they are seeing and not seeing. If divers aren't seeing anything, they need to remain patient and relaxed. Often, becoming impatient and anxious and trying too hard makes spotting more difficult. Remember that spotting helps achieve the most important goal in diving—consistency.

Besides spotting, two other factors contribute to knowing when to come out of a dive. The first is the diver's proprioceptive (internal) feedback from kinesthetic (feel) and vestibular (spatial orientation) senses. Some divers have a keener kinesthetic sense than others do. Through repeated practice, however, divers can develop a better feel for when to come out of dives by practicing simple drills.

The other factor that helps divers know when to come out of a dive is timing. A certain tempo, or timing, is associated with each somersault. For example, the board makes a tapping sound as it bounces off the fulcrum after a diver leaves the board, and then taps with each somersault for a 107B. Some divers mentally say "1-2-3" during a 107B to gain a sense of timing and anticipation for coming out of the dive. Divers should use all three factors—spotting, feeling, and timing—when coming out of their dives.

The sidebar Spotting Drills provides some simple but effective drills for learning to spot.

Spotting Drills

1. *Basic dives tuck in all directions.* The diver uses the pike-out come out, looks over or at the toes, and then spots the entry point on the water surface. When first using this as a spotting drill, emphasize spotting and don't worry so much about technique.

2. *Backward and reverse somersault.* The diver focuses on a spot into the dive, picks it up early, and looks at the spot when entering the water. This can be done in a tuck or pike, or straight, on a 1-meter springboard or in a spotting belt on a trampoline.

3. *Backward 1 1/2 somersault straight in spotting belt.* This is a phenomenal drill for practicing seeing everything during the dive rotation. The straight position makes it much easier than the tuck or pike positions for divers to see their spots. Most divers see their spots after only a few attempts at this drill. Notice the head movement (tracking) in figure 5.19.

4. *Spot progression for backward and reverse somersaulting.* The diver starts with a backward somersault, comes out, and sees the tip of the board. Next, the diver does a backward 1 1/2 somersault, sees the board, and then kicks out. Next, the diver does a backward double, sees the board at the first somersault, releases at the double, and sees the board while entering the water. The progression is the same for reverses. No spotting belt is required. This is a good drill for preparing to spot 205 and 305.

5. *Spot progression for forward and inward somersaulting.* The diver starts with a double-bouncing forward somersault. Next, the diver does a forward 1 1/2 and sees the water when coming out. Next, the diver does a double-bouncing forward double, sees the water at the 1 1/2 somersault, and then comes out.

(continued)

Spotting Drills *(continued)*

Figure 5.19 The backward 1 1/2 somersault straight in spotting belt drill.

6. *Double-bouncing reverse 1 1/2 somersault.* The diver takes two bounces and does a 303 on a 1- or 3-meter springboard. The double bounce provides more air time to spot which allows the diver to relax and not try too hard.

7. *Spotting aids.* The coach uses a plastic placard with different colors on each side or a banner with large numbers that hangs vertically from the ceiling. Spotting aids give divers an exact point in space on which to spot and anchor their feet on the come-out.

8. *Verbal cues.* The coach shouts a verbal cue such as "Look!" before each of the diver's spots. The cue should slightly precede the spot so the diver has time to look for it.

Come-Outs

An overriding concept for performing great optional dives is *get into the dive early, move it fast, get out early, and stop the dive.* In this sense, diving is simple: get after the dive and make it; control it at the end of the dive not at the beginning; you can't hit a dive you don't make. This credo has served many a diver well in competition. So, KISS: Keep It Simple and Smart. But how does a diver stop or control the dive at the end?

The come-out is important because it slows the dive rotation. It's like applying the brakes to a speeding car. The diver creates rotational momentum and then must stop it or at least slow it down to enter the water. Four types of come-outs control the end of a dive: pike-out, straight-out, kick-look-look-reach, and square-out.

Pike-Out

The pike-out is used for coming out of all forward and inward somersaulting dives. The **pike-out** involves shooting the legs straight and placing the arms laterally in a T position from a tuck position as shown in figure 5.20.

When starting the pike-out, the upper body remains motionless and the head stays neutral. The legs snap up as though kicking a ball with both feet. The diver keeps a small tuck and tight core muscles *before* the pike-out; otherwise, the legs drop and the pike-out is too open. The more open the pike-out is, the more likely the dive will be short of vertical on entry. There also is a pike-out for somersaulting dives in the pike position. The pike-out for these dives is achieved by letting go of the legs but still holding the pike position, as indicated in figure 5.21.

The pike-out occurs between approximately 3 and 4 o'clock or sooner depending on the speed of the rotation and the height of the dive above the water. Many elite divers pike out even earlier than 3 o'clock depending on the dive. The advantage of

Figure 5.20 The pike-out position for forward and inward somersaulting dives from a tuck position.

Figure 5.21 The pike-out for forward and inward somersaulting dives from a pike position.

the pike-out is that it gives the diver a choice. If the dive is rotating slowly, the diver simply remains in the pike-out position until the hips rotate up to approximately 12 o'clock and then lines up vertically. If the dive is rotating quickly, the diver opens early to elongate the body, slow the rotation, and line up vertically. The pike-out also gives the diver more time to grab the hands and prepare for the entry.

A diver should not pike out at 6 o'clock. For example, if performing a 105C, the diver should not pike out at 2 1/2 somersaults because the dive will rotate well past vertical by the time the body is straight. The pike-out has a great advantage over the straight-out come-out, discussed next.

Straight-Out

The **straight-out** involves shooting straight out of a tuck or pike immediately into a straight body alignment. I refer to this as the "one-shot come-out" because the diver gets only one shot at hitting the dive. The straight-out is either on time or not, as opposed to the pike-out, in which the diver can either maintain or come out of the position depending on the speed of rotation and proximity to the water surface.

If a dive is rotating slowly and finishing on top of the water, the diver may not have time to execute a pike-out. In this case, the straight-out can be a useful come-out. Before the Olympic trials, one of my divers was struggling to pike out of her 407C on 10-meter platform. When we changed to a straight-out, she consistently nailed her 407C throughout the trials.

Kick-Look-Look-Reach

The come-out for backward and reverse somersaulting dives is much different from the come-out for forward and inward somersaulting dives. The **kick-look-look-reach** is a sequential movement for coming out of backward and reverse somersaulting dives in which the legs *kick* out first and the diver *looks* at the feet, then *looks* back for the water, and then *reaches* for the water. This sequence of movements is shown in figure 5.22.

After the first look, the diver tilts the head back and looks for the water (preferably the entry spot) before moving the hands from the thighs. After spotting the water, the diver moves the arms to a line-up position while moving the head to a neutral position, as shown in figure 5.23.

Some elite divers perform a pike-out for reverse and backward optional dives. They come out of the tuck or pike with their hands down by their ankles or shins in a pike position, as shown in the series of pictures in figure 5.24. After the pike-out, they perform the remainder of the kick-look-look-reach.

The kick itself is a series of movements that involves the following sequence: knees-legs-hips. From the tuck position (figure 5.25a) the diver straightens the *knees* (figure 5.25b), then presses out the *legs* (figure 5.25c), and then slightly opens the *hips* (figure 5.25d). As in the forward somersault pike-out, during the kick the upper body remains motionless so there is a pike or hollow position after the kick, the head is neutral, the arms are straight, and the core muscles are tight. Unlike the forward pike-out, the hands are placed on the front of the thighs. Keeping the arms down on the thighs and opening the hips lengthens the body and effectively slows down the dive rotation. If the arms whip out with the kick, the dive will continue rotating and move past vertical on entry. During the kick, the diver looks at the feet.

Many diving contests come down to who hits backward and reverse optional dives. The forward and inward optional dives are easier because divers can see the water much sooner before entry. In contrast, backward and reverse optional dives are considered blind dives because divers don't get much of a look at the water before entry. For this reason, backward and reverse come-out drills should be heavily emphasized in practice. I typically wanted most of my divers practicing backward and reverse come-out drills 60 to 70 percent of the time so that their kick-look-look-reach motor response would be proficient and automatic, especially in competition.

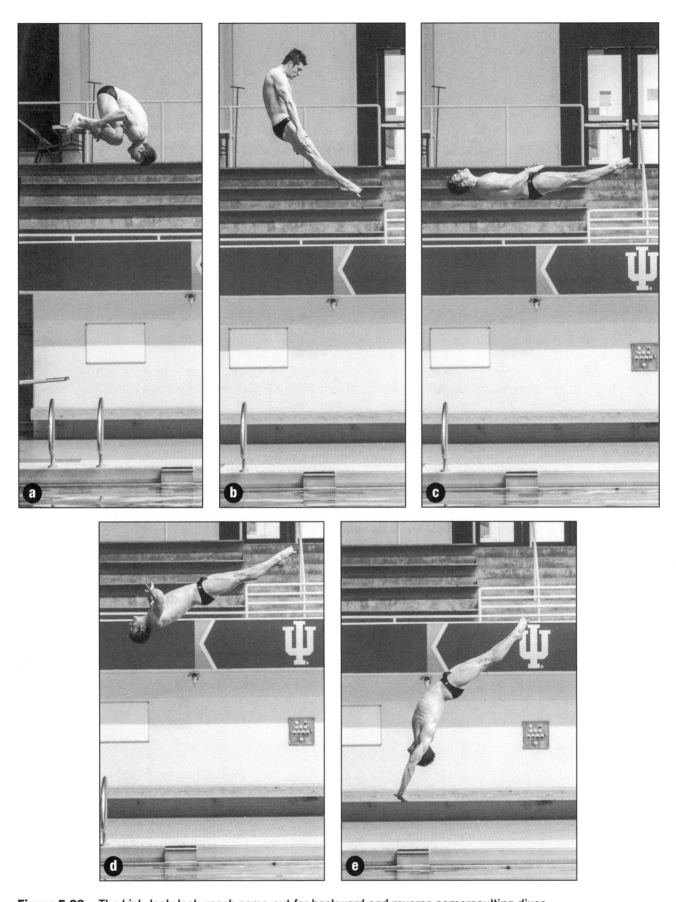

Figure 5.22 The kick-look-look-reach come-out for backward and reverse somersaulting dives.

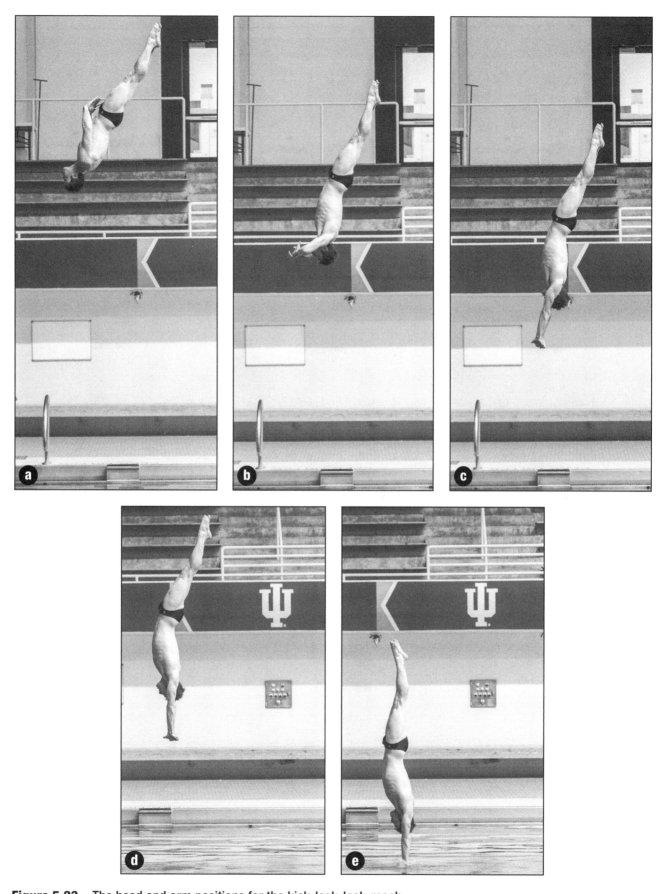

Figure 5.23 The head and arm positions for the kick-look-look-reach.

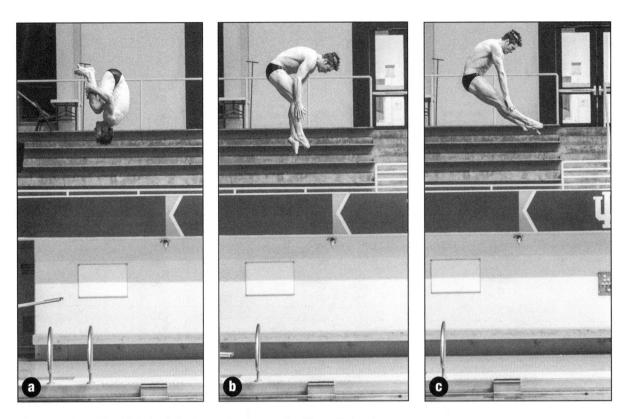

Figure 5.24 The kick-look-look-reach come-out with a pike-out.

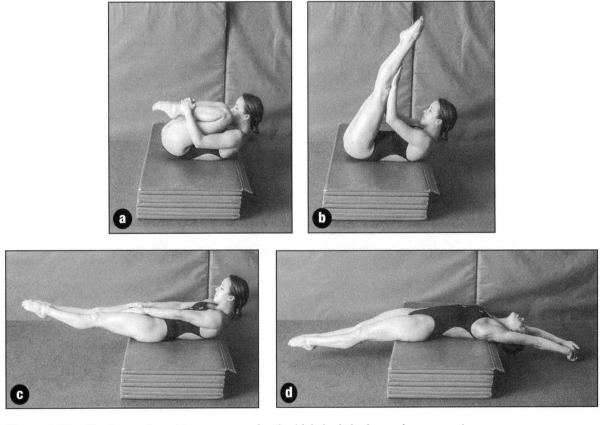

Figure 5.25 The knees-legs-hips sequence for the kick-look-look-reach come-out.

Square-Out

The **square-out** is the come-out for twisting dives and like the kick-look-look-reach, it stops the dive. Beginning from the twist position, the square-out involves a series of movements performed in the following sequence.

1. Twist position (figure 5.26a)
2. One up, one down (figure 5.26b)
3. Turn to a T arm position (5.26c)
4. Sit (figure 5.26d)

Note that the square-out is initiated before the completion of the entire twist. Initiating the square-out after the twist is completed causes the dive to over twist. As in the other come-outs, a certain amount of anticipation is necessary for performing the square-out. The arms come out before completing the twist so that they are ready to T when the body turns to complete the correct number of twists.

Why "one up, one down" with the arms? When twisting, a slight tilting of the body occurs on the vertical axis. From the one-up, one-down position, the diver turns and moves the arms into a T position thereby bringing the hips back in line on the vertical axis. The next position, the sit, involves pushing the upper body down *and* lifting the legs up. Many divers believe that this position is achieved only by pushing the upper body down, but both must occur to achieve the sit position. The pike (sit) position is what stops the twist. From the sit or pike position, the diver then moves the legs (not the upper body) upward into a straight position and closes laterally with the arms for the line-up.

The sidebar Come-Out Drills outlines some time-tested exercises for learning the various come-outs.

Figure 5.26 The sequence for the square-out for twisting dives.

Come-Out Drills

Pike-Out and Straight-Out Drills

1. *Forward dive roll.* The diver does a forward tuck dive roll on a mat and finishes in a pike-out position (figure 5.27).

2. *Forward somersault to seat drop.* The diver does a standing somersault and finishes with a seat drop in a pike position onto a landing mat (figure 5.28).

3. *Hanging pike-out with hold.* The diver hangs from a bar, does a tuck-up, pikes out, and then holds the pike-out position. This drill is good for strengthening the core and learning how to hold the pike-out position. The diver can also do a pike-up and hold that position to learn how to hold the pike-out for somersaulting dives in the pike position.

4. *Roll-off with pike-out.* The diver sits on the end of a 3-meter springboard in a tight tuck position, pikes out, and then rolls off and lines up for the entry. This drill is most effective when the diver starts with a tight tuck, kicks the legs up into a pike position before rolling off, and then keeps the chest down and the arms in a T position on the roll-off.

5. *Standing somersault with pike-out.* The diver stands on the end of a 1-meter springboard and pikes out of a somersault and then straightens out for a feet-first entry.

6. *Forward 1 1/2 somersault in tuck with pike-out.* The diver performs this drill standing, double bouncing, or with a hurdle. This is a nice progression from the standing somersault with pike-out drill.

Figure 5.27 The forward dive roll drill.

Figure 5.28 The forward somersault to seat drop drill.

7. *Basic dives in tuck position.* The diver does forward, backward, reverse, and inward dives in tuck position and comes out with the pike-out and the straight-out.

8. *Backward roll to handstand.* The diver does a backward roll on a mat and then presses to an armstand to practice the straight-out. The coach can spot the diver.

9. *Seated pike-out with shoulder hold.* The diver sits on the edge of a bench or mat in either the tuck or pike position with a coach holding the diver's shoulders. The diver activates the core muscles and then releases the legs while the coach continues to hold the shoulders and the diver holds the pike-out position (figure 5.29).

10. *Forward 1 1/2 somersault without grabbing legs.* The diver maintains a tuck with the core muscles rather than grabbing the legs with the hands (figure 5.30) and then performs the straight-out come-out. This is an effective drill for teaching the straight-out for divers who need this type of come-out.

(continued)

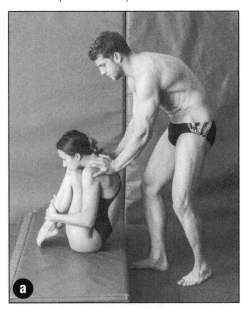 

Figure 5.29 The seated pike-out with shoulder hold drill.

Figure 5.30 Forward 1 1/2 somersault without grabbing legs.

Kick-Look-Look-Reach Drills

1. *Backward roll-off with kick-look-look-reach.* The diver sits on the end of a 3-meter springboard in a tight tuck position (figure 5.31*a*) and then rolls off backwards and performs the kick-look-look-reach. Notice that the diver first rolls off the board (figure 5.31*b*), then attains a straight position (figure 5.31*c*), *then* looks back for the water (figure 5.31*d*), and *then* reaches (figure 5.31*e*). This is a deceptively challenging drill when done as outlined. Most divers want to immediately reach during the kick and often don't look back for the water. The drill can also be done from the pike position.

2. *Backward and reverse tuck dives.* The diver practices the kick-look-look-reach coming out of backward and reverse dives. Even at the Olympic Games, the best divers in the world do these basic dives.

3. *Backward and reverse somersaults.* The diver comes out of a tuck or pike somersault on a 1-meter springboard and enters the water with the hands on the thighs. Divers learning to kick-look-look-reach on reverse and backward 2 1/2 somersaults should enter the water with the hands on the thighs on a double somersault. This is a good drill for overcoming the innate human tendency to put the hands overhead when landing headfirst.

4. *Reverse and backward 1 1/2 somersaults.* Divers should do hundreds of these to practice the tuck and pike positions, spotting, and the kick-look-look-reach.

5. *Standing back fall from pike position.* The diver stands backward on the end of a 3-meter springboard or platform in the pike position. The diver falls off the board and presses out with the legs (not the upper body), looks at the feet, looks back, and then reaches. This is a good drill for practicing pressing out with the legs rather than the upper body. This drill can also be done with a slight jump.

6. *Jumping back dive.* The diver starts with the head down and looking at the feet with the hands on the thighs. The diver then jumps off the board looking at feet, looks back for the water, and then lines up.

7. *Kick-look-look-reach on mat.* The diver performs a come-out from a tuck or pike position. This drill should be part of every diver's prepractice warm-up routine.

8. *Double-bouncing reverse 1 1/2 somersaults.* The diver does this drill on a 1- or 3-meter springboard. It gives the diver more air time in which to practice the kick-look-look-reach, especially keeping the hands down on the out.

9. *Backward and reverse dives and 1 1/2 somersaults with no reach in belt* (figure 5.32). The diver kicks with a flat body alignment, looks back for the trampoline or dryboard and leaves the hands on the thighs. The diver does not reach for a line-up. The coach holds the diver in the air. This is another good drill for overcoming the innate human tendency to put the hands overhead when landing headfirst.

10. *Reverse and backward entries with hands down.* The diver enters the water headfirst with the hands on the thighs. This is a good drill if you don't have a trampoline for the preceding drill. Perform only on a 1-meter springboard.

(continued)

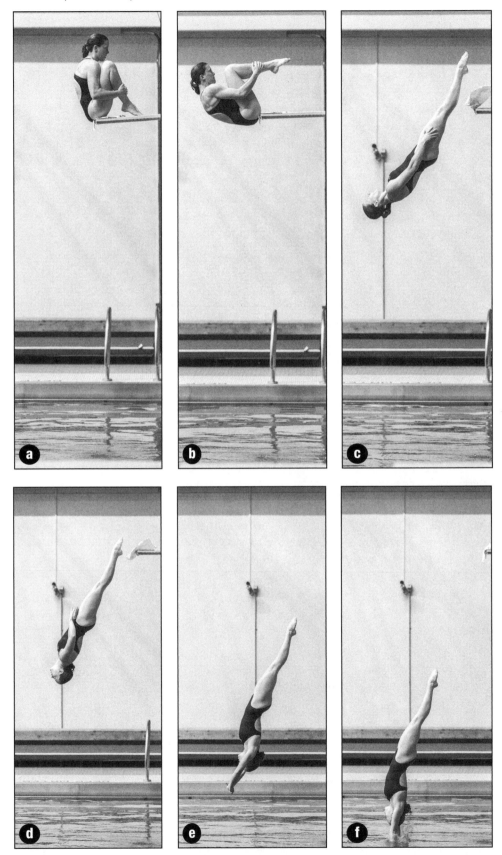

Figure 5.31 The roll-off with kick-look-look-reach drill.

Figure 5.32 The backward 1 1/2 somersault with no reach drill.

Square-Out Drills

1. *Jump and square-out to seat drop on trampoline.* The diver stands on a trampoline facing the side of the trampoline with the arms in a twist position; jumps up; does one up, one down and a quarter twist; assumes a T arm position (figure 5.33); and lands in a seat drop position. The diver then puts the hands on the trampoline bed on landing. This can also be done effectively onto a landing mat.

2. *Jump and square-out to the feet on 1-meter springboard.* This is the same as the preceding trampoline drill except that the diver straightens out of the seat drop to finish to the feet.

3. *Jump and square-out off poolside.* This is also the same as the first trampoline drill, except that it is performed poolside. The diver finishes to a seat drop into the water. Once proficient, the diver can finish to the feet.

4. *Quarter twist roll-off on 3-meter springboard or platform.* The diver lies on the side in a twist position, does a quarter twist, squares out, and then rolls off and does a line-up (figure 5.34).

5. *Square-out feet-first entry.* The diver does a feet-first twisting lead-up (e.g., full twisting somersault), squares out, and enters the water in a slight pike position. This is good preparation for helping divers learn to perform the sit position on the square-out before reaching for the water on a head first entry twisting dive.

(continued)

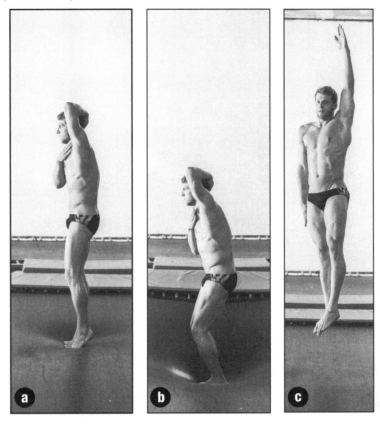

Figure 5.33   The jump and square-out to seat drop on trampoline drill.

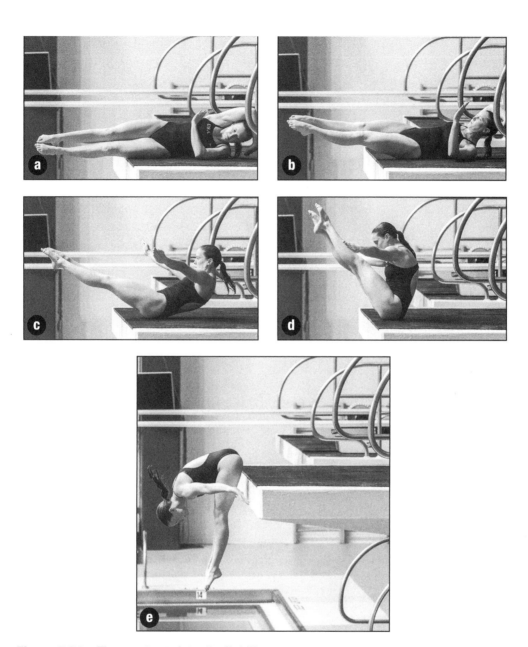

Figure 5.34 The quarter twist roll-off drill.

6. *Dryland modeling.* The diver performs the four-step sequence (figure 5.28) for a square-out in slow motion on a mat. As proficiency increases, the diver increases the speed of modeling until actual performance speed is achieved.

7. *Backward armstand half twist.* The diver does an armstand half somersault with a half twist to a seat drop on a mat or to the feet on a 1-meter platform.

8. *Forward somersault full twist.* The diver does this drill on a 1-meter springboard or 3-meter platform.

9. *Double-bouncing 5132D.* The diver does this drill on a 1-meter springboard. The double bounce gives the diver more air time to practice the square-out.

(continued)

Come-Out Drills *(continued)*

10. *Backward somersault 1 1/2 twists.* The diver does this drill on a 1-meter springboard or a 3-meter platform and should focus on squaring out of the twist.

CHAPTER 6

Line-Ups and Entries

So, the takeoff was masterfully performed, the connection quick as lightning, and the come-out rock solid. Now it's time to lay the baby to bed, put the icing on the cake, tie the bow on the box . . . you get the picture. Simply put, it's time to finish the dive: to line up and rip the entry. **Rip** means entering the water with little or no splash, and the better the rip is, the better the judges' scores will be. It is called a rip because a great rip entry has a distinctive sound like that of a large sheet of paper being violently ripped apart. The rip is the big tamale of our sport and the ultimate mind eraser. Divers can make minor mistakes during dive performances and still receive good scores by ripping the entry, because the rip often causes judges to forget about the earlier miscues. *Ninety percent of performing a great dive involves establishing a good takeoff, but 90 percent of gaining a great score involves performing a good line-up and entry.* Of course, elite coaches emphasize both great technique and a great line-up and entry, but consistency in competition is often achieved by being able to rip a dive even after an imperfect takeoff.

This chapter tears (rips?) away the veil of mystery surrounding the rip entry by revealing the essential movements that occur above and below the waterline. These essential movements are based on high-speed video analyses as well as personal conversations with some of the best rippers in the world. In truth, performing a rip entry is easy, and anyone can do it. Every diver I coached learned to rip with some degree of proficiency. Before we examine the rip, however, let's reconsider something that precedes the rip and plays an influential role in creating a stellar rip—the come-out.

But first, a short story . . .

At the World Championship in Rome, less than 2 points separated the top four divers heading into the final round. Battling were the defending Olympic champion, two Olympic medalists, and a world champion. Sitting in a distant fifth place was young teen sensation Thomas Daley from Great Britain. Thomas's last dive was his 307C. As he left the platform, it was apparent that his jump was somewhat low and the dive slightly too far from the platform, so it appeared the dive wouldn't be quite good enough to win the contest. However, Thomas used the mind eraser on the judges. He absolutely obliterated his entry—by far the day's best entry—and received all 10s from the judges to win the World Championship at the precocious age of 15. No judge remembered his less-than-perfect takeoff.

The Come-Out Revisited

Just as the magic position is critical for contributing to a good takeoff, the come-out is important for a good line-up and entry. The **line-up** is the body position the diver assumes before contacting the water. The **entry** is the movement of the body breaking the surface of the water as well as the movement under the water. If a tight core isn't established before and during the come-out, it is impossible to recapture and establish it on the line-up and entry. A tight body core contributes to dive control on the line-up and entry and to creating the holy grail of diving—the rip.

A simple but effective drill for teaching a tight body core before and during the come-out is the seated pike-out with shoulder hold drill outlined earlier in chapter 5, figure 5.29. Recall that the diver starts in a tight tuck or pike position on a bench or mat. Next, she rolls slightly forward and pikes out while her coach holds her shoulders. The diver's goal is to keep the pike-out as deep as possible. Divers performing this drill discover quickly that they must keep the core tight *before* releasing the legs and performing the pike-out; otherwise, their legs will drop and the pike-out will be open.

Often, divers don't realize that they can be tighter during the come-out, line-up, and entry. A good way to determine body tightness is to ask divers to rate their tightness on a scale of 1 to 10, with 10 being the tightest. They generally respond honestly and accurately, often suggesting a 6. There isn't any reason for being less than 10 tight. It doesn't take talent, just effort. Although 6 out of 10 may not seem deficient, would 60 percent on an exam earn a passing grade?

In China, young divers begin their training on platforms and only later train on springboards. The platform teaches them to line up correctly and tightly. If divers aren't tight on a platform line-up, they definitely feel it. A lack of tightness is less conspicuous on a 3-meter springboard entry and even less so on a 1-meter springboard entry.

Forward and Inward Line-Ups and Entries

The essential elements are the same for forward and inward line-ups and entries. The only difference, obviously, is the direction of the dive rotation. Forward somersaulting dives move horizontally away from the springboard or platform and somersault forward. Inward somersaulting dives also move horizontally away, but somersault toward the board. Although this difference may seem obvious, it has implications for forward and inward line-ups and entries that are discussed at the end of this chapter.

Above Water—The Line-Up

The rip entry is separated into two parts—above-water movements (the line-up) and below-water movements (the entry). The dive isn't fully completed once the diver's hands hit the water, although some divers and diving coaches think so. On the contrary, there is as much action below the water as above it. Let's begin with the above-water line-up. There are five essential elements that encompass the line-up. The first is the concave position.

Concave Position

I am indebted to former diver Marc Carlton for helping me more fully understand the dynamic interplay between body positioning and ripping. Before graduating, he developed one of the best rips in the country and it served him well, helping him set conference records on both the 3-meter springboard and the 10-meter platform. As a parting gift, he sketched the body position he formed to create his rip. Figure 6.1 displays his original drawing.

The **concave position** for forward and inward line-ups involves forming a curved body shape like the inner shape of a circle or sphere that curves inward, as opposed to a **convex** body shape that curves outward like the exterior shape of a circle or sphere. This concave body alignment is depicted in figure 6.2.

Notice that the hips are rolled under and the body forms a concave position from the toes to the fingertips, not just from the waist to the fingertips, as some

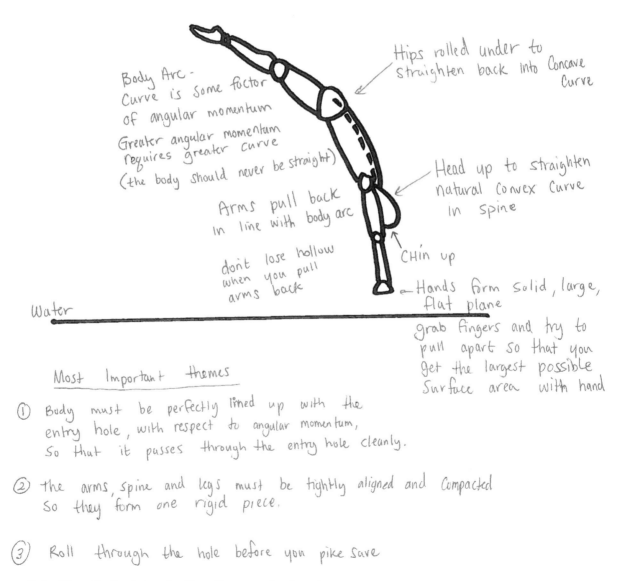

Figure 6.1 Marc Carlton's handwritten diagram of a rip entry.

Courtesy of Marc Carlton.

Figure 6.2 The first essential position for forward and inward line-ups: the concave position.

Figure 6.3 Core tightness for forward and inward line-ups.

divers mistakenly conceptualize. Notice also that the lower rib cage is pulled in so that the front of the body makes a clean, smooth concave surface. Figure 6.3 shows a front view of what the core should look like immediately before contact with the water. Notice how incredibly tight the core muscles are.

To learn to form the concave body position, divers should start by standing on the end of the springboard in a pike position with the low back rounded, hands grabbed, and arms over the ears. They then slowly open up as depicted in figure 6.4 into a concave position. Notice that the hips are positioned slightly behind the ankles in the curve, but there is no bending or piking at the hips, which some divers mistakenly do when first learning to achieve this position.

A dive follows a parabolic curve from the board to the water and through the water. The concave body shape nicely matches the shape of this parabolic curve as it travels along the curve to the water and through the water. For this reason, divers must maintain the concave position through the water, at least until the hips are below the waterline. The next essential element for the line-up is the lateral close.

Lateral Close

The **lateral close** occurs as the arms move along the plane of the body toward the hand grab, as shown in figure 6.5. Notice that the thumbs are turned up.

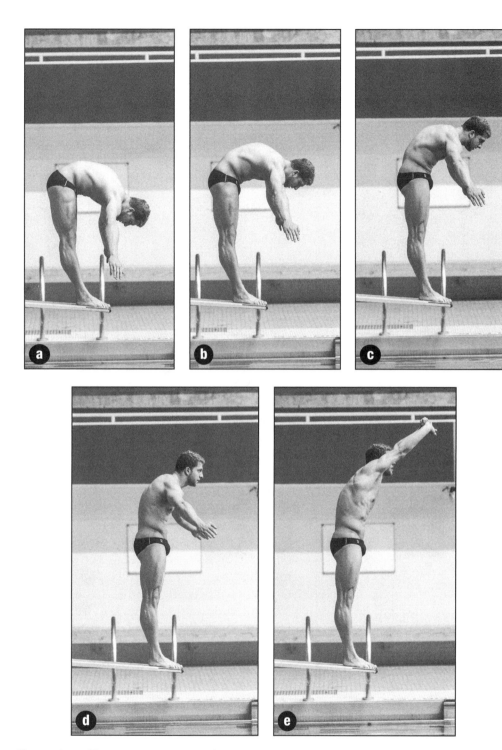

Figure 6.4 The sequence for forming a concave body alignment position.

Turning the thumbs up opens the shoulders, allows for external rotation, and makes the lateral close easier to perform. As an experiment, turn your thumbs down and try closing laterally. Your arms will close underneath. One factor that separates elite from nonelite divers is the lateral close. Elite divers T out with their arms and close laterally, which gives them a sharper look, greater body control, and ultimately, a better rip.

Figure 6.5 The second essential position for forward and inward line-ups: the lateral close.

Closing under instead of laterally causes the dive to rotate past vertical because the force of the arms swinging under and up causes the legs to move in an opposite and equal reaction. However, if the diver is rotating slowly and about to enter the water short of vertical, swinging the arms underneath causes the legs to move closer to vertical.

To attain a lateral close, divers slightly bend the elbows and relax the trapezius muscles. Notice that before the close the elbows are slightly bent, the hands are relaxed, and the shoulders are dropped and relaxed, all of which contribute to a lateral close. Relaxed shoulders also allow the diver to shrug the shoulders before the hands contact the water.

Shoulder Shrug

During my many conversations with great rippers, they always seem to emphasize one aspect of the entry, the **shoulder shrug.** This is the process of grabbing the hands and then simultaneously pushing the shoulders up into the neck and locking out the elbows just before the hands contact the water, as depicted in figure 6.6.

Figure 6.6 The third essential position for forward and inward line-ups: the shoulder shrug.

Notice that there is no daylight (gap) between the shoulders and the head after the shoulder shrug. Pushing through the shoulders locks out the elbows and forms a rigid and solid projectile that knifes through the water. Notice in figure 6.7 that the scapulae are turned down to give a "chicken wing" appearance. A slight hyperextension of the elbows provides a ripping advantage by allowing the arms to wrap around the head to create a tight seal.

During the lateral close and shoulder shrug, the diver should maintain the concave position. Shrugging upward causes the body to arch and shrugging downward causes the body to round beyond the concave position. After the shrug, the diver should remain motionless. Movement causes the body to throw water and reduces the quality of the rip. Movement on the entry is connected to head positioning.

Neutral Head Position

The **neutral head position** involves keeping the head back, rather than forward, and the chin level, as shown in figure 6.8. The head remains still and neutral throughout the entry. As in the shrug, moving the head upward causes the body to arch, and moving the head downward causes the body to bend or round. *A rule of thumb is that the body goes where the head goes.* In other words, if the head goes down, the body curves downward underwater. If the head goes up, the body arches upward underwater.

When the diver looks for the water, the eyes should move, not the head. The diver looks for the water as though looking over a pair of sunglasses, looking up past the eyebrows. Keeping the head neutral and motionless allows the flat hand to remain still and to make solid contact with the water.

Flat Hand

We now arrive at the pièce de résistance, the element that gives the rip its sound and its moniker. The **flat hand** is the bottom hand of the hand grab, and its palm is flat and level with the surface of the water on contact. Keeping the hand still allows the flat hand to forcefully strike the water to make the rip sound and open a hole for the diver to enter the water. Shifting the flat hand before contact with the water causes body movement and a heavy (splashy) entry.

Typically, but not always, a diver's dominant hand is the top grab hand and the nondominant hand is the bottom flat hand. Just as they do when learning the direction in which to twist, divers can determine their grab hand by not thinking and automatically putting their hands together. They typically grab in the way that is most natural and comfortable to them.

Notice in figure 6.9 that the top hand grabs the flat (bottom) hand and the fingers wrap around the bottom hand. Part of what determines the effectiveness of the flat hand is wrist flexibility. The more flexible the wrist is, the easier it is to pull

Figure 6.7 The line-up position after the shoulder shrug.

Figure 6.8 The fourth essential position for forward and inward line-ups: the neutral head.

  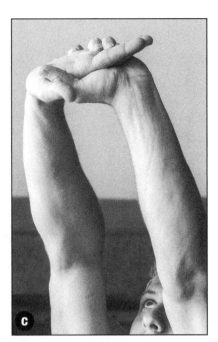

Figure 6.9 The fifth essential position for forward and inward line-ups: the flat hand.

the flat hand back so that it is parallel to the surface of the water. Therefore, improving and maintaining wrist flexibility creates a great rip entry. Some divers with less wrist flexibility grab farther out on the hand toward the fingertips, which allows them to bend the fingers back.

There are several effective hand grabs, and coaches and athletes should experiment to see which works best for the individual diver. For example, a former U.S. national champion with a nasty rip grabbed only two fingers because he had lost two fingers in an accident when he was a small child. Another diver grabbed only three fingers and won an Olympic gold medal. Still another diver with a phenomenal rip grabbed high on the hand and was U.S. national champion. The diver should delay squeezing the flat hand with the grab hand until just before or during the shoulder shrug. Squeezing the hand earlier causes the shoulders to tighten up and interferes with an effective shrug. So what happens underwater after the flat hand?

Below Water—The Entry

As mentioned earlier, there is as much technique under the water as there is above it. Like the line-up, the entry for forward and inward entries can be broken down into five easily comprehended essential elements.

Quick Swim

The first essential element of the entry is the **quick swim,** in which the hands quickly release and the arms separate (swim) as rapidly as possible to a T position, as shown in figure 6.10. The T position is held throughout the entry. To conceptualize the quick swim, think of the surface of the water as a piece of paper that the diver rips open with the quick swim as soon as the flat hand contacts the water. There are two dimensions to executing the quick swim: speed and timing.

Ideally, the quick swim and resulting T arm position should be established 2 to 3 feet (60 to 90 cm) below the waterline. For this to occur, the diver must anticipate and initiate the swim quickly on contact with the water. Some divers make the mistake of starting the swim too late but executing the swim quickly. Other divers make the mistake of starting the swim at the right time but executing the swim too slowly. Either mistake results in a late rather than quick swim and a less-than-perfect rip. Some divers make both mistakes, resulting in an especially poor entry.

Another mistake divers make when executing the quick swim is bending the elbows and then straightening them. The goal of the quick swim is to establish a T arm position as quickly as possible,

Figure 6.10 The first essential position for forward and inward entries: the quick swim T arm position.

but bending the elbows delays establishing this T position. Keeping the arms straight during the entry is critical for producing a good rip. Notice how divers can often enter the water feet first and achieve an impressive foot rip. That is because they get a flat-foot line-up and keep their knees locked during the entry.

Quick 90

After the quick swim comes the quick 90-degree position, or **quick 90**, which is achieved by bending at the waist so that the upper body and legs form a right angle, as shown in figure 6.11.

Underwater video analysis indicates that elite divers achieve the quick 90 as soon as their toes are below the waterline. Consequently, initiating the quick

Figure 6.11 The second essential position for forward and inward entries: the quick 90.

90 has to happen quickly and as soon as the hips are below the waterline. Bending at the waist above the waterline creates a noticeable splash along with a break in the line-up position. And bending at the waist too late in the water negates the positive effect of the quick 90. The positive effect is that the quick 90 sucks the water down with the diver. The quick 90 is an important part of the rip effect.

Pike Save

The third essential position is the **pike save**, which involves pushing the legs down into a pike position to keep them from moving past vertical on the line-up. How is the pike save different from the quick 90? Both positions form a 90-degree body position. The difference is that the quick 90 is achieved by moving the *upper body* down into the 90-degree position. In contrast, the pike save is performed by moving the *legs* down into the 90-degree position. Another difference is that the pike might be deeper than the quick 90 depending on how much of the pike save is needed to save the dive. For slow rotating dives such as the 101B or 401B, a pike save is generally not needed.

The pike save is a diver's best friend because it does exactly what it says it does—saves the dive from going over. I have observed elite divers in major competitions start to go over on an entry and use the pike save to score 9s and even 10s on their dives. That is how effective the pike save is. Knowing this, and knowing that there is no truly effective save for a dive that lines up short of vertical, elite divers rarely perform a short dive.

Many divers make the mistake of feeling vertical 3 or 4 feet (90 to 120 cm) underwater. The vertical position, however, has to be attained above water. Judges want to see a vertical entry as the hands contact the water. As the body enters the water, however, a certain amount of rotational momentum continues. For this reason, a pike save is necessary for every forward and inward somersaulting dive that lines up vertically on the surface of the water. When performed correctly, the dive should feel as if it is lining up slightly past vertical.

Some divers make the mistake of moving the upper body instead of the legs during the pike save. A good drill for correcting this mistake is to slap the water with the feet on the pike save. Another mistake often made is saving too late. Anticipation is necessary for an effective pike save. If a diver waits to feel the dive go over before saving, the dive will already be past vertical. This is like waiting to get hit on the head before ducking. Another mistake some divers make is not piking enough. The more the dive moves past vertical, the deeper the pike position must be.

6 Position

Following the pike save, the diver continues somersaulting back into the plume of bubbles created by the entry. This action should feel like a forward somersault in an open pike position. It is called the **6 position** because the direction of the body underwater follows a pattern of the number 6. If performed correctly, the diver's head should enter the plume of bubbles. The 6 position is shown in figure 6.12.

Figure 6.12 The fourth essential position for forward and inward entries: the 6 position.

Figure 6.13 The fifth essential position for forward and inward entries: the straddle.

The somersaulting action of the 6 position continues to suck the water underneath to further accentuate a rip entry. As we will see, a similar action occurs in the opposite direction for backward and reverse entries.

Straddle

After the 6 position there remains one final element for the entry. It is almost an afterthought and occurs so late that most diving observers never see it. The **straddle** involves spreading the legs past the shoulders, as depicted in figure 6.13, once the diver's body is fully underwater.

The straddle is a simple action performed during the latter part of the 6 position. The purpose of the straddle is to diffuse the plume of air bubbles and prevent bubbles from rising to the surface of the water.

How to Teach the Forward Line-Up and Entry

As mentioned earlier in this chapter, the entry is the most critical part of the dive in terms of acquiring a good judge's score: the cleaner the entry, the higher the score. But gaining a quality rip entry takes time, patience, and persistence. It also may take some experimentation to discover the type of hand grab that works best for each diver. Begin teaching the forward line-up by using the dryland drills previously outlined in this chapter. Specifically, begin by having divers close laterally, grab the flat hand, lock out the elbows, and shrug. During this phase, emphasize the importance of a tight, hollow body position. Once proficient with these skills, divers may then practice the swim.

The next step is pushing off the side of the pool into a torpedo dive and working on body position, followed by sliding off a mat into the water from poolside and then sliding off the mat from the 1-meter springboard. Next, divers practice a standing concave fall-in from the side of the pool. Once this is mastered, they perform the same drill from the 1-meter springboard. They should pay particular attention to keeping the flat hand parallel to the water surface and to maintaining a concave body position going through the water. Only after the preceding skills have been mastered should divers begin practicing the below-water skills (e.g., quick swim, quick 90).

Forward and Inward Line-Up and Entry Drills

1. *Standing concave fall-in.* The diver stands on the end of a 3-meter springboard or platform in a concave position, grabs the hands, and falls into the water (figure 6.14). This can be performed with a slight jump off a 1-meter springboard. The diver can bend over and then slowly uncurl the upper body into a concave position. The goal of this drill is to fall into the water without shifting the concave position or loosening up in any way. It is a highly effective drill.

2. *Concave standing fall-in from T position.* This is similar to the previous drill except that the diver starts with the arms in a T position. The diver begins the fall-in and then grabs the flat hand before the feet leave the board. This is a good progression from the preceding drill. The point of this drill is to learn to move the arms to the flat hand while maintaining that concave position and body tightness and remaining motionless while going through the water.

Figure 6.14 Standing concave fall-in drill.

3. *Seated roll-off.* The diver starts in an open pike position (i.e., a deep pike with the arms in a T position) and the upper body in a concave position while sitting on the end of a springboard or platform. The goal of the drill is to roll off the board and maintain the concave shape while opening up at the waist. The diver can practice this drill on the mat by simply standing in an open pike position, lifting the upper body, and grabbing the flat hand while maintaining a tight, hollow core position.

4. *Line-up off poolside.* This drill involves no arm swing; the diver starts with the arms overhead. This is a simple but effective drill for several reasons: divers can perform this drill quickly and get in a high number of repetitions; divers of any age and proficiency level can practice this drill; coaches get an up-close view of what divers are doing underwater and can clearly see the swim, pike, save, and straddle; and divers can experiment and more easily make changes to the line-up (e.g., change the hand grab, swim sooner, or swim more in front). Divers must remember to jump out to avoid hitting the pool wall.

5. *On-the-mat swim pike save modeling.* The diver simply stands with the hands overhead in a line-up position and then swims with the arms into a T position and lifts one leg off the ground into a 90-degree position. Bringing one leg up rather than bringing the upper body down emphasizes moving the legs, not the upper body, to perform the pike save.

6. *Touch hands and swim.* The diver sits on the ground in an L position with the arms in a T position; then closes to an overhead flat hand grab. Another diver or coach stands behind the seated diver and taps the diver's flat hand. The diver reacts as quickly as possible with a quick swim to a T position while maintaining a tight core.

7. *Push on arms.* The diver stands in a concave position with the arms overhead and a flat hand grab, and the coach grabs the diver's arms and forcefully pushes down. The push simulates the force of the diver entering the water. The diver must hold the concave position during the push. When first performing this drill, most divers arch the low back during the push. The purpose of the drill is to practice keeping the core tight during the entry.

8. *Armstand forward wall shrug.* The diver does an armstand with the feet against a wall, the abdomen facing the wall, and the body in a concave position. The diver then repeatedly shrugs up in an armstand. This is a good drill for practicing the shoulder shrug for forward and inward entries.

9. *Forward and inward dives.* This drill brings divers back to the basics. Done in tuck, in pike, and even straight, these unassuming dives have everything: the hollow position, the lateral close, the quick swim, and so on. World-class divers do these simple dives routinely.

10. *Hollow hold.* The diver rests the heels on a stack mat and the upper back on another stack mat and holds the concave position with arms overhead. This is a great drill for strengthening the core and getting used to holding a concave position.

11. *Forward somersault underwater.* The diver does an extra somersault underwater after the quick 90 and 6 position. This is a quick and effective drill for learning the 6 position.

Backward and Reverse Line-Ups and Entries

The five essential elements are almost identical for both backward and reverse line-ups and entries. The only difference that must be factored into the equation, of course, is the direction of rotation in relation to the springboard or platform. Backward somersaulting dives rotate away from the board, whereas reverses rotate toward the board. Backward and reverse entries are comprised of above-water (the line-up) and below-water (the entry) elements similar to the elements for forward and inward entries.

Above Water—The Line-Up

After the kick-look-look-reach come-out for backward and reverse entries, the diver lines up the body in preparation for the entry. There are five essential elements of the above-water line-up for backward and reverse entries. The first is the convex position.

Convex Position

After the come-out, the diver maintains a flat body alignment. However, after reaching for the water, the body forms a **convex position** in which there is a slight outward curvature from the hands to the toes like the exterior shape of a circle or sphere. The convex position is shown in figure 6.15.

Like the concave position for forward and inward entries, the convex position is formed with the entire length of the body from hands to toes. The diver remains still and holds the convex position upon contact with the water. Many divers impatiently shift their hands past their entry point before contact, which increases body curvature, loosens the body core, causes the dive to move past vertical, and contributes to a splashy entry.

The diver may arch more if the dive is lining up short of vertical, but the arch must occur *after the hips are below the waterline*. Many divers miss backward and reverse entries because they overreact and arch too much or too soon (or both) on dives that are slow or short of vertical, or both. It is not uncommon to see divers rotate past vertical on slow rotating dives. Obviously, if they could go past vertical, the dive wasn't that short or difficult to make. Note that since there is very little somersaulting motion for simple voluntary dives, such as reverse and backward dives, the diver should assume a flat body line position rather than a convex position for the line-up.

Lateral and Midline Closes

There are two options for moving the arms to the line-up position. The first is the **lateral close,** in which the arms move along the plane of the body, as indicated in figure 6.16.

Notice in the sequence of photos that, as in the lateral close for forward and inward entries, the trapezius muscles are relaxed and the elbows are slightly bent making it easier to perform the lateral close. The lateral close makes it easier to maintain the convex position.

The second option is the **midline close,** in which the hands come through the middle of the body as shown in figure 6.17. As in the lateral close, the

Figure 6.15 The first essential position for backward and reverse line-ups: the convex position.

Figure 6.16 The second essential position for backward and reverse line-ups: the lateral close.

Figure 6.17   The second essential position for backward and reverse line-ups: the midline close.

shoulders and arms should be relaxed and the hands grabbed as soon as possible. The diver should wait to squeeze the flat hand until after the arms have pushed over the ears. Squeezing the flat hand causes the shoulders to tighten and restricts the arms from moving freely and easily overhead. The hands should stay near the body as they reach for the water and then push forward toward the end of the convex curve.

One advantage of the midline close is the opportunity to grab the hands sooner, which provides more preparation time for the all-important flat-hand rip entry. It is not unusual, for example, to observe elite divers grabbing their hands immediately after the kick-out and well before they reach for the water on a 307C. The disadvantage of the midline close is that it is easier to whip the arms, arch too much, and reach past vertical on entry.

Some divers use both lateral and midline closes depending on the dive or the condition of the dive. For example, Olympic gold medalist Mark Lenzi closed laterally for the 307C but midline for the 305B. For dives rotating slowly or lining up short (or both), whipping the arms overhead with a midline close increases rotation and causes the body to achieve a more vertical entry, which is similar to closing under on forward and inward entries.

Shoulder Shrug

The trapezius and shoulder muscles should be relaxed until the arms are overhead. Just before contact with the water, the **shoulder shrug** occurs, in which the shoulders push into the neck and head and as shown in figure 6.18. The shoulder shrug for backward and reverse entries serves the same purpose that it does for forward and inward entries.

Neutral Head Position

For backward and reverse dives, the head is often tilted up and back before the line-up because of the second "look" during the kick-look-look-reach. Some elite divers don't look back, or if they do, it is slight. Others, however, look back far enough to advantageously see their entry point on the water surface. As the arms reach for the water, the head smoothly tilts back to a **neutral head position** in which the chin is approximately 90 degrees with the neck and the head is pulled back so that the cervical spine is roughly straight, as shown in figure 6.19. The diver should avoid snapping the head down into the neutral position because the downward force causes the feet to move upward and the dive to move past vertical (action–reaction).

Notice that when the head is neutral, the arms are slightly behind the ears and the scapulae are turned down and in to give a "chicken wing" appearance. Tilting the chin and head back forces the arms in front of the ears, as shown in figure 6.20. This unstable position distorts the convex position, makes it difficult to maintain a rigid upper body on contact with the water, and causes a splashy rather than rip entry. It also prevents the diver from getting a good flat hand on top of the water, as we will see in the next section.

Figure 6.18 The third essential position for backward and reverse line-ups: the shoulder shrug.

Figure 6.19 The fourth essential position for backward and reverse line-ups: the neutral head.

Figure 6.20 The incorrect head position for backward and reverse line-ups.

Flat Hand

The **flat hand** depicted in figure 6.21 for backward and reverse entries is the same as it is for forward and inward entries. Some divers achieve a better flat hand on backward and reverse entries than they do on forward and inward entries because, as they reach slightly back for the entry, they tend to turn the palm back more so that it is parallel to the water surface on contact. For forward and inward entries, some divers mistakenly turn the palm down.

Below Water—The Entry

As in the forward and inward entries, a great deal of movement occurs below the water on backward and reverse entries. Much of this action is similar, but there are some differences as well. Let's look at the five essential elements for backward and reverse entries and how they are similar to and different from those for forward and inward entries.

Quick Swim

The **quick swim** occurs immediately and rapidly upon contact with the water, just as it does for forward and inward entries. The arms remain straight throughout the swim, and the arms swim in front of rather than behind the body. Swimming behind the body can cause serious shoulder injury. The arms swim to a T position (figure 6.22). Some elite divers swim to more of a V position.

Figure 6.21 The fifth essential position for backward and reverse line-ups: the flat hand.

Figure 6.22 The first essential position for backward and reverse entries: *(a)* the quick swim to the *(b)* T position.

Scoop

The **scoop** involves putting the head back underwater, arching the back, and letting the body move in a backward somersaulting action, as shown in figure 6.23. Because the body tends to go where the head goes, the head must remain back; otherwise, the scoop won't fully occur. The scoop is equivalent to the quick 90 and serves the same purpose of sucking the water down on entry. The scoop begins as soon as the hips are underwater. Scooping before the hips are underwater causes a loose core, splashy entry, and potential sore low back. The scoop involves much more of an arched position than many divers and diving coaches realize.

Knee Save

The **knee save** involves bending the knees underwater and pushing the feet back above water to prevent the lower legs and feet from moving past vertical. Like the pike save, the knee save is an incredibly effective save that elite divers perform routinely on virtually all backward and reverse somersaulting dives. The knee save is shown in figure 6.24.

Similar to the pike save, anticipation is necessary for performing the knee save. The diver must not wait to feel the dive go over before saving. At that point the dive is already past vertical and can't be saved. The knee save must occur before the dive goes over but not before the knees are below the waterline. If performed above the waterline, the judges will see the knees break position and apply a major deduction. No deduction is applied when the knees bend underwater. The timing, speed, and amplitude of the knee bend are determined by how far and fast the dive is rotating past vertical.

Tilting the head down into the chest during the knee save draws the knees into the torso (action-reaction effect) and produces the inferior **tuck save**. The tuck save is moderately effective for dives moving just slightly past vertical but totally ineffective for dives moving significantly past vertical. Divers should always keep the head back underwater and execute a knee save.

Figure 6.23 The second essential position for backward and reverse entries: the scoop.

Figure 6.24 The third essential position for backward and reverse entries: the knee save.

6 Position

The **6 position** for backward and reverse entries involves continuing the scoop back into the entry bubbles to form a 6 as shown in figure 6.25. The head should tilt backward so the body continues scooping back into the bubble stream. If the head moves down into the chest, the body stops rotating into the 6 position. Just as it does for forward and inward entries, the 6 position keeps the body moving through the water in the same direction and speed and sucks the water down to contribute to a rip entry. When the 6 position is done correctly, the diver's upper body should be approximately parallel to the surface of the water.

Figure 6.25   The fourth essential position for backward and reverse entries: the 6 position.

Straddle

The **straddle** (figure 6.26), the fifth essential position for backward and reverse entries, occurs after the knee save and involves pulling the legs apart but not as far apart as in the straddle for forward and inward entries as shown in figure 6.13. For forward and inward entries, the straddle exceeds the width of the shoulders, but typically, the straddle for backward and reverse entries is approximately shoulder width. The straddle for backward and reverse entries serves the same purpose as it does for forward and inward entries—diffusing the plume of entry bubbles.

Most divers spread their knees slightly apart but keep their feet together during the knee save. Pulling the feet apart above water during the knee save would result in a major deduction from the judges. Late in the 6 position, the feet come apart to create the straddle.

Saving Dives Short of Vertical

Note that forward and inward dives lining up short of vertical can be saved by using a scoop save, and backward and reverse dives lining up short of vertical can be saved with a pike save. In both cases the movement of the body underwater brings the legs closer to vertical. These saves are, at best, only moderately

Figure 6.26   The fifth essential position for backward and reverse entries: the straddle.

effective and should be used only as a last-ditch effort. I never taught divers to use these saves on short dives because I didn't want the saves to be an option for them. As we discuss in the final section of this chapter, divers should focus on making their dives and getting vertical. Leaving a dive short of vertical is a big no-no in the sport of diving and should be avoided at all cost.

How to Teach the Backward Line-Up

The backward line-up is somewhat more difficult to learn than the forward line-up because most people find putting the head back when falling to be an unnatural movement. Consequently, the backward line-up often requires more acclimation time than does the forward line-up. Begin by having divers practice the dryland drills outlined in this chapter. The backward wall shrug is especially effective for preparing divers for a backward line-up into the water.

For a water entry, begin by having divers push off the side of the pool, putting their arms overhead in a line-up position, and doing a scoop save. Next, use a mat and have divers slide off the mat into the water first off poolside and then off a 1-meter springboard. Next, have them stand backward in a line-up position on the 1-meter springboard and hand spot them as they fall backward into the water. Hand spot by holding divers by the hips as they arch their backs and fall into the water. Once comfortable with this drill, divers can perform the line-up without assistance, then with a jump, and then with a backward press.

USA Diving offers some excellent resources for hand spotting and teaching beginning skills, such as their Aerial Training Process and Trampoline Skill Progression videos. For more information, go to www.usadiving.org.

Backward and Reverse Line-Up and Entry Drills

1. *Dryland kick-look-look-reach.* The diver sits on a mat in a tuck or pike position, does a kick-look-look-reach, and then closes either laterally or midline to a line-up position. This is an easy drill for practicing the close, shoulder shrug, neutral head position, and flat hand.

2. *Standing backward fall.* The diver stands on a 3-meter springboard in a backward convex line-up position, arms overhead, and simply falls. This is a great drill for helping divers at all levels learn to stay still and feel the correct body, head, and arm positions for the backward line-up.

3. *Backward roll-off in tuck and pike positions.* This drill is performed from a 3-meter springboard seated or from the feet.

4. *Backward dive with jump and no arm swing.* The diver starts by looking at the feet with the arms straight and the hands grabbed and touching the body. This drill can also be done starting with the hands apart and on the thighs.

5. *Armstand backward wall shrug.* The diver holds an armstand with the feet on a wall, the back facing the wall, and the body in a convex position. The diver then repeatedly shrugs up. This is the same as the wall shrug for forward and inward entries except that with the back to the wall, the diver can attain a slight convex position rather than a concave position.

6. *Backward and reverse dives.* Everything divers need to do for a line-up and entry on backward and reverse optional dives can be practiced on these simple dives. Olympic and world champions do these dives tuck, pike, and sometimes straight on 1-meter and 3-meter springboards and platforms. Basics, basics, basics.

7. *Arched layout backward somersault underwater.* This is a good drill for learning the 6 position. After the underwater scoop, the diver does an additional somersault in the arched layout position. Divers quickly discover that they can't perform this drill without keeping the head back. Most divers lower the head on the scoop and then the body stops somersaulting and bends at the waist into a tuck position.

8. *Push-off from wall in water.* The diver holds on to a gutter with the hands, bends the legs, puts the knees into the chest, and then pushes off the pool wall. The diver then does an arched layout somersault underwater and practices the scoop knee save, 6 position, and straddle. This is a great drill for beginning and intermediate divers.

9. *Mat scoop.* The diver lies on the abdomen in a line-up position on a mat and then swims, arches the back, lifts the chest and legs, looks up at the ceiling, and bends the knees (figure 6.27). This is an effective drill for establishing the correct scoop knee-save position.

10. *Backward slide off mat into water.* In this great beginner drill, the diver assumes a correct backward line-up position and holds it into the water. This can be done on a 1-meter springboard or platform.

Figure 6.27 Mat scoop.

Evaluating Underwater Movement

Using an underwater camera is superb for analyzing divers' below-water actions, but most diving coaches don't have funds for or access to such equipment. No worries. Often, coaches can determine what occurred underwater on an entry by analyzing the entry bubbles and where the diver's head pops up out of the water.

Analyzing Entry Bubbles

A classic telltale three-bubble pattern emerges on a great rip entry. This pattern is shown in figure 6.29. The middle bubbles are the entry point of the diver's body, and the other two bubbles are the swim bubbles from the right and left arms. Notice that the distance between the two swim bubbles is approximately the length of the diver's wingspan. Also notice that the swim bubbles are in front of the body and the entry bubbles. The swim bubbles should always be in front of the body for entries in all directions so that the diver doesn't incur a shoulder injury. What can we deduce that the diver has done underwater from the following bubble patterns?

Figure 6.29   The classic three-bubble entry pattern.

Bubbles are too close together. Bubbles too close together may indicate that the elbows bent during the quick swim. It may also indicate that the diver pulled the arms into the body on the swim rather than holding a T position with the hands toward the water surface.

Swim bubbles are behind entry bubbles. This bubble pattern usually means that the diver shifted the hands behind the head and swam behind the body instead of in front. Take heed of this pattern because it can foreshadow shoulder soreness and injury, such as shoulder dislocation.

Swim bubbles come up late. This occurrence suggests that the diver swam too slow, too late, or both.

Diffused swim bubbles. This pattern indicates that the arms collapsed underwater because the diver didn't lock out the arms or lacks triceps strength to keep the arms straight on impact.

Mistimed swim bubbles—one swim bubble comes up before the other. This pattern indicates that one arm swam before the other, probably because one elbow was bent.

Asymmetrical swim bubbles. The preceding patterns can be used to determine what each arm is doing underwater. For example, if one swim bubble is too close to the entry bubble, then that elbow was bent on the quick swim.

Analyzing the Diver's Return to the Surface

Where the diver comes up in the water after an entry often indicates what is occurring underwater. Consider the following scenarios.

Diver comes up in the entry bubbles. The 6 position was successfully completed underwater (for entries in all directions).

Diver comes up behind the entry bubbles. The diver failed to complete the 6 position. Instead of a 6, the diver did a C, L, J, or U underwater. These underwater shapes can be observed from the pool deck by watching carefully what the diver is doing underwater.

Diver comes up in front of the entry bubbles. The diver incorrectly scooped on a forward or inward entry or pike saved on a backward or reverse entry. These actions are bad habits divers should avoid in practice.

Diver comes up late. The diver performed the quick 90 too late for a forward or inward entry or performed the scoop too late for a backward or reverse entry.

Diver comes up early. The diver performed the quick 90 or the scoop too soon. These actions usually result in bending at the waist above water for forward and inward entries and excessively arching the back above water on backward and reverse entries.

Diver comes up to the side of the entry bubbles. The diver turned underwater and, most likely, above water, which results in a major deduction. Coach and diver need to monitor and fix this before it becomes a bad habit.

Concepts and Heuristics for Diving

Heuristic is a fancy term that means "rule of thumb." Following are some simple concepts and heuristics for line-ups and entries that elite divers use. We touched on some of these lightly earlier in this chapter.

Reach in front of the entry point. Every dive has a certain amount of **rotational momentum** that is referred to as **angular momentum**. Coming out of a tuck or pike slows momentum because the body lengthens (the radius is lengthened), but momentum doesn't completely stop. Consequently, the diver must reach approximately 3 or 4 inches (about 8 to 10 cm) in front of the entry point (i.e., the point where the body's center of gravity passes through the surface of the water) and allow the angular momentum to rotate the dive to vertical.

Perform line-up drills in all directions. There is a subtle but perceptible difference between forward and inward line-ups and between backward and reverse line-ups. When first attempting a forward line-up, most divers rotate past vertical; when first performing an inward line-up, most rotate short of vertical. A comparable phenomenon occurs when learning backward and reverse line-ups. Divers rotate past vertical on backward line-ups and short of vertical on reverse line-ups. This difference is connected to two effects: the distance over effect and the distance short effect.

Distance over effect. The **distance over effect** occurs when the direction of the dive matches the direction of the rotation—in other words, when the dive moves away from the board *and* somersaults away from the board. Thus, the distance over effect applies to all forward and backward somersaulting and twisting dives. The farther out the dive travels, the more the dive will tend to rotate past vertical on entry.

Come out early and reach out. The distance over effect is counteracted by two simple and easily executed actions: coming out of the dive earlier and reaching out in front of the entry point. Coming out early lengthens the body sooner to slow rotation. However, both actions must be initiated. If a diver comes out early but reaches straight down instead of out for the water, the dive will still overrotate. Many divers, even experienced divers, fail to fully comprehend the necessity of performing both actions. Note that these two actions may also be applied to reverse and inward somersaulting and twisting dives that rotate too fast.

The farther the distance from the board and the faster the speed of rotation, the sooner and farther out the diver must reach for forward and backward somersaulting and twisting dives. To automatize these two actions, the diver should purposely jump too far out on forward and backward dives and purposely somersault too fast on dives in all directions.

Distance short effect. The **distance short effect** occurs when the direction of the dive and the direction of the rotation are opposite—in other words, when the dive moves away from the board but somersaults toward the board. It is the opposite of the distance over effect and applies to all reverse and inward somersaulting and twisting dives. The farther out the dive moves, the shorter the dive is likely to be on entry.

Come out late and kick up. Like the distance over effect, the distance short effect is counteracted by two simple and easily executed movements: coming out later and kicking up. Again, both actions are necessary because if the diver comes out later but kicks down, the dive will line up short of vertical. Only these two corrections are needed. Nonelite divers often add an unnecessary third correction, such as ducking the head on inwards and arching too much on reverses, which causes the dive to overrotate.

Get vertical. Successful diving is surprisingly simple when divers set a goal to get vertical. Judges love vertical dives and hate short dives. Getting vertical is a mind-set: vertical, good; over, good (the dive can be saved, right?); short, bad. This heuristic ties in with the next one.

Make the dive. Before performance, divers need to commit to aggressively going after the dive from the outset. Divers can't get vertical on dives they don't make.

Get to the tip of the board. This heuristic ties in with the preceding two. It is much easier to make a dive and get vertical when the dive is initiated from the tip of the board or platform. The converse is also true. Landing back on the end makes the dive much more difficult than it needs to be.

Use the three Gs. The three Gs make for great line-ups and entries: Get the dive moving, Get out early, and Get the dive vertical. In other words, control the dive at the end, not the beginning. For example, a diver should rotate a 303B fast enough on 1-meter springboard so she can get out early, stop the dive with the kick-look-look-reach, and then get it vertical by using rotational momentum and pulling it through the water with the scoop knee save. Similarly, for a forward somersaulting dive such as a 105C on 1-meter springboard, a diver should rotate fast enough to pike out early, get vertical, and then use a pike-save. Many divers make the mistake of trying to cautiously control a dive at the beginning and then don't make it to vertical at the end of the dive.

CHAPTER 7

Skill Progression: Putting It All Together

The essential elements are the building blocks for all well-executed dives, and the better they are performed, the better the dive will be. For this reason, preceding chapters examined the essential elements of the forward approach, backward press, takeoff, connection, come-out, line-up, and entry. This chapter explains how to take all of these essential elements and put them together to create outstanding dives.

But first, a brief story . . .

Some years ago while in Beijing, China, I had the opportunity to observe renowned diving coach Professor Yu Fen at Tsinghua University as she coached her divers who ranged in age from 6 to 16. During my visit, Olympic gold medalist Tian Liang was also training with Yu Fen while he pondered making a comeback. It was intriguing to watch his practice, because it entailed many of the same drills that his much younger training partners were rehearsing. There, side by side, Tian Liang was practicing some of the same skills and drills as 6 and 9-year-old divers. On occasion, when a more experienced diver was having difficulty with an optional dive, such as a forward 3 1/2 somersaulting dive, Yu Fen would direct the diver to the trampoline to practice a simple forward somersault.

As scientists, writers, and coaches have made clear, helping someone become really good at something has less to do with identifying talent and more to do with nurturing excellence (e.g., Bloom, 1985; Coyle, 2009; Ericsson, 1996; Gladwell, 2008; Huber, 2013). Given the appropriate environment, people can develop into great athletes. This environment, much like Professor Yu Fen's practices, includes a clearly defined progression and mastery of essential skills. What follows is a step-by-step outline for progressing athletes from level-1 introductory divers to level-3 elite divers.

Keep in mind that each level and each progression serves as a scaffold for the subsequent level and progression. Great diving is built from the ground up. Cutting corners, by skipping skills or advancing before mastery, results in a faulty and shaky dive, just as laying a shoddy and weak foundation leads to a poorly constructed house.

Level 1: Introductory and Beginning Divers

Level 1 is the entry level for the sport of diving. It is perhaps the most important level because the primary coaching objectives are to hook young kids on the great sport of diving and begin laying a rock-solid foundation for success. Building this foundation involves providing deliberate play; creating a warm and accepting environment that engenders a positive physiological response to the sport; presenting diving-related concepts; teaching simple mental and cognitive skills (chapters 9 and 10); initiating introductory stretching and conditioning routines (chapter 8); being mindful of an annual training plan (chapter 9), and teaching simple dryland, trampoline, and diving skills.

Recall from chapter 1 that **deliberate play** is a loosely structured activity that uses flexible rules, de-emphasizes improving performance, and emphasizes fun. In contrast, **deliberate practice** is a highly structured activity that emphasizes improving performance (e.g., error detection, skill development) and giving maximal physical, mental, and emotional effort. Deliberate play and deliberate practice are equally important for developing expertise (Côté, Baker, & Abernethy, 2003).

Level 1 Introductory Diver

The **introductory diver** is someone brand new to the sport. These divers are most likely very young children who have had no experience with diving and little if any experience with other sports. The main emphasis at this level is to help these newbies become excited and enthusiastic to the point that they go home and tell mom and dad that they want to continue in the sport and practice more often. Coaches promote such a response and attitude by making sure introductory divers experience fun, find success, interact positively with other divers, receive positive reinforcement, and practice in an inviting and nurturing environment.

The introductory stage should be relatively brief. The diver should advance fairly quickly from this stage to the subsequent stage—the beginning diver stage.

Level 1 Introductory Diver Concepts

1. Diving is fun!
2. Learning new skills is fun!
   * Level 1 introductory diver deliberate practice: 20 percent
   * Level 1 introductory diver deliberate play: 80 percent

The goal here is to keep it fun and playful. Young divers will have plenty of time to become more serious about the sport later in their careers.

Level 1 Introductory Diver Games

1. Silly dives
2. Simon says
3. Play time—Divers are allowed to do whatever they like during the last 10 minutes of practice.

Level 1 Introductory Diver Practice Frequency and Duration

1. Two or three days per week
2. Each practice should be approximately 30 to 45 minutes in duration.
3. Level 1 introductory diver should transition to the beginning diver level after four to six weeks.

Level 1 Introductory Diver Mental Skills

1. Have fun.
2. Think positively.
3. Positive self-talk—Talk positively to oneself and to teammates.

Level 1 Introductory Diver Cognitive Skills

1. Pay attention and remember the coach's instructions.
2. Be mindful of and courteous to other athletes.

Level 1 Introductory Diver Warm-Up Routine

This warm-up routine is used with minimal additions by all levels of divers. Starting with the level 1 beginning diver (the subsequent section), a stretching routine is introduced. The following warm-up routine should be done as a group with coach supervision.

1. Jump rope or jumping jacks for 30 seconds.
2. Lace the fingers and swivel the hands (loosen up wrists and forearms): eight clockwise and eight counterclockwise. Simultaneously swivel the foot with the heel up and toes on the ground, and then switch to the opposite foot.
3. Hands on hips and roll hips: eight clockwise and eight counterclockwise.
4. Head circles (loosen up neck muscles): eight clockwise and eight counterclockwise.
5. Swing arms back and forth eight times.
6. Swing each leg back and forth eight times.
7. Bend the knees, hands on knees, and circle the hips eight times clockwise and eight counterclockwise.
8. Bend the knees, place the palms on a mat, and then straighten the legs with the palms remaining on the mat.
9. Sit on the mat, bend the knee, grab the foot, and rotate the ankle with the hands. Then switch to the opposite foot.
10. Pull the hands back to stretch the wrists and prepare for a flat-hand water entry.
11. Lateral leg swings: While holding on to a bar, swing one leg eight times from side to side, and then switch and swing the other leg.
12. Medial leg swings: Hold on to a bar, bend over, and kick one leg up and behind eight times; then switch legs.
13. Upper body twists: With the arms in a T position, twist from side to side eight times.

14. Butterfly stretch: Seated on a mat, bend the knees, push the bottoms of the feet together, and pull the feet into the body.

15. Quad stretch: From a standing position, bend one knee and grab the foot from behind.

Level 1 Introductory Diver Coach Reminders

1. Keep it fun, playful, and social.
2. Create slight challenges, but ensure success.
3. Create a positive conditioned response.
4. Keep practices short—not all skills and drills can be performed at each practice.
5. Include deliberate play.

A checklist is provided for each level that outlines the dryland, dryboard, and trampoline drills for skill development and physical conditioning, as well as the springboard and platform drills and dives to be performed by the diver at each level. The checklists presented in this chapter are also available for download in fillable .pdf form. Visit www.humankinetics.com/products/all-products/Springboard-and-Platform-Diving for access. The checklist for the level 1 introductory diver follows.

LEVEL 1 INTRODUCTORY DIVER PROGRESSION CHECKLIST

Skill	Skill Description	Pass-P	Redo-R	Comments
CONDITIONING				
Hollow rocks	Holding hollow shape during each rock			
Squat jumps	Hands on hips, chest up, hips rolled under			
Supermans	Feet together, legs and arms straight, toes pointed			
Pike-ups lying on mat	Touch toes, slide hands along side of legs, look at feet			
Hollow barrel rolls	Hold hollow shape while rolling			
Single-leg pelvis lifts	Hold for 5 seconds			
Double-leg pelvis lifts	Hold for 5 seconds			
Crunches	Knees bent, hands behind head, bring back off floor			
Supine lifts	Lift by feet, shake, alternate letting go right foot, then left foot			
Prone lifts	Lift by feet, shake, alternate letting go right foot, then left foot			
DRYLAND—FLOOR				
Forward rolls	Tuck jump between somersault rolls			
Backward rolls	Tuck jump between somersault rolls			
Flat hand grab	Bottom hand flat, top hand fingers and thumb grab flat hand			
Seated lateral close to hand grab	Thumbs up, shoulders relaxed, lateral close, flat hand			
Hurdle position against wall	Back and arms against wall, knee 90°, foot pointed and back			
Jump from squat position	Arms overhead, hips rolled under			
Kick-look-look-reach	Hold for 5 seconds			
Continuous straight jumps	Across floor, arms overhead, tight core			
Toe crackers	Coach stretches toes			
DRYLAND—DRYBOARD				
Standing 100A from squat position	Hips rolled under, arms overhead, swing arms			
200A	No arm swing, straight body position, bend knees on landing			
Standing 100A	With arm swing			
200A	With arm swing			
Forward dryboard rocking	Stand on end of board and gently rock with feet on board			
DRYLAND—TRAMPOLINE				
Standing jump with no arm swing	Straight body alignment			
Standing jump with arm swing	Straight body alignment			
Single jump seat drop	Palms touch trampoline on seat drop, finish to feet			

(continued)

Level 1 Introductory Diver Progression Checklist *(CONTINUED)*

Skill	Skill Description	Pass-P	Redo-R	Comments
DRYLAND—TRAMPOLINE *(continued)*				
Single jump with half twist	No arm swing, arms in T position entire time			
Open tuck jump	Jump straight up and finish to feet			
Open pike jump	Jump straight up and finish to feet			
Handstand hold	Straight body position in belt or coach spot			
Tuck jump	Grab legs, finish to straight body line			
Pike jump	Touch toes; finish to straight body line			
Consecutive jumps	3-5 in belt, with arm swing			
Double-bouncing tuck jumps	In belt; finish each jump with straight body position			
DIVING—SPRINGBOARD 1M				
100A—arms overhead	Poolside, no arm swing, hips rolled under			
200A—arms overhead	Poolside, no arm swing, hips rolled under			
100A—arms overhead	1M, standing, no arm swing, hips rolled under			
200A—arms overhead	1M, no arm swing, hips rolled under			
100C to cannonball	Poolside, land in water in tuck position			
Forward surface torpedo	Push off pool wall, hand grab, maintain straight body line			
Backward surface torpedo	Push off pool wall, hand grab, maintain straight body line			
101	Poolside, kneeling or track start			
101 mat slide	1M, hand grab and straight arms overhead			
201 mat slide	1M, hand grab and straight arms overhead			
100A	1M, standing, with arm swing, straight body position			
200A	1M, with arm swing, straight body position			
100C, B	Poolside, with arm swing, kick to straight body position			
200C, B	Poolside, with arm swing, kick to straight body position			
400A	1M, no arm swing, enter water with slight inward lean			
300A	1M, no arm swing, enter water with slight reverse lean			
101	1M, from squat position, hand grab, arms overhead			
101	1M, from open pike, hand grab, arms overhead			
101	1M, from half squat, slight jump			
101	1M, from hollow position and fall to water			

Skill	Skill Description	Pass-P	Redo-R	Comments
	DIVING—SPRINGBOARD 1M *(continued)*			
101	1M, stand sideways, arms in T, one leg up, turn to 101			
201	1M, fall with coach spot			
401	1M, hand grab, arms overhead, no press, open pike			
Tear Drop	Poolside, jump out, land on seat with hands touching toes			
102C	In water, circle arms to somersault			
202C	In water, circle arms to somersault			
	DIVING—SPRINGBOARD 3M			
100A step-off no arm swing	Start with arms in T position; enter water with arms at sides			
	DIVING—PLATFORM			
100A	1M, with straight body position			
200A	1M, with straight body position			
100C, B	1M, kick to straight position			
200C, B	1M, kick to straight position			
101 mat slide	1M, hand grab and straight arms overhead			
101	1M, from squat position, arms overhead			
101	1M, from open pike, hand grab, arms overhead			
101	1M, from hollow position			
201 mat slide	1M, hand grab and straight arms overhead			
201	1M, with spot from coach			
400A	1M, no arm swing, enter water with slight inward tillt			
300A	1M, no arm swing, enter water with slight reverse tillt			
401	1M, hand grab, arms overhead, spot from coach			
100A running	1M, jump up off platform; straight body position			
100A step-off	3M, start arms in T position, enter water with arms at sides			

Notes:

1. Skills are listed in order of learning progression.
2. All skills and dives performed with arm swing unless "no arm swing" is noted.
3. Coach spot on jumps to make sure diver is safe distance from board.
4. At least 80-85% proficiency required to pass each skill.

Coach Final Comments:

From J. Huber, 2016, *Springboard and Platform Diving* (Champaign, IL. Human Kinetics).

Level 1 Beginning Diver

The **beginning diver** is someone who has found enjoyment in the introductory practices and wishes to further pursue the sport of diving. These divers are intrigued and curious enough about the sport to want to spend additional practice time discovering and learning.

Level 1 Beginning Diver Concepts

1. The sport of diving consists of essential elements that are the foundation for performing great dives.
2. Flexibility and physical conditioning are important aspects of practice for improving and advancing as a diver.
3. The coach's comments are helpful suggestions for getting better and should be eagerly accepted. They should not be interpreted as personal criticism.
   - Level 1 beginning diver deliberate practice: 40 percent
   - Level 1 beginning diver deliberate play: 60 percent

Level 1 Beginning Diver Games

1. Follow the leader
2. Tuck or pike jump: After the diver jumps from the springboard, the coach calls out "tuck" or "pike," and the diver has to perform that position before entering the water.
3. Pretend meet: The coach announces a dive (e.g., forward jump) and gives a score.

Level 1 Beginning Diver Practice Frequency and Duration

1. Three or four days per week
2. Each practice should be approximately 45 to 60 minutes in duration.
3. The transition to the next level depends on mastering the skills, drills, and dives.

Level 1 Beginning Diver Mental Skills

1. Cognitive structuring: Practice is a privilege, not a right. I don't *have* to practice; I *get* to practice.
2. Mental imagery: Visualizing is part of motor learning and motor performance.
3. Energy management: Physical relaxation is part of motor learning and performance.

Level 1 Beginning Diver Cognitive Skills

1. Pay attention to the coach's comments.
2. Incorporate the coach's comments on the next performance attempt.
3. Cognitive organization: The six dive categories are forward, backward, reverse, inward, twisting, and armstand.

Level 1 Beginning Diver Stretching Routine

After the warm-up routine is performed (outlined in the preceding introductory diver level), divers do the following stretching routine (a warm-up routine always precedes the stretching routine).

1. Split with one knee on the ground.
2. Hip flexor stretch: One leg is forward and bent, and the back leg is straight. Then switch legs. This may be done with the back leg bent and the foot against a wall.
3. Toe point squeeze: diver curls toes and foot down into a toe point using hands.
4. Pike sandwich: The legs are straight, the head is between the knees, the hands are past the dorsiflexed feet, and a teammate or coach pushes on the rounded part of the back.
5. Grab a railing with thumbs touching and arms straight. Bend down and stretch the shoulders. The coach or another diver may push down on the middle back to create more stretch.
6. Hamstring and side stretch: With the foot on a bar, hamstring stretch each leg, and touch the elevated foot with the opposite hand.

Level 1 Beginning Diver Coach Reminders

1. Keep it fun, playful, and social.
2. Create challenging but attainable tasks to ensure success.
3. Practice now should be slightly longer and more structured. The diver works even more closely with the coach. Deliberate play, however, is still important and accounts for much of practice.
4. Consider individual developmental differences. Athletes vary in their level of physical, emotional, social, and cognitive development.
5. Consider individual learning differences. For example, some divers benefit more from visual presentations and observations, some divers benefit more from verbal explanations, some diver benefit more from guided instruction, and so on. Of course, all types of presentations have merit.
6. Support divers' efforts to participate in other sports. The experiences they gain from those sports contribute to their development and, ultimately, to their diving success should they choose to someday focus exclusively on diving.

The checklist for the level 1 beginning diver follows.

LEVEL 1 BEGINNING DIVER PROGRESSION CHECKLIST

Skill	Skill Description	Pass-P	Redo-R	Comments
CONDITIONING				
60-second squat hold	90° knee bend with back against wall, arms overhead			
50 sit-ups	Knees bent, hands behind head, touch knees with elbows			
Headstand	10 seconds			
Armstand	10 seconds with spot and straight body alignment			
Hanging tuck-up	Knees together, 90° or higher			
Kneeling double-arm swing	Hips rolled under, tight core, no shoulder movement			
Hollow hold	Prop feet and shoulders and hold hollow			
Push-up	Flat back, hips slightly elevated, chest touches ground			
Body squat	Hips under, knees in front of toes, 90° knee bend			
Back extension	Arms in T position, heels together, hold position			
Leg scissors	Straight legs, good toe point, sitting up slightly			
Kick-look-look-reach	With pike out			
Tuck jumps	Knees to chest or close to, legs straight before touch ground			
DRYLAND—FLOOR				
One-step hurdle to hanging bar	Straight arms and hold stretch position on bar			
Hurdle step-up	One-step hurdle to low box, legs straight on contact			
Armstand pop-up	Forward & back rolls to armstand with spot; 5 second hold			
Lateral arm close	Seated and standing, tight core			
Pike-open-close-swim-pike save	From standing pike position; draw one leg up for pike save			
Tuck position	Lay on back, draw knees to shoulders, then V position			
Tuck position pick-up	Diver rolls back in C position & coach picks up diver by heels			
Pike position push down	Coach pushes diver's back to flatten pike			
Twist position pick-up	Diver in D position and coach picks up diver by heels			
Inward heel kick	Quick ankle snap and pop heels into mat			
Model twist sequence	1-2-3-4: reach, drop, turn, arms into tight twist			
Model forward hurdle	With arm swing, good body alignment, and hurdle foot back			
Armstand holds	Against wall, forward and backward entry position			

Skill	Skill Description	Pass-P	Redo-R	Comments
DRYLAND—DRYBOARD				
Floppy feet	From end of board, slightly bounce high enough to point toes			
100A, B, C	Standing, finish to feet with straight body			
100A, B, C to seat drop	Finish to seat drop with palms on mat for support			
200A, B, C	Finish to feet with straight body			
200C, B to seat drop	Finish to seat drop with palms on mat for support			
400A	With arm press, slight inward tilt			
300A	Standing, with arm press, slight reverse tilt			
100A, B, C	One-step hurdle, finish to feet with straight body			
100A, B, C	Full approach, finish to feet with straight body			
100A	Double bounce from end of dryboard			
DRYLAND—TRAMPOLINE				
Two-bounce jump	Stay in center of trampoline and finish to straight body line			
Single jump to back drop	Straight legs and body, land with arms in T position			
Single jump to stomach drop	Straight legs and body, land with arms in T position			
Single jump with half twist	Arms remain in T position the entire time			
Single jump full twist	Arms remain in T position the entire time			
Triple jump with arm swing	Stay in center of trampoline, finish to straight body line			
Hurdle jumps	Lift hurdle knee with each jump, foot back in hurdle			
One-step hurdle	Finish to straight body line in middle of trampoline			
100C, B	With one-step hurdle; finish in middle of trampoline			
101C to armstand	In belt, double bounce			
201C to armstand	In belt, double bounce			
401C to armstand	In belt, double bounce			
301C to armstand	In belt, double bounce			
5111A	In belt, double bounce			
5211A to armstand	In belt, double bounce			
102C	In belt or coach spot, double bounce			
202C	In belt or coach spot, double bounce			
402C	In belt or coach spot, double bounce			
Back drop	In belt, double bounce, watch feet, hold hollow position			

(continued)

Level 1 Beginning Diver Progression Checklist (CONTINUED)

Skill	Skill Description	Pass-P	Redo-R	Comments
DIVING—SPRINGBOARD 1M				
100B, C	Standing, double bounce, full approach			
200B, C	Jump with no press then full press			
400A, B, C	Jump with no press then full press			
300A, B, C	Standing, double bounce, full approach			
101 hollow	Arms overhead, falling, single jump, double jump			
101C, B	Standing, double bounce, full approach			
201C, B	Jump with no press then full press			
401C, B	Jump with no press then full press			
301C, B	Single & double bounce, coach spot if desired			
102C, B	Standing, double bounce, full approach			
103C, B	Double bounce, full approach			
5111A	Standing, double jump, full approach			
5211A	Standing from quarter twist, then full press			
5101A	Standing, double bounce, full approach			
5102A	Standing, double bounce, full approach			
5201A	With arms in T position, no press			
5301A	With arms in T position, slight reverse lean, no press			
5122D	Underwater, slight pike, snap, wrap			
5223D	Float on back, arms T position, wrap twist			
101 with pike save	Poolside, arms overhead, pike save			
201 with scoop knee save	Push off pool wall, scoop, knee save			
DIVING—SPRINGBOARD 3M				
100A, B, C	Standing, double bounce, full approach			
200A, B, C	Standing without press, with press			
300A, B, C	Standing, double bounce, full approach			
400A, B, C	Standing without press, with press			
101C, B	Open pike, seated, standing, double bounce, full approach			
401C, B	No press, arms overhead, then with press			
201A, C, B	Arms overhead, back fall with spot, then with full press			
301C, B	Standing, single bounce, double bounce, full approach			
DIVING—PLATFORM				
100A, B, C	1M and 3M standing, then two hop			
200A, B, C	1M and 3M with press			
300A, B, C	1M and 3M with slight reverse tilt			
400A, B, C	1M and 3M with slight inward tilt			
101C, B	1M and 3M standing, then two hop			

Skill	Skill Description	Pass-P	Redo-R	Comments
DIVING—PLATFORM *(continued)*				
201 C	1M, coach spot			
101B	3M pike roll off line-up			

Notes:

Coach Final Comments:

1. Remember individual differences in rate of mastery attainment.
2. Utilize drills cited throughout the textbook.
3. Bend knees on all feet first dryland landings.
4. At least 80-85% proficiency required to pass each skill.

From J. Huber, 2016, *Springboard and Platform Diving* (Champaign, IL. Human Kinetics).

Level 2: Novice and Intermediate Divers

Level 2 is distinguished by a noticeable decrease in deliberate play and an increase in deliberate practice. At this level divers are somewhat more committed to the sport, yet still may have an interest in other sports—an interest that at this level should be respected and supported.

Level 2 Novice Diver

The **novice diver** is someone who continues to enjoy the sport and would like to pursue it further and engage in low-level (i.e., novice) competition. These divers are curious to learn more about the sport and discover what more they can accomplish and how good they can become. At this level the coach continues to be an influential role model for all types of behavior: social behaviors, learning behaviors, motor behaviors, and champion behaviors. The 3-meter is introduced, and physical conditioning is significantly increased.

Level 2 Novice Diver Concepts

1. Beauty is defined in diving as straight lines, simplicity of movement, and smoothness of performance.
2. Working closely with a coach is important for improving diving.
3. The 3-meter springboard and 10-meter platform are our premier Olympic events.
4. Great diving is built on sound fundamentals.
   - Level 2 novice diver deliberate practice: 60 percent
   - Level 2 novice diver deliberate play: 40 percent

Level 2 Novice Diver Games

1. Jump or dive: As the diver is coming off the board, the coach calls out "jump" or "dive," and the diver has to do whatever the coach calls out.
2. Jump or dive and catch: As the diver leaves the springboard, the coach throws something (e.g., a pull buoy) for the diver to catch and hold while entering the water. The diver earns 1 point for a jump, 2 points for a dive, 3 points for a somersault, 4 points for a 1 1/2 somersault, and so on. The diver must emerge still holding the pull buoy to receive points.
3. Watch videos of great dives.

Level 2 Novice Diver Practice Frequency and Duration

1. Three or four days per week
2. Each practice should be approximately 60 to 90 minutes in duration.

Level 2 Novice Diver Mental Skills

1. Mental imagery: Visualize dives before dive performance and at night in bed before falling asleep (chapter 10).
2. Self-talk: Make it positive, motivating, directional, and responsive to self-doubt (chapter 10).
3. Other skills for handling the fear of learning new dives: see chapter 10 and discussion on handling fear.

Level 2 Novice Diver Cognitive Skills: RIPS (chapter 1)

R: *Review* briefly the coach's comments on your last dive, and make the corrections on the next dive.

I: *Immediately* look at and listen to the coach after performing the dive.

P: *Pose* questions if unclear about the coach's comments.

S: *Strategize*: Rehearse, elaborate, organize, and return to the first step. Novice divers can use the following simple strategies for staying cognitively engaged during practice.

1. Simple rehearsal: repeat the coach's comments, repeat physical movement of correction to be made on subsequent dive.
2. Simple elaboration: consider the meaning of and the reason for the coach's comments.
3. Simple organization: consider how the coach's comments relate to other aspects of the dive or drill you are working on.

Level 2 Novice Diver Stretching Routine

At this level, divers work on gaining a full range of flexibility, because this is the time in their careers when they can become the most flexible.

1. Full splits on the floor.
2. Partner leg lift with the back against a wall with dorsiflexion: The ultimate goal is to raise the leg to the chest.
3. Shoulder stretch: Lie on the abdomen with the arms straight overhead; a coach or teammate lifts up on the arms.
4. Calf stretch.
5. Triceps stretch.
6. Forward lunge with lean.
7. Side lunge with lean.
8. Straight-leg kicks: Kick one leg up and touch the toes with the hand.
9. Arm butterfly stretch: Sit on the ground and put the hands behind the head; a coach or teammate stands behind and pulls the elbows back.

Level 2 Novice Diver Coach Reminders

1. Keep it fun, playful, and social.
2. Create challenging but attainable tasks to ensure success.
3. Introduce more mental skills and associate them with diving performance and success.
4. Remember that young children think in concrete terms and may not fully understand abstract concepts such as Newton's third law. Nevertheless, these concepts are worth introducing now.
5. Physical conditioning is a high priority and should be a significant part of practice.
6. Sound fundamentals (X's and O's) build great divers, so be patient and promote mastery of these basic building blocks.

The level 2 novice diver checklist follows.

LEVEL 2 NOVICE DIVER PROGRESSION CHECKLIST

Skill	Skill Description	Pass-P	Redo-R	Comments
CONDITIONING				
Armstand hold	90 seconds against wall			
Armstand shrugs	Against wall--both forward and backward			
Wall sit 90° knee bend	90 seconds, back flat against wall, arms overhead			
Hanging tuck-ups	Knees up together and then V position			
Hanging pike-ups	Keep knees locked, legs to head			
Tuck jumps	Consecutive jumps on crash mat or port-a-pit, knees to chest			
Lunge jumps	Consecutive jumps on folding mat			
Single-leg jump	Consecutive jumps on folding mat			
Upper-body extensions	Torso hangs over mat; teammate holds legs, 4 ways			
DRYLAND—FLOOR				
Tuck somersaults in all directions	Start on elevated mat, coach spot			
Armstand split-leg hold	Hand spot, use wall or bench for control, see chapter 2			
Armstand tuck & pike hold	Hand spot, use wall or bench for control, see chapter 2			
Armstand pop-ups	From armstand, pop up and finish to feet			
Hanging C position	Arms next to ears, open hips to C position, chin on chest			
Hanging hurdle	One-step hurdle to hanging bar			
Hang-drop punch jump	Drop from bar, punch jump to elevated mat			
Hang-drop punch somersault	Drop from bar, punch somersault to seat drop on mat			
One-step hurdle to bench	Arms straight and overhead, legs straight before contact			
Four-step hurdle	Consecutive four-step hurdles across floor			
102C to seat drop	Standing & running, land legs straight, use hands for landing			
Forward armstand fall to flat back	Off mat to mat of same height			
Forward armstand fall to seat drop	Off elevated mat to lower mat			
Back armstand to abdomen	Off mat to mat of equal height			
Forward approach to magic position	On springfloor or mat; full approach			
Platform backward press drills	See chapter 3			

Skill	Skill Description	Pass-P	Redo-R	Comments
DRYLAND—DRYBOARD				
Two-bounce jump A, B, and C	Straight body line, bend knees on landing			
201C, B	Landing on back in open pike position			
301C, B	Standing, landing on back in open pike position			
102C to seat drop	Standing; use hands for landing; spot from coach			
202C	In belt			
302C	In belt			
402C	In belt			
103C, B	In belt; double bouncing; finish to armstand			
403C, B	In belt; arms overhead; no arm swing; finish to armstand			
203C, B	In belt, finish to armstand			
303C, B	In belt, finish to armstand			
DRYLAND—TRAMPOLINE				
Three-bounce 100A, B, C	Stay in center of trampoline and finish to straight body line			
Barrel roll	Straight tight body line with hands in twist position			
Swivel hips	Arms overhead and body straight off mat before twisting			
Full twisting backdrop	Show proficiency in belt, then out of belt with coach spot			
101C, B	In belt, pike out, finish to armstand			
201C, B	In belt, pike out, finish to armstand			
102C and B	In belt, out of belt, coach spot, finish to feet & seat drop			
202C and B	In belt, then out of belt, coach spot, finish to feet			
103C and B	In belt, pike out, finish to armstand			
203C with two bounces	In belt, spot, finish with hands on thighs			
303C with one-step hurdle	In belt, spot, finish with hands on thighs			
104C with two bounces	In belt; start with arms overhead; no arm swing, spot			
204C with two bounces	In belt, spot, finish with straight legs, hands on thighs			
Backdrop to pike position	Land on back in pike, legs straight; hands on mid shins			
102A and 202A	In belt, spot			
5122D	In belt, establish straight position early before twist			
5223D	In belt, use down and in twist technique to teach			

(continued)

Level 2 Novice Diver Progression Checklist *(CONTINUED)*

Skill	Skill Description	Pass-P	Redo-R	Comments
DIVING—SPRINGBOARD 1M				
101C	With pike-out and straight out			
201C	With pike out and straight out			
201B	Header with hands on side			
301C	With pike-out and straight out			
301B	Header with hands on side			
401C	With pike-out and straight out			
102C	With pike-out			
103C, B	Double bounce then full approach			
202C	With pike-out and straight out			
302C	With pike-out and straight out			
402C	With pike-out and straight out			
102B	Open pike with snap to straight position			
202B	Open pike and closed pike			
302B	Open pike and closed pike			
402B	Closed pike			
102A	Straight body position immediately off board			
202A	Straight body position immediately off board			
5121D	Straight body off board, 1/2 twist with arms in T position			
5122D	Straight body off board, arms into body at 1/2 twist			
5221D	Straight body position immediately off board, half twist with arms in T position			
5223D	Straight body, down and in twisting			
DIVING—SPRINGBOARD 3M				
103C, B	With pike out, single jump, double bounce, full approach			
Back fall line-up	Start with arms overhead in line-up position			
Forward roll off	Start in open pike position			
301C, B	Emphasize kick-look-look-reach			
DIVING—PLATFORM				
101C, B	1M, full approach			
102C, B	1M, standing, coach spot, then with full approach			
103C, B	3M, standing, running, with pike out			
201B	3M			
202C, B	1M, full press, coach spot			
401C, B	1M, full press, coach spot			
402C	1M, full press, coach spot			
301C and B	3M, coach spot			

Skill	Skill Description	Pass-P	Redo-R	Comments
DIVING—PLATFORM *(continued)*				
302C	1M, full press, coach spot			
Armstand dive	1M, coach spot			
611A	1M, coach spot			
612B	3M, fall first, then pike			
621A	1M, arms locked out on fall			
6211A	1M, arms up first before 1/2 twist			
101B	5M, roll off, then standing			
401B	5M			

Notes:

1. Skills are listed in order of learning progression.
2. Emphasize using eyes to spot, even on simple drills and dives.
3. Utilize drills cited throughout the textbook.
4. At least 80-85% proficiency required to pass each skill.

Coach Final Comments:

From J. Huber, 2016, *Springboard and Platform Diving* (Champaign, IL. Human Kinetics).

Level 2 Intermediate Diver

The **intermediate diver** is someone who now takes the sport more seriously and engages in more deliberate practice. These divers are interested in competition and learning more difficult dives. At this level, mental training becomes important for handling fear and maintaining composure and mental focus during dive performance both in practice and competition.

Level 2 Intermediate Diver Concepts

1. Diving is fun. Yes, this concept is worth repeating and emphasizing at this level—and at all levels.
2. Competition is fun. Competition is something to embrace, to enjoy, to give your best effort, and to perceive as an opportunity to gain something positive, not something negative.
3. Mental training is as important as diving skills and is a significant part of performing well under pressure.
4. Learning is defined as change that persists over time.
5. A significant connection exists between relaxation and performance.
6. Effort and ability are changeable and self-directed.
7. An internal locus of control means that each diver has control over success and failure through increased effort and increased ability.
   * Level 2 intermediate diver deliberate practice: 80 percent
   * Level 2 intermediate diver deliberate play: 20 percent

Level 2 Intermediate Diver Games

1. Challenge another diver to a contest.
2. Hit a cold turkey dive.
3. Take part in a best rip entry contest.
4. Challenge another diver to learn a new dive.

Level 2 Intermediate Diver Practice Frequency and Duration

1. Five or six days per week
2. Each practice should be approximately 60 to 90 minutes in duration.

Level 2 Intermediate Diver Mental Skills

1. Energy management of three sources of energy: physical, emotional, and mental
2. Relaxation techniques: breathing and muscle control
3. Cognitive restructuring
4. Self-monitoring
5. Preperformance routine: A specific routine done before dive performance that includes all five pillars of mental training. See chapter 10 for more details about these mental skills.

Level 2 Intermediate Diver Cognitive Skills

1. Complex rehearsal: Involves rehearsing corrections mentally (imagery), verbally (self-talk), and physically while focusing on specific details of the movement as well as the actual intensity of the movement.

2. Complex elaboration: Using analogical processes (i.e., relating something new to something old, something already understood) such as "Hey, the forward platform take-off is kind of like my punch front in gymnastics!"

3. Complex organization: Forming relationships of new information with old information, such as "Hey, the C position on reverse somersaulting dives also works for backward somersaulting divers, so reverses and backs are kind of in the same group of dives!"

Level 2 Intermediate Diver Stretching Routine

Stretching is critical at every level, but especially at the intermediate diver level. This level occurs at an optimal time when divers have decided to more fully engage in the sport and when their bodies are most malleable and adaptable to increased flexibility. The stretching routine at this level is the same as at the preceding level; however, the volume and intensity are significantly higher, and the emphasis is on maximal flexibility.

Level 2 Intermediate Diver Coach Reminders

1. Reserve some practice time for mental training.

2. Provide divers with relaxation audio files.

3. Emphasize mastery learning. Divers should not progress to a subsequent skill until they have achieved at least 80-85 percent mastery on the current skill. This reminder is true for all levels.

4. Fundamentals are the critical building blocks on which all dives are built, and you are the most significant coach for establishing this foundation.

5. Now is an appropriate time to teach a preperformance routine.

6. The most influential role model for your divers is you. They are always watching you, so lead by example.

The level 2 intermediate diver checklist follows.

LEVEL 2 INTERMEDIATE DIVER PROGRESSION CHECKLIST

Skill	Skill Description	Pass-P	Redo-R	Comments
CONDITIONING				
Incline sit-ups	Knees bent, hands behind head, touch knees with elbows			
Hanging pike-up window wipers	Bring legs up and then move side-to-side			
Armstand pike-ups	Back against wall, raise and lower lets to 90°			
Armstand push-up	Bend elbows more than for shrugs, use landing mat			
Leg curls	Sit on bench, teammate provides resistance			
Leg extensions	Lay on stomach, teammate provides resistance			
Hollow hold	Feet and shoulders propped up			
Board push downs	Push board up and down, no jump			
Squat	With teammate on back			
DRYLAND—FLOOR				
Somersaults tuck all directions	Hand spot from coach from elevated mat if necessary			
102C	Hand spot from coach from elevated mat if necessary			
102C	Running and finish to seat drop onto elevated mat			
102B	Running to seat drop on mat			
Back armstand 1/2 twist to back	From mat to mat of equal height			
Back armstand 1/2 twist to seat	From elevated mat to lower mat, finish to seat drop			
Armstand hold	45 seconds			
Armstand press-up	Using pike-up, tuck-up, split-leg press to straight line			
DRYLAND—DRYBOARD				
Somersaults tuck all directions	Out of belt; coach spot			
5122D	Standing and land in seat drop			
DRYLAND—TRAMPOLINE				
402, 202—C & B	Out of belt; coach spot			
102, 302—C & B	Out of belt; one-step hurdle; coach spot			
102A	In belt, out of belt, two bounce, arms overhead on start			
202A	In belt, out of belt, two bounce, arm swing, spot			
5122D	From knee drop; finish to seat drop			
5122D	One-bounce; finish to seat drop			
5112D	From backdrop and finish to feet			
105C, B with two bounces	In belt; finish to armstand			

Skill	Skill Description	Pass-P	Redo-R	Comments
DRYLAND—TRAMPOLINE *(continued)*				
One-step hurdle 305C and B	In belt; finish to armstand			
5223D with two bounces	In belt, arms overhead; no arm swing; finish to seat drop			
5323D with one-step hurdle	In belt, arms overhead; no arm swing; finish to seat drop			
5122D with two bounces	In belt; arms overhead; no arm swing; finish to feet			
5124D with two bounces	In belt; arms overhead and no arm swing; finish to feet			
Ball out	First back-to-feet and then back-to-back			
Forward 3/4 somersault	Finish to flatback			
Back 3/4 somersault	Finish to stomach, hands on trampoline			
DIVING—SPRINGBOARD 1M				
101A, B, C with two bounces	Good body alignment on bounces, pike out of B and C			
301A, B, C with two bounces	Good body alignment on bounces, pike out of B and C			
401A				
201A				
103C, B	Two-bounce and with hurdle			
104C	Position B also if ready			
105C				
203C	Position B also if ready			
204C				
303C	Position B also if ready			
304C				
302A				
403C	Position B also if ready			
5132D				
5132D				
5124D				
5231D				
5233D				
5225D	If ready			
5321D				
DIVING—SPRINGBOARD 3M				
103C, B	Two-bounce			
105C, B	Two-bounce and full approach			
301C, B	Two-bounce			
203C, B				
303C, B	Two-bounce and full approach			
403C, B				
5132D				

(continued)

Level 2 Intermediate Diver Progression Checklist (CONTINUED)

Skill	Skill Description	Pass-P	Redo-R	Comments
DIVING—SPRINGBOARD 3M *(continued)*				
5231D				
5233D				
5331D				
DIVING—PLATFORM				
Jumps all directions	7.5M, 10M			
201C, B	5M			
301C, B	5M			
103B	5M, standing, then running			
203C	3M			
303C	5M			
403C	5M			
102B	3M, open pike			
202A	3M			
5122D	3M			
5132D	5M			
5221D	3M			
5223D	3M or 5M			
5231D	5M			
613B	5M			
623B	5M			
101B	7.5M, 10M, roll off, then from standing pike position			
401B	7.5M, 10M			
103B	7.5M, 10M, standing			
301B	7.5M			
612B	7.5M			

Notes:

1. Skills are listed in order of learning progression.
2. Utilize drills cited throughout the textbook.
3. Coach spotting on all drills.
4. At least 80-85% proficiency required to pass each skill.

Coach Final Comments:

From J. Huber, 2016, *Springboard and Platform Diving* (Champaign, IL. Human Kinetics).

Level 3: Advanced and Elite Divers

Perhaps the defining feature of **level 3** is the diver's willingness to commit more fully to diving at the expense of other sports. Level 3 divers may start off at this level still participating in another sport but soon dedicate themselves exclusively to diving. The other defining feature is the amount of deliberate practice. At this level divers find satisfaction through deliberate practice. They still engage in play time, but they are increasingly interested in learning more difficult dives, perfecting new skills, and developing consistency.

Level 3 Advanced Diver

The **advanced diver** is someone who has decided to become even more committed to the sport and engage almost exclusively in deliberate practice. These divers want to set loftier goals, participate in challenging competitions, and make big strides in their diving performances.

Level 3 Advanced Diver Concepts

1. Newton's third law of motion
2. Mental training is as important as physical training.
3. The 13 characteristics of deliberate practice (see chapter 1) are necessary for advancement to the elite diver level.
4. The strength of the effort is the measure of the result.
5. Goal setting: daily, weekly, monthly, and longer-range process and outcome goals
6. Good nutrition and recovery are necessary for good training and adaptation.
   * Level 3 advanced diver deliberate practice: 90 percent
   * Level 3 advanced diver deliberate play: 10 percent

Level 3 Advanced Diver Games

At this level games become more competition oriented.

1. Coach challenge (e.g., everyone has to do a 305 for a score of 7 or better).
2. Hit a dive three consecutive times.
3. Change practice routine (e.g., do everything in the reverse order of normal practice).

Level 3 Advanced Diver Practice Frequency and Duration

1. Five or six days per week
2. Each practice should be approximately 90 to 120 minutes in duration.
3. Divers may begin practicing twice a day.

Level 3 Advanced Diver Mental Skills

1. Energy management
2. Cognitive restructuring
3. Self-monitoring

Level 3 Advanced Diver Cognitive Skills: MURDER

M: Set your *mood* before practice.

U: *Understand* what you want to accomplish during practice.

R: *Recall* what you learned from your last performance or last practice.

D: *Digest* your coach's comments.

E: *Expand* the information.

R: *Review* your mistakes.

Level 3 Advanced Diver Stretching Routine

Divers should continue performing a stretching routine both before and after practice. This is a good time to consider individual differences so that divers are working individually on areas where they might be deficient in flexibility and need extra work.

Level 3 Advanced Diver Coach Reminders

1. Remedial work may be necessary. If some of the building blocks (fundamentals) are incorrect, divers will need to regress and relearn the fundamentals in which they are deficient.

2. Remember the importance of developing the individual as both an athlete and a human being. Athletes who develop as people are more empowered and more successful both during and after their diving careers.

3. Self-discipline is important at all levels but especially at this and the subsequent level for both athlete and coach. Remember the adage: What you hope to see in others, may you see in yourself.

4. You should be creating and following an annual individualized training plan (see chapter 9) as well as providing divers with a daily individual practice plan (chapter 1). These plans are increasingly more important at each level. Elite coaches always have a master plan.

The level 3 advanced diver checklist follows.

LEVEL 3 ADVANCED DIVER PROGRESSION CHECKLIST

Skill	Skill Description	Pass-P	Redo-R	Comments
CONDITIONING				
Prone trunk lift	Teammate holds legs, use weight vest			
Prone leg lift	Weight vest on legs			
Prone lateral lift	Lift legs and upper body simultaneously, use weight vest			
Incline sit-up	Keep legs straight			
Prone pike-up	From curved surface			
Squat with we ight	Maintain good form, head up			
Plyometrics with body weight	Use ballistic movement			
DRYLAND—FLOOR				
Somersault all directions	On landing mat, bend knees on landing			
Back 3/4 somersault half twist	Straight body, finish to flat back, from elevated mat, with spot			
Drop-down punch somersault	Drop from box and forward somersault to landing mat			
DRYLAND—DRYBOARD				
Somersaults pike all directions	Out of belt, coach spot			
203C, B	To back drop open pike			
303C, B	To back drop open pike			
102A	Out of belt, coach spot			
202A	Out of belt, coach spot			
302A	Out of belt, coach spot			
104C, B	Pike out, finish to seat drop and feet, coach spot			
DRYLAND—TRAMPOLINE				
2 1/2 somersaults all directions	In belt, spot, finish to armstand			
5223D with two bounces	Out of belt, finish to feet, then to seat drop, coach spot			
5122D with two bounces	Out of belt, finish to feet, then to seat drop, coach spot			
5142B	In belt, two bounces, arms overhead on start			
5225D	In belt, two bounces, arms overhead on start			
5243B	In belt, two bounces, with arm swing			
6233D	In belt, see chapter 4			
Forward 3/4 with full twist	Finish to backdrop and arms on trampoline bed			
Cody	Keep head neutral on cody, land with palms on mat			
Cody with 1 1/2 twist	Initiate cody before twisting			
Full twisting ball-out	Begin with full twist back-to-feet then back-to-back			
Forward 1 3/4 somersault	C and B to seat drop			

(continued)

Level 3 Advanced Diver Progression Checklist *(CONTINUED)*

Skill	Skill Description	Pass-P	Redo-R	Comments
DIVING—SPRINGBOARD 1M				
105B	C for women but B if ready			
203B				
204C, B				
303B				
304C, B	C for women but B if ready			
403B				
5134D	If ready for women			
104B	If ready for women			
5142B	If ready for women			
5225D				
5323D				
5333D	If ready for women			
5325D	If ready for women			
DIVING—SPRINGBOARD 3M				
107C	105B for women, but 107C if ready			
205C	205B for men if ready			
305C				
405C				
5134D				
5152B	If ready for women			
5235D				
5335D	5333D for women, but 5335D if ready			
DIVING—PLATFORM				
Men:				
105C, B	5M, running			
107C	7.5M and 10M, B if ready			
204C, B	3M in C, 5M in B			
205C or B	7.5M in C 10M in B			
304C	5M			
305C	10M, 7.5M if ready			
403B	3M or 5M			
405B	10M			
5223D	3M			
5233D	5M			
5243B	7.5M with bubbles			
5225D	5M			
5235D	7.5M, 10M if ready			
104B	3M, running			
5142B	5M with bubbles			
5152B	7.5M or 10M if ready			
614B	10M			

Skill	Skill Description	Pass-P	Redo-R	Comments
DIVING—PLATFORM *(continued)*				
623A	7.5M			
6233B	7.5M			
624B	10M			
Women:				
105C	5M, running			
105B	7.5M or 10M			
204C, B	5M,			
205C, B	7.5M, B on 10M if ready			
304C	5M			
305C	10M			
404C	3M			
405C	7.5M or 10M, B on 10M if ready			
5223D	3M			
5225D	5M			
5235D	10M			
5233D	5M			
614C, B	10M			
624C, B	10M if ready			

Notes:

1. Always use coach spot and good landing mat for safety.

2. There will be individual differences regarding mastery of optional dives.

3. If problem with dive, regress to easier lead-up dive or drill.

4. At least 80-85% proficiency required to pass each skill.

Coach Final Comments:

From J. Huber, 2016, *Springboard and Platform Diving* (Champaign, IL. Human Kinetics).

Level 3 Elite Diver

The **elite diver** is someone who is all in—heart and soul—fully vested, and able and willing to do whatever it takes to reach the highest level of performance. Elite divers are willing to train as much and as long as it takes to reach their greatest potential. At this level the focus is on improving competition performance. Consequently, everything these divers do in practice has one overriding purpose—to improve competition performance. Their goals are to continually improve their skill level, be consistent, and be competitive. They have dropped other sports and focus exclusively on diving.

Level 3 Elite Diver Concepts

1. Diving is fun. Never forget this, even at the elite level.
2. Practice is connected to competition: The more challenging practice becomes, the less challenging the competition will be.
3. Play the inner game of diving: Practice mental skills as much as diving skills.
4. Consistency is the key to dive performance success.
5. Physiological adaptation and the training effect (chapter 9).
6. Recovery: A training effect won't occur without recovery (chapter 9).

- Level 3 elite diver deliberate practice: 95 percent
- Level 3 elite diver deliberate play: 5 percent

Level 3 Elite Diver Games

Games are important at every level, but at this level the type of games changes. At the elite diver level, it is all about competition.

1. Practice dives in random order and list order.
2. Mock meets and imagined meets (e.g., during practice announce the dive to oneself and imagine being in a meet situation)
3. Challenge another diver to a dive-off.
4. Hit the first attempt at a drill or dive.
5. Ask the question: "What can I do right now on this drill or dive to improve?"

Level 3 Elite Diver Practice Frequency and Duration

1. Six days per week
2. Each practice should be approximately 120 minutes in duration.
3. Typically, elite divers train approximately two hours twice a day for five days, and practice once on the sixth day.

Level 3 Elite Diver Mental Skills

1. The five pillars of mental training continue to be critical for high-level performance.
2. Individual zone of optimal functioning (IZOF): finding individual emotions and range of emotions for optimal performance. See chapter 11 for more information.

3. Responding to adversity and implementing the seven Rs. See chapter 11 for more information.
4. Detailed preperformance routine.
5. Detailed precompetition plan. See chapter 11 for more information.

Level 3 Elite Diver Cognitive Skills

1. Practice mental imagery at home.
2. Mentally review and analyze each practice immediately afterwards.
3. Mentally review the previous practice a second time immediately before the subsequent practice.
4. Set goals for each phase of each practice.
5. Review the success or failure to reach these goals after each practice, and reset goals for the next practice.

Level 3 Elite Diver Stretching Routine

Elite divers continue performing a stretching routine both before and after practice. At this level, flexibility has hopefully been established and the purpose of the stretching routine is to maintain that flexibility.

Level 3 Elite Diver Coach Reminders

1. This level of diver has completely committed to the sport of diving and strives to reach her highest level and fulfill her cherished dreams. Consequently, you need to be equally committed. To assist your athletes in becoming elite divers, you need to continually improve your coaching knowledge and effectiveness. In other words, you need to up your coaching game so that you are an elite-level coach. For a more in-depth discussion of the elite (expert) coach, see *Applying Educational Psychology in Coaching Athletes* (Huber, 2013).
2. The coach–diver relationship changes somewhat at this level. The coach and diver work closely together, and the relationship may be described as somewhat of a collaborative effort. You develop an annual plan and daily individualized practice plans, continually evaluate, provide remedial skill learning where necessary, and look for small but significant changes to improve diver performance. However, individual athlete input is genuinely welcomed and considered.

The level 3 elite diver progression checklist follows.

LEVEL 3 ELITE DIVER PROGRESSION CHECKLIST

Skill	Skill Description	Pass-P	Redo-R	Comments
CONDITIONING				
Inverted sit-up	From hanging bar with coach spot			
Heavy squat	Emphasize for springboard divers			
Plyometrics with weighted vest	Emphasize for platform divers			
DRYLAND—FLOOR				
Somersault all directions	To elevated mat			
Somersault all directions	With weight vest			
DRYLAND—DRYBOARD				
12 consecutive good hurdles	Consistency for competition			
12 consecutive good hurdles	With somersaults; practice list order			
Somersault to X	Somersaults in all directions, land on X on pit			
DRYLAND—TRAMPOLINE				
107B	In belt, spot, finish to armstand			
109C	In belt, spot, finish to armstand			
206C, 207C	In belt, spot, finish 207 to armstand			
306C, 307C	In belt, spot, finish 307 to armstand			
406C, 407C	In belt, spot, finish 407 to armstand			
Forward 2 3/4 somersault	Tuck and pike and finish to seat drop and flat back			
Back 2 1/2 twist somersault	Finish to seat drop and feet			
Front somersault 2 twists	Finish to seat drop and back			
Cody with 2 1/2 twists	Use crash pad for safety			
Cody double	C, B if ready			
5245D	In belt			
DIVING—SPRINGBOARD 1M				
107C	105B for women			
205C	Men			
206C	Men			
305C	Men, women if ready			
306C	Men			
405C	Men, women if ready			
5126D	Men			
5136D	Men			
5152B	Men			
5144B	Men			
5235D	Men, women if ready			
5227D	Men			
5335D	Men, women if ready			
5327D	Men			
5343B	Men			

Skill	Skill Description	Pass-P	Redo-R	Comments
	DIVING SPRINGBOARD 3M			
107B	C for women, B if ready			
205B				
207C	Men			
305B				
307C	Men			
405B				
407C	Men			
5136D	Men, women if ready			
5154B	Men, 5152B for women			
5237D	Men			
5337D	Men			
5253B	Men			
5353B	Men, 5335D for women			
	DIVING—PLATFORM			
Men:				
107B	10M			
107C	7.5M			
109C	10M			
205C	5M			
206C	7.5M			
207C	10M			
304C	3M			
305C	5M			
306C	7.5M			
307C	10M			
403c, 404C	3M			
405C	5M			
407C	10M			
5152B	10M			
5237D	10M			
5253B	10M			
5235D	5M			
5255B	10M			
6243B	10M			
6245D	10M			
626C	10M, B if ready			
6142D	10M			
Women:				
107C	10M			
105B	5M			
107B	10M if ready			

(continued)

Level 3 Elite Diver Progression Checklist *(CONTINUED)*

Skill	Skill Description	Pass-P	Redo-R	Comments
	DIVING—PLATFORM *(continued)*			
205B	10M			
204C	3M			
205C	5M			
206C	7.5M			
207C	10M			
304C	3M			
305C	5M			
306C	7.5M			
307C	10M			
403C	3M			
405C	5M			
407C	10M			
5152B	10M			
5237D	10M			
5253B	10M			
623C	3M			
624C	5M			
625C	7.5M			
626C	10M			
623A	7.5M			
6233D	7.5M			
6243D	10M			

Notes:

1. Follow your governing body's guidelines for all drills and dives.
2. Utilize drills cited throughout the textbook.
3. Trampoline drills may only be done if allowed by certifying organization.
4. 80-85% proficiency required to pass each skill.

Coach Final Comments:

From J. Huber, 2016, *Springboard and Platform Diving* (Champaign, IL. Human Kinetics).

Here we are at the end of the skill progression line, from the introductory diver to the elite diver. Throughout this chapter, the importance of physical preparation was emphasized. Let's now look at chapter 8 and the critical aspects of strength, conditioning, nutrition and recovery for diver development.

CHAPTER 8

Strength, Conditioning, Nutrition, and Recovery

As a coach, I was frequently approached by divers at competitions and at my summer diving academy asking me what they could do to improve their diving, learn more difficult dives, and reach their performance goals (e.g., win a state championship). Unfortunately, many of these divers lacked the physical readiness necessary for moving to the next level. For example, some wanted to learn a 203B on the 1-meter springboard or a 205B on the 3-meter springboard, yet could not do one hanging pike-up. Some wanted to learn a 105B, but lacked the flexibility to get anywhere near an acceptable pike position. Some wanted to learn more difficult 1-meter springboard dives, yet lacked the leg strength to jump high enough to perform them. And others lacked the appropriate body weight to learn harder dives and reach their long-term goals.

This chapter examines aspects of physical readiness that divers need to reach their greatest diving potential.

But first, a short story . . .

Becki was a talented diver but was missing a key ingredient—strength. More precisely, she was missing **power,** which consists of strength and speed. At the time, she could barely make a 104C on a 1-meter springboard. So she committed religiously to a rigorous strength training program for a full semester. Three days each week, she made her way to the weight room where she did squats, leg presses, leg extensions, and leg curls. Then, she moved to the indoor track where she performed plyometric (jumping) exercises. After one semester, her leg strength had significantly increased and her vertical jump had grown from 14 to 21 inches (35.6 to 50.8 cm)! Her newfound power dramatically changed her diving. She no longer struggled with her 104C. In fact, she was able to make a 105B on the 1-meter springboard!

Like Becki, Karen was a talented diver who lacked power. Unlike Becki, however, Karen wasn't willing to commit the time and energy to strength training. Karen believed that the only real training she needed was diving practice, and that anything other than diving was unnecessary. Although Karen was a talented diver, she never progressed beyond her current level of diving; even though she had the talent to become a champion, she never did.

Many divers—and diving coaches—limit their perspective on what it takes to become a proficient diver. Like Karen, these divers and coaches perceive that the route to diving success runs to the diving well but not the weight room or dryland training. However, for divers like Becki who see the bigger picture and are willing to put in the work outside the pool and do the auxiliary activities such as strength training, cardio training, and stretching, diving success is truly attainable and just around the corner. It was no coincidence that the divers who returned to my diving academy the following summer and said that they had added strength and conditioning to their training during the past year also reported having a highly successful diving season.

This chapter, then, is perhaps the most critical in the book, because no matter how technically correct the fundamentals might be, divers can't reach their greatest diving potential without attaining their greatest degree of physical readiness. Physical deficiencies will restrain even the most talented diver from reaching full potential. The good news, however, is that the body is adaptable and therefore capable of getting stronger and quicker as well as leaner and more flexible. In this chapter we consider the specific strength and conditioning programs that can help divers achieve physical readiness. We also discuss two additional aspects critical for achieving physical readiness—nutrition and recovery.

Strength

Springboard and platform diving have slightly different strength demands. Following are some aspects of strength training to incorporate into training programs for springboard and platform divers.

Strength Training for Springboard Divers

For springboard divers, leg strength is critical and perhaps the key component for this event. It was said that 3-meter springboard Olympic gold medalist He Chong could squat over 1,000 pounds (454 kg). Whether or not this is true, his legs certainly looked as though he could squat that much weight and he pressed the board as though he could! A number of successful springboard divers have average vertical jumps but can load the springboard because of their exceptional leg strength. Because leg strength is important for loading the springboard, strength training for springboard divers should emphasize increasing leg strength through exercises such as the heavy squat, leg press, leg extension, and leg curl.

Plyometric Training for Platform Divers

In contrast to springboard divers, platform divers need more quickness and greater vertical jump. Consequently, their strength training should emphasize plyometric exercises such as the box jump, bounding, and other types of explosive drills. **Plyometric training** is a type of training developed by the Russians that involves a maximal loading of the muscles to increase speed. Plyometric exercises, such as a box jump, shock the muscles. Upon landing, the knees bend (eccentric contraction) and as quickly as possible push (concentric contraction) to jump upward. The goal of plyometric exercises is to land and then jump off the landing mat as quickly as possible.

Injury Avoidance

Strength training is important for avoiding injuries. For example, some divers have hyperflexible shoulders, which can result in subluxation. For this type of diver, strengthening the peripheral stabilizing muscles around the shoulders keeps the shoulders stable during dive performance. Another area in which strength training can promote injury avoidance is the low back. Exercises such as the hang clean strengthen the low back.

Before beginning any strength and conditioning exercises, divers should follow these guidelines to avoid injury during lifting:

- Stretch before exercising.
- Consult with your coach regarding the amount of weight and the number of repetitions and sets.
- Use good form.
- Wear appropriate socks and shoes, especially for plyometric training.
- Start light and gradually work up to heavier weight while maintaining good form.
- Use a spotter when squatting.

At-Home Strength Program

Figure 8.1, called the Program Constructor, is based on a program by Schwartz (2012) and outlines the exercises to choose from when constructing a strength program for springboard and platform divers. The program is the same for core, posterior, and shoulders for both springboard and platform divers. However, for springboard divers, the percentage of heavy weight training to plyometric training should be approximately 70 percent heavy weight and 30 percent plyometric. For platform divers, the percentages should be reversed—approximately 70 percent plyometric and 30 percent heavy weight. Demonstrations of many of these exercises can be viewed on YouTube.

The four strength training phases are base, foundation, building, and peak. The training phase the diver is currently experiencing determines the volume and intensity of each exercise. The strength program is in addition to dryland training exercises.

On-the-Road Strength Program

An on-the-road strength program is important, especially if competition duration is considerable and the diver is accustomed to doing strength training

Core

- Hanging tuck-up and pike-up
- Hanging 90-degree pike or tuck hold, or both (3-5 seconds)
- Ball roll-out
- Armstand tuck-up and pike-up
- Front and lateral bridge
- Hollow hold with shoulders and feet propped and weight on abdomen
- Pike-up on floor
- Incline sit-up with weight
- Hollow hold with weight between ankles
- Sit-up with knees bent
- Tuck kick-out keeping low back pressed into floor
- Seated twist with weight and knees bent

Posterior

- Back extension
- Reverse hyper
- Glute-ham
- Back bridge with band

Lower Body

- Squat
- Squat hold: Hold at bottom 3 to 5 seconds and then push up.
- Squat-hold-jump: Hold for 3 to 5 seconds and then jump up off floor.
- Front squat
- Leg press
- Bulgarian squat
- Step-up with weight (dumbbells or bar on shoulders)
- Lunge with dumbbells
- Leg extension: Hold weight at top for 5 seconds.
- Leg curl

Upper Body

- Band face pull
- Seated row
- Hang clean
- Romanian deadlift
- Front raise with band or dumbbells

(continued)

Figure 8.1 Program Constructor for springboard and platform divers.

■ Lateral raise with band or dumbbells

■ Bent-over rear deltoid raise with band or dumbbells

■ Bent elbow pull-back with band or dumbbells

■ Crossover with band

■ Armstand shrug against a wall

■ Dip

■ Curl

■ Triceps extension

Plyometrics

■ Box jump

■ Box squat jump

■ Depth drop < 2ft

■ Double-leg jump

■ Double-leg pike jump (touch toes)

■ Single-leg jump

■ Lunge jump

■ Jump on 8 inch or higher landing mat

■ Bounding

■ Consecutive forward somersaults

■ Consecutive backward somersaults

■ Somersault to landing mat working up to weighted vest

Figure 8.1 *(continued)*

before or during the competition (or both). At the 2004 Olympic Games, for example, I observed 3-meter springboard Olympic gold medalist Guo Jingjing doing 315-pound (143 kg) shallow squat presses in the Olympic Village weight room several days before her competition. As divers improve, they attend more and more competitions. For example, in the United States, junior elite divers often attend both the junior national championship and the senior national championship. In this circumstance, they easily can be on the road for three weeks or more.

At some competitions, it may be difficult to find a weight room. Consequently, the on-the-road strength program outlined in figure 8.2 lists exercises that use body weight, elastic bands (that divers can carry with them in their travel bags), and an exercise partner (i.e., another diver or a coach). Both diver and coach can determine the exercises and number of repetitions depending on the competition schedule and the diver's needs. If a weight room is available, divers may follow a modified version of their normal strength program. I use the word *modified* because on-the-road conditioning should be used as a maintenance workout rather than a full-blown workout intended for making gains in strength.

Warm-Up

- ▦ Stretch
- ▦ Quick feet
    - ◦ 10 seconds on, 10 seconds off: front and back, feet together; front and back, switching legs; side to side, crisscross
    - ◦ Jump rope (instead of the preceding)

Lower Body

- ▦ 1 × 10 (each leg) ballistic lunge jumps
- ▦ 2 × 6 partner body squats if no squat racks (springboard divers only)
- ▦ 2 × 10 (each leg) single-leg vertical jumps with arm circle (platform divers only)
- ▦ 2 × 10 partner hamstring curls, or with elastic band
- ▦ 2 × 15 single-leg calf raises
- ▦ 2 × 5 single-leg squats

Upper Body

- ▦ 2 × 10 handstand shrugs against a wall
- ▦ 2 × 15 push-ups
- ▦ 2 × 15 elastic band shoulder exercise (diver's choice; e.g., internal, external, elevated internal/external, rear deltoid)

Core

- ▦ 2 × 25 partner sit-ups
- ▦ 50 V-ups
- ▦ 15 hip extensions with legs on a raised surface (about 3 ft, or 90 cm, high)
- ▦ 25 leg lifts (from headstand)

Cardio

- ▦ 15-20 minutes, diver's choice

Figure 8.2 On-the-road strength program.

Conditioning

Conditioning consists of stretching and cardio training, two types of exercises important for helping divers reach their greatest diving potential. Consider the following story about stretching.

Sage's story is perhaps one of the most remarkable examples I can recall about personal commitment and physical adaptability. At my summer diving academy, I tested Sage's flexibility and found him to be the most inflexible diver I had ever worked with—great kid, but incredibly inflexible. On a sit-and-reach test, he could not touch his knees, let alone his toes. But Sage wanted to be a good diver, no matter what it took. And he had the self-discipline to go home and work on his flexibility before and after each practice and even on his off day. The following summer, with a smile on his face, Sage touched his toes on the sit-and-reach test. The next summer, he collapsed into an amazing pike position. Sage went on to become an accomplished collegiate diver.

Stretching

Stretching is critical because increased flexibility allows divers to more efficiently perform movements such as the quick connect, the tuck and pike positions, and the lateral close for a line-up. Following are some concepts related to stretching that are invaluable in helping divers become more flexible. Use them as guidelines for stretching effectively and safely.

When the central nervous system sends a message to the agonist muscle (the muscle causing the movement) to contract (tense, or tighten up), the tension in the antagonist muscle (the muscle opposing the movement) is inhibited by impulses from motor neurons and, thus, must simultaneously relax. This neural phenomenon is referred to as **reciprocal inhibition**. For example, when stretching the hamstring, contracting (tightening up) the quadriceps (in this case, the agonist muscles) causes the hamstring (the antagonist muscles) to relax resulting in an increased stretch. Reciprocal inhibition stretching is based on **Sherrington's law** of reciprocal innervation, which states that when a muscle contracts, its direct antagonist muscle relaxes to an equal extent. Reciprocal inhibition is an extremely effective method of stretching to create greater diver flexibility and range of motion.

Autogenic inhibition refers to the sudden relaxation of a muscle that has previously been highly tensed. Muscle tensing activates the **Golgi tendon organ** (GTO), which relaxes the muscle after a sustained contraction (i.e., longer than six seconds). For example, to apply autogenic inhibition when stretching the hamstrings, tighten them up for six to eight seconds and then release the tension and stretch the muscles.

Proprioceptive neuromuscular facilitation (PNF) is a common stretching technique that uses both autogenic and reciprocal inhibition. One PNF technique, called *contract-relax,* involves the following process:

1. Tense the muscle (isometric contraction) being stretched for six to eight seconds.
2. Relax the muscle being stretched.
3. Tense the opposing muscle.
4. Move the limb to elicit a greater stretch.

Stretching before diving practice, conditioning, and strength training is important for preparing the body for the exertion that is about to occur. Perhaps the best time to stretch again is immediately after practice when the body's connective tissues are warmed up. Think of these connective tissues as being made of Silly Putty. Remember playing with Silly Putty? If you simply pick it up and pull on it, it snaps into two pieces. But if you roll it in your hands to heat it up, it stretches. The connective tissues in your body react in a similar fashion when warmed up.

Stretching Program

Stretching should be thought of as part of diving practice, not simply as an insignificant or meaningless social activity before practice. If divers perceive stretching as an integral part of the overall training program for improving diving and attaining long-term goals, they will give it the attention, effort, and focus necessary for becoming flexible. They can even work on their flexibility between practices. Olympic gold medalist Laura Wilkinson stretched frequently throughout the day. I remember talking to her while she was sitting on the ground; she suddenly collapsed into a pike position and talked to me in that position for 10 minutes. Figure 8.3 outlines a stretching program.

It can be beneficial to stretch with a partner. Figure 8.4 outlines a partner stretching program.

Warm-Up Stretches

- ▦ Jump rope, jumping jacks, etc., for two to three minutes
- ▦ Neck: eight neck rolls clockwise, eight counterclockwise
- ▦ Trapezius: eight shoulder shrugs, rolling shoulders
- ▦ Shoulders: eight arm swings back and forth, eight side to side
- ▦ Triceps: behind-the-head bent-elbow stretch
- ▦ Biceps: swing arms back and forth while bending the elbows
- ▦ Wrists: with palm forward, pull fingers toward body
- ▦ Middle back: band middle pull
- ▦ Low back: eight hip rolls clockwise, eight counterclockwise
- ▦ Hamstrings: hamstring stretch
- ▦ Quadriceps: bend the knee and hold the foot behind the back
- ▦ Hip flexors: kneeling hip flexor stretch, pigeon pose
- ▦ Glutes: glute bridge stretch
- ▦ Calf and Achilles tendon: kneeling calf stretch or equivalent stretch
- ▦ Ankles: eight ankle rolls clockwise, eight counterclockwise

Flexibility Stretches

- ▦ Split
- ▦ Over split (with front leg on raised surface)
- ▦ Front lunge (stretches hip flexors)
- ▦ Straddle
- ▦ Pancake
- ▦ Hanging shoulder stretch: hang from bar with hands touching
- ▦ Straight-arm bent-over shoulder stretch: grab low bar with hands touching and bend over
- ▦ Ballet one-foot toe-point stretch: toes on mat and heel up

---

Figure 8.3 Stretching program for divers.

- Warm-up: jump rope, jumping jacks, etc., for two to three minutes
- Pike stretch: push on hump of back
- Small straddle: push on back
- Large straddle: push on back
- Hamstring wall stretch: stand with back to wall; partner lifts one leg up and keeps the bottom leg straight; then does the same thing with the other leg
- Seated overhead straight-arm stretch: partner wraps arms around arms and pulls backward
- Seated hands-behind-head stretch: partner wraps arms around arms and pulls backward
- Single arm behind head: partner pulls elbow toward back of head
- Pike with arms straight out: partner sits on back and pulls arms upward
- Lie on front: partner pushes ankles to butt (single leg and double leg)
- Lie on front: partner lifts bent knee off ground while sitting on butt

Figure 8.4 Partner stretching program.

Cardio Exercise

Athletes don't need to be terrific runners, swimmers, or cyclists to become great divers. However, because the pace of diving practice doesn't burn a great deal of calories, divers may find it necessary to engage in these or other types of cardio activities to maintain an appropriate body weight. Consider Cassandra's story.

Cassandra wasn't the most talented, accomplished, or highly recruited high school diver in the United States. In fact, she flew well below the recruiting radar. However, she was bright, optimistic, coachable, and most important, willing to accept advice and make changes. Upon entering college, she recognized that to get to the next level, she needed to reinvent herself. She wasn't in bad physical shape, but she wasn't in elite diver shape either. And an elite diver is what she aspired to become. So, she changed. She changed her eating habits, changed her fitness program (adding daily cardio exercise), and changed her mind-set (she wanted to look and feel like an elite diver). Slowly, over time, her body changed. With her new physical readiness, she became an elite athlete and U.S. Olympian.

Cardio exercise (also called aerobic exercise) refers to sustained cardiorespiratory exercises, such as running, jogging, walking, swimming, and cycling, which elevate heart rate and burn additional calories. Cardio exercise is an important part of a training plan for divers like Cassandra who want to achieve or maintain lean body mass. Maintaining a lean body is important for aesthetic reasons in the sport of diving. It also is important for maintaining an ideal strength-to-weight ratio.

The **strength-to-weight ratio** is the relationship, or proportion, between a diver's body strength and body weight. All divers have an optimal strength-to-weight ratio that gives them maximal body control. Changing this optimal ratio by gaining or losing too much weight or by losing strength negatively affects body control. Following are benefits of maintaining an appropriate strength-to-weight ratio:

- Economy of movement (less effort and more efficiency of movement)
- Improved metabolic function
- Decreased injuries
- Hastened recovery
- Improved mechanical efficiency

Cardio Exercise Program

A host of cardio exercises are available, including running, jogging, jumping rope, circuit training, playing basketball, and cycling. Divers should find what works best for them, what they enjoy, and therefore what they will continue doing. Cassandra liked to run, but other divers prefer to cycle or swim or perhaps use a cardio machine such as a stair stepper or elliptical trainer. Some like to cross train. Divers should find the appropriate type and amount of cardio exercise to incorporate into their training plans.

Another effective cardio program is a team dryland circuit. Most divers find this fun because it is a social activity they can do with their teammates while keeping their heart rates up and burning calories. Figure 8.5 outlines a 20-station team circuit. Notice that the circuit requires very little equipment other than a folding mat and landing mat.

Staying Motivated for Cardio

For many divers who need to include cardio in their training, the challenge is staying motivated to do cardio on a weekly basis. For cardio to be effective, it has to be done consistently. It doesn't do a diver much good to do cardio one week and then not at all or sporadically the next week. Following are some simple but effective tips for staying motivated for cardio.

- Find ways to make it enjoyable (e.g., bring headphones and favorite music).
- Remember, sometimes it takes time to learn to enjoy it.
- Keep it fun (e.g., exercise with a teammate or friend).
- Reward yourself for engaging in cardio exercise (e.g., buy a new exercise outfit).
- Mix it up: cross-train—if that is what you like.
- Strive to make it part of your weekly training routine.
- Remember, it is a healthy habit for later in life after diving.
- Think in terms of *I get to* not *I have to.*
- Start easy so you feel like doing it again the next day.
- Consult with your diving coach, conditioning coach, or personal trainer.
- Remember, half the battle is just showing up.

Nutrition

Besides cardio exercise, nutrition plays a key role in achieving an increased strength-to-weight ratio and contributing significantly to improved diving

Team Dryland Circuit

- Wall armstand with shrug
- Jump on port-a-pit (or landing mat)
- Inverted pike-up
- Lunge
- Jump rope
- Incline sit-up with weight
- Tuck jump
- Push-up
- Trampoline jump (or use springboard or landing mat again)
- Kick-out with low back pressed into floor
- Full-squat jump
- Stretching: shoulders and hamstrings
- Twisting bicycle crunch
- Hanging pike-up three ways (or pike-up hold on ground)
- Consecutive forward somersaults
- Lunge jump
- Consecutive backward somersaults
- Hollow hold with weight held between ankles
- Single-leg jump
- Log roll with four-way crunch

Circuit Progression

- 30 seconds on, 15 seconds off; two rounds, two minutes between rounds; one week
- 30 seconds on, 10 seconds off; two rounds, two minutes between rounds; one or two weeks
- 40 seconds on, 15 seconds off; two rounds, two minutes between rounds; one or two weeks
- 40 seconds on, 10 seconds off; two rounds, two minutes between rounds; one or two weeks

Figure 8.5 20-station team circuit.

performance. The following story highlights how both cardio exercise and proper nutrition are important for reaching one's greatest diving potential.

Coming out of high school, Dwight was talented but fairly unknown by college coaches. He loved to eat, which of course, is a good thing. However, he could overindulge on occasions. On a road trip his freshman year, he became famous among team members for eating three enormous supreme sandwiches on the bus! During his sophomore year he competed at the U.S. indoor national qualifying meet in December and finished 50th out of 55 divers. For Dwight, that dismal experience forced him to ask the question every diver eventually asks: How good do I want to become? He realized that he was uncommitted and overweight. So, he decided to change. He recommitted to his goals, started playing basketball for his cardio exercise, modified his daily diet, and perhaps most important, quit overeating. Over several months he lost 18 pounds (8 kg). With his new chiseled look, he not only performed better, but felt better mentally and physically. In late February he was crowned conference champion, and in March he earned All-American by making top eight in two events at the collegiate national championship.

Good nutrition means fueling the body correctly to have enough energy to train, recover, and compete. Many athletes' energy expenditure also includes additional activities such as attending classes, studying, holding a part-time job, and volunteering. The following sections offer some simple nutrition guidelines for training and competing. Much of this information comes from USOC sport dietitian Jennifer Gibson (2012).

Nutrition for Training

Carrie was a hardworking diver and student. Every day she gave her very best effort, both on the springboard and in the classroom. The only problem was that she would always break down physically before the championship, a frustrating and disheartening experience for Carrie and her coach. Before her senior season, her coach recommended that she have her blood and daily diet evaluated. The evaluation revealed that she was iron deficient. By changing her diet and taking iron supplements, she was able to maintain her vigor and health throughout the season and enjoy the most successful championship of her career.

Good nutrition creates and maintains an energized, lean, healthy, and strong physique throughout the season, especially during the heavy training phases. Gibson (2012) offers seven guidelines for establishing a solid foundation for a healthy diet.

- Mentally or physically map out meals, and be sure this food is available. Healthy nutrition starts with planning.
- Eat at regular intervals during the day. Don't go longer than four hours without food.
- Choose whole foods rather than processed foods for the majority of your diet (90 percent of the time). See figure 8.6.
- Balance meals and snacks with carbohydrate, protein, antioxidants, and healthy fat.
- Maintain a healthy relationship with food and your body. Eat for health and performance, not out of boredom, guilt, or stress.
- Choose liquids with minimal sugar such as water; a milk, soy, or almond beverage; and tea. Avoid juice, soda, and energy drinks.
- Enjoy treats in moderation—they taste better that way!

Pre- and Postpractice Snacks

Divers should develop the habit of fueling their bodies before and after practice. Some divers make the nutritional mistake of sleeping an extra 15 to 20 minutes and then skipping breakfast, the consequence of which is running out of gas in the middle of a morning workout. If they fail to bring a lunch and have class immediately after a morning practice, now they are really in nutritional trouble and running on fumes—no breakfast and no lunch. By the afternoon practice, they are completely out of gas. Gibson (2012) recommends the following top five pre- and postdiving snacks:

- 1/2 to 1 cup of rice cereal or oatmeal + skim or soy milk
- Banana or apple + 1 Tbsp peanut butter
- 6 oz (175 g) Greek-style yogurt
- Fruit + protein (milk, whey) smoothie
- Sport nutrition bar

Competition-Day Nutrition

Some divers make the mistake of overlooking a simple but critical and easily controllable variable: competition-day nutrition. During a long contest, they suddenly say, "Coach, I'm starving. Can you get me something to eat?" These divers may have had a plan for competition day, but their plan did not include nutrition. Gibson (2012) offers a well-thought-out and detailed nutritional plan for competition day, shown in figure 8.6.

7:00-7:30 a.m.
- Eat breakfast, ideally two to four hours before the first session.
- Aim for easy-to-digest, low-fat foods and a combination of carbohydrate and protein for a sustained energy release (e.g., one or two packets of oatmeal + Greek-style yogurt).
- Check urine color. Dark colored urine indicates dehydration.

7:30 to 9:00 a.m.
- Take frequent sips of water.
- Check urine color. It should be pale yellow (1 or 2 on a urine chart).

9:00 a.m. to 12:00 p.m. (warm-up and diving preliminaries)
- Have nutrition fuels available on deck (e.g., applesauce).
- Aim to take a few small bites every hour.
- Take frequent sips of water or a diluted sport drink.

12:00 to 1:30 p.m.
- Eat lunch, ideally two to four hours before the next session.
- Aim for easy-to-digest, low-fat foods and combinations of carbohydrate and protein. Following are examples:
  - Broth or vegetable-based soup + half or whole turkey sandwich or wrap

(continued)

Figure 8.6 Competition-day nutritional plan.

- Chicken salad with fruit
- Meal replacement smoothie
- Fish or chicken + steamed rice + carrots
- Minimum 8 oz (240 ml) of water (check urine color)

1:30 to 4:00 p.m.
- Take frequent sips of water.
- Check urine color. It should be pale yellow (1 or 2 on a urine chart).

4:00 to 6:00 p.m.
- Have a prediving snack, ideally one to two hours before competing.
- Aim for easy-to-digest, low-fat foods and a combination of carbohydrate and protein (e.g., a banana or apple + 1 Tbsp peanut butter).
- Take frequent sips of water.
- Check urine color. It should be pale yellow (1 or 2 on a urine chart).

6:00 to 9:00 p.m. (warm-up and finals)
- Have nutrition fuels on deck (e.g., banana).
- Aim to take a few small bites every hour.
- Take frequent sips of water or a diluted sport drink.

Dinner (9:00 p.m.)
- Aim to follow the healthy plate model for this meal (veggies, lean protein, and a carbohydrate).
- Take frequent sips of water at dinner.

Figure 8.6 *(continued)*

Excerpted from "Sport Nutrition for Diving: A Practical Guide for Athletes and Coaches," and reprinted with permission from the United States Olympic Committee, Colorado Springs, Colorado.

On-Deck Nutrition

Many divers are unsure about what foods to consume while on deck. Gibson (2012) offers the following top five on-deck fuels:

- Water + a diluted sport drink
- Banana
- 1/2 cup dried fruit
- Applesauce (in squeezable tube)
- 1 package sport gels, bites, or blocks

Sample Meals

Many divers (and often diving coaches) don't know what a healthy meal consists of, which becomes especially problematic when they leave home and are on their own. Figure 8.7 outlines examples of some healthy meals and snack (Gibson, 2012).

Best Breakfasts

- Oatmeal, one or two eggs, handful of almonds
- Shake: 2 cups skim, soy, or almond milk; 1 banana; 1Tbsp natural peanut butter
- Mix: 6 oz (175 g) Greek-style yogurt + 1/3 cup whole granola + 1-2 tsp dried cranberries
- One or two slices whole grain toast with natural peanut butter + 1 cup skim chocolate milk or soy milk
- 1-2 cups high-protein cereal (e.g., Kashi) + 1 cup skim, soy, or almond milk

Best Snacks

- 6 oz (175 g) Greek-style yogurt + small fruit
- 1/2 scoop whey + 1 1/2 cups skim or soy milk
- 1 cup of vegetable sticks + 2 tsp hummus
- 1/2 cup skim cottage cheese + 1 fruit
- Natural nutrition bars (look at ingredients list)

Best Lunches and Dinners

- Chicken breast salad with low-fat dressing + fruit
- Tuna salad mixed with low-fat ranch salad dressing on wheat pita + 1 cup celery sticks
- 1-2 cups vegetable soup + turkey sandwich on whole-grain bread
- Tofu, chicken, or beef stir-fry with veggies and brown rice
- Salmon, trout, or whitefish + couscous + steamed vegetables
- 1-2 cups of vegetarian, turkey, or lean beef chili + 1 cup carrots
- Lean beef steak + baked potato or sweet potato + side spinach salad

Figure 8.7 Examples of healthy meals and snacks.

Excerpted from "Sport Nutrition for Diving: A Practical Guide for Athletes and Coaches," and reprinted with permission from the United States Olympic Committee, Colorado Springs, Colorado.

Travel Nutrition

Eating healthy on the road presents a challenge to divers and coaches. However, although it is a challenge, it is not an insurmountable one. Following are some suggestions for good travel nutrition.

Plan ahead. Know ahead of time what may or may not be available during the trip. If certain foods won't be available, bring them with you. Many elite divers, for example, bring food such as nutrition bars, peanut butter, applesauce, oatmeal, and dried cranberries.

Make good choices. Make choices you would make if you were eating at home. When you sit down with the team and pick up a full menu, make healthy choices. After all, you have gotten into incredible physical shape. Stick with your nutritional game plan.

Avoid overeating. Maybe the food is free because someone else is paying for it. Or maybe you are a little stressed about the upcoming championship. Both of these situations make it easy to overeat. Remind yourself of the work you have put in thus far to arrive at the upcoming competition, and continue eating your normal portions of food.

Eat periodically. Practice and competition schedules on the road are often much different from home schedules. To stay fueled, try as much as possible to eat at regularly scheduled times, even if it is just a snack.

Recovery

During a presentation to coaches, a noted physiologist declared that after working with the U.S. Navy SEALs, everything he thought he knew about the limits of training the human body had to be expanded. He was truly amazed at the volume and intensity of training the SEALs could endure. But what I thought was going to be a presentation on training turned out instead to be an hour-long discourse on recovery.

Coaches and athletes tend to focus on the volume and intensity of training. Yet, there can be no high volume and no high intensity without a commensurate level of recovery. The secret to the U.S. Navy SEALs' training in part is their meticulous attention to recovery. Effective recovery helps prevent roadblocks to training such as injury, physical deterioration, chronic fatigue, mental and emotional fatigue, staleness, and burnout.

Nutrition for Recovery

Eating right plays a major role in promoting recovery. The body is like a car. As fuel is expended, refueling becomes necessary. Proper refueling involves putting in the right type and amount of fuel as well as refueling at the right times throughout the day. To refuel and promote recovery, divers should follow the seven tips for a healthy diet cited earlier in this chapter. They should take the time to get up 15 to 20 minutes earlier to eat breakfast before practice, and pack a snack and a lunch before leaving home. They also should eat at regular intervals throughout the day (go no longer than four hours without food), eat soon after practice, and make healthy food choices.

Sleep

Jon was an outstanding diver, team leader, role model, and captain. Over the course of several weeks, however, Jon's demeanor, outlook, diving, and overall behavior became quite odd. In talking with him before practice one day, I noticed that things he was saying made no sense. I finally asked him if he had been getting enough sleep. He said, "Coach, for the past three weeks I haven't been getting more than three or four hours of sleep each night. I am a wreck." Once Jon reset his body clock and slept through the night again, his diving took off and he enjoyed his best season.

Consistent lack of sleep (**sleep deprivation**) results in symptoms such as fatigue, daytime drowsiness, cognitive impairment, weight gain or loss, depression, irritability, and increased stress hormone levels, all of which impair physical, mental, and emotional recovery. The most important stage of sleep for recovery occurs during **rapid eye movement** (REM) sleep. REM sleep typically occupies approximately 20 to 25 percent of total sleep, or roughly 90 to 120 minutes of a night's sleep. During a normal night of sleep, humans experience about four or five periods of REM sleep. REM periods are quite short at the beginning of the night and longer toward the end of the sleep cycle.

Athletes who stay up late reduce their amount of sleep and upset their sleep cycles, both of which decrease REM and recovery. To recover fully, divers need to maintain a consistent nightly sleep pattern and receive an adequate amount of sleep. What constitutes an adequate amount of sleep varies among athletes, but a minimum of eight hours of sound sleep per night is recommended. Following are 10 tips for getting a good night's sleep.

- Prepare for bed, as you would any event that affects your health and happiness, with appropriate clothing, a nurturing environment, and a positive mind-set.
- Turn the lights down and turn all screens off before going to bed. Bright light suppresses the pineal gland's production of the sleep hormone melatonin.
- Leave computers, phones, and televisions outside of your bedroom.
- Eat earlier, and drink less alcohol and caffeine.
- Get up at the same time every day.
- Exercise daily.
- Keep the bedroom cool and dark.
- Don't check the clock; just let it happen.
- Read up on other tips for getting a good night's sleep.
- Get counseling for anxiety and depression.

Drug and Alcohol Use

Without question, drug and alcohol use impedes athlete recovery. Consider, for example, the following negative aspects of alcohol.

- Is high in calories and contributes to weight gain.
- Suppresses the body's ability to burn fat.
- Provides little or no nutritional value.
- Interferes with the absorption of nutrients.
- Acts as a toxin that the body must eliminate.
- Dehydrates the body because it is a potent diuretic.

Athletes of legal drinking age, when consuming alcohol, should do so sensibly without seriously compromising recovery. They should factor alcohol calories into their daily caloric intake, keep hydrated, limit themselves to two drinks per sitting, never binge drink, and drink only occasionally.

Mental and Emotional Recovery

Conor was an accomplished diver. He won conference and finished third at the NCAA championship. But as good as he was, it was time to learn 307C on the 10-meter platform. He knew he was ready, but he delayed learning the dive, inventing several reasons for not being ready. Over time, he became sullen, fatigued, and unhappy. Upon learning the dive, however, he was instantaneously his old self. Physical, mental, and emotional well-being feed off each other. Procrastination had diminished Conor's physical, mental, and emotional recovery. Mental and emotional imbalances are often indicators of inadequate recovery.

Mental and emotional recovery can be enhanced by actions such as avoiding rumination and procrastination, practicing mindfulness, dealing with small problems before they become big ones, engaging in positive self-talk, taking short breaks, developing healthy hobbies, and cultivating friendships. For more examples, see *Applying Educational Psychology in Coaching Athletes* (Huber, 2013) and the chapter on The Emotional Athlete.

Differences in Recovery

Athletes differ in their ability to recover. Some, for example, recover from sustained high-volume and high-intensity training much more quickly and easily than do others. Some athletes require 10 hours of sleep, whereas others need only 8 to recover. Some require more calories to recover than others do. It is the coach's responsibility to identify these differences and carefully monitor each athlete's recovery to ensure good health for all athletes throughout the season and especially leading up to the championship.

CHAPTER 9

Creating an Annual Individualized Training Plan

Great achievements never occur by accident. Their genesis is a well-contemplated and clearly defined deliberate plan that serves as a road map to success. In diving this plan is called an **annual individualized training plan** (AITP). This chapter outlines the step-by-step process of creating a plan for goal attainment for each training phase that comprises an AITP: preseason, early season, midseason, championship season, and postseason. Let's begin by considering the concept of periodization.

But first, a short story . . .

At the U.S. national collegiate championship, a diver fairly new to the sport hoped to contend for the 3-meter springboard title. Instead, she failed to even make finals. Sitting in the stands with tears in her eyes, she and her coach began mapping out a plan for the following year. When they arrived home, her coach continued working on the plan, spending many hours in his office poring over every detail of each training cycle. No detail was too small for consideration. Details such as stretching, strength and conditioning, early season goals, new dives, and periods of intense training were all factored into the plan.

Soon after the plan was developed, the diver resumed training. She and her coach worked on refining skills, incorporating new drills, and learning more difficult dives. Each of her training phases was perfectly choreographed, and time passed quickly. Before she knew it, she was back at the national collegiate championship. Everything was different this time. She felt better prepared than she had the previous year. And it showed in her performance. She won the 3-meter springboard event with a record-setting performance.

Periodization

Periodization is the process of varying a training program at specified intervals during the season to bring about optimal gains in performance. In other words, coaches alter athletes' training depending on the time of season. These alterations include changes in work volume and intensity, drills and skills, types of dives (i.e., basic dives versus optional dives), dryland training, strength training, and mental training.

Coaches shouldn't be put off by the term *periodization*. It simply means doing different things at different times (periods) throughout the season. Some diving coaches have their divers do the same things in practice every day for the entire season. Although modest performance gains can occur using such a predictable and monotonous seasonal practice plan, research suggests that significantly more gains occur through periodization (e.g., Bompa, 1994).

Periodization is predicated on the concept of a **training effect,** which states that when the body is consistently required to do more physically than it is accustomed to doing, it responds by adapting. Anyone who has ever exercised has experienced a training effect. Let's say you make a New Year's resolution to get back in shape. The first day of training is somewhat rough. This stage of training is referred to as the **alarm stage**—the initial shock of the stimulus (exercise) on the system (your body). When you get out of bed the next day, you feel those aching muscles.

But what happens after you hold steadfast to your resolution and continue exercising for a week or two? Your body adapts and you are no longer sore from performing the exercise routine. This adaptation is referred to as the **resistance stage**. Let's suppose now that you are totally psyched about your improved physical fitness and you decide to up the ante: during *every* practice you try to do more than you did in the preceding practice. It makes sense, right? If you saw big improvements the first few weeks, why stop there? Why not shoot for big improvements every week? But then, something starts to happen. Your body breaks down; you feel exhausted, you incur injuries, and your body refuses to adapt anymore. Because it can't repair itself, physical development ceases or even regresses. This stage, not surprisingly, is called the **exhaustion stage**.

The purpose of periodized training is to keep athletes in the resistance stage in which the body experiences **beneficial stress** (i.e., stress that induces adaptation) and avoid the exhaustion stage in which the body undergoes **detrimental stress** (i.e., stress that causes tissue damage, disease, and so on). This feat is accomplished by creating cycles of training.

There are three types of training cycles worth understanding: macrocycles, mesocycles, and microcycles. The **macrocycle** is the annual plan that encompasses the entire season and emphasizes peaking the athlete for the season-ending major competition(s). The **mesocycle** is a period of training within the macrocycle that lasts around two to four weeks. Each of the weeks within a mesocycle is considered a **microcycle**, a relatively short training cycle.

Following are five simple but critical coaching guidelines for creating an AITP.

Monitor your athletes and keep them in the resistant (adaptation) stage when training. It's deceptively easy for hungry, ambitious, dedicated, and well-meaning coaches and athletes to believe that if a lot of training is good, then even more training is better. Not long ago, the number-one-ranked U.S. collegiate swimmer in the 1650 yard freestyle event pulled out of the national collegiate championship a week before the meet because of illness. Of course, the illness could have been for any number of reasons, and any exceptional coach can and most likely will experience such an occurrence. Nevertheless, as coaches, we must assume responsibility for maintaining the health of our athletes. Monitor athletes so you know when to spur them onward and when to pull in their reins during training so that they avoid the exhaustion stage in which they encounter detrimental stress.

Keep in mind the time of season. Ask yourself, *What mesocycle are we in?* For example, as the championship looms nearer, don't fall into the trap of overtraining. Ask yourself, *Is it training time, or is it championship preparation time?* After qualifying for a championship, some divers over train and arrive at the championship injured. In the preseason, don't have your athletes dive (pardon the pun) headfirst into full-blown training without first establishing a prephysical training base. Such an approach causes preseason injury and delays training. Not too long ago, several U.S. Major League baseball players seriously injured themselves in early preseason training. In their zeal to excel, some coaches and athletes overestimate the volume and intensity of training given the time of the season, which often results in athlete injury. A well-thought-out annual individualized training plan that includes periodization prevents such injuries.

Consider individual differences. Part of the fun—and challenge—of coaching is determining the differences among athletes. For example, because of past illnesses and injuries, Cassidy has to be closely monitored with regard to volume and intensity of training. On the other hand, Amy can endure much higher volume and intensity of training. Both athletes are similarly talented, but dissimilarly suited for high training volume and intensity. Other differences to consider include physical durability (some athletes are hardier than others and can endure more sustained physical stress), physical maturation (some early-maturing athletes can endure more physical stress than late-maturing athletes), psychological readiness, diving experience (more experienced divers can endure more stressors than less experienced divers), and outside stressors (e.g., a diver who has recently experienced a deep personal loss of a family member).

Create an annual plan that includes periodization. USA Diving requires every Coach of Excellence to develop and submit an annual plan that includes periodization. This plan ensures that coaches and athletes have a clear plan for improvement. Shouldn't every coach and every diver at any level have such a plan? Creating this plan may seem like extra work on top of everything else you do during your busy day, but you accrue two advantages by taking that extra time to develop a periodization plan.

One advantage is that a periodization plan makes your job easier and less time-consuming throughout the season. Once created, it is a roadmap for success, and all you have to do is follow it. This roadmap gives you and your divers directions for what to do during the seasonal phases. Because you took the time before the season to set your course of sail, you don't have to second-guess yourself, backtrack on training, or suddenly work on something you overlooked. A periodization plan insures smooth sailing.

Another advantage to a periodization plan is that you and your divers gain a sense of abiding confidence and calm because you have a plan to follow. From the season's outset, you know where you are going, what you are going to do, and when you are going to do it. Sure, with individual monitoring there will be some changes, some alterations to the plan, but by and large everyone is on the same page; they know what is going to happen, when it is going to happen, and how it is going to happen. A periodization plan provides peace of mind.

Training cycles can be altered. Coaching is an amazing adventure. You never know what is around the next bend after you set sail. Circumstances change: an athlete gets sick, a grandmother passes away, or a new dive is more difficult to learn than previously thought. Be prepared to make changes to your carefully crafted periodized plan. Coaches should take tap dancing lessons, because just when we think we have everything planned, something mucks up the works and we have to tap dance our way out of it. Some coaches stick to their plan, even though circumstances change, because that is the plan and nothing is going to make them alter their course or deviate from their sacred holy grail of a plan. However, nothing should be set in stone. A plan is important, but so is the ability to deviate from it. A plan is only as good as the circumstances it serves. When the circumstances change, so must the plan. Great coaches are able to adapt, just like great divers. Poor takeoff from the springboard or platform? Adapt. Training circumstances change? Adapt.

Now that we understand the concept of periodization, let's develop an AITP by looking at the postseason. Postseason?

Developing an Annual Individualized Training Plan

In truth, every season begins with the postseason. The **postseason,** which begins after the conclusion of the championship season, is a time for reflection and introspection for both diver and coach, just like the diver and coach in the story at the beginning of this chapter did after the disastrous U.S. national collegiate championship. What worked well? What didn't work? What new goals should we set? What could we do better? What changes do I need to make in my coaching, in my diving, in my attitude, in my level of effort? What changes need to be made in conditioning, stretching, fundamentals, and mental training?

The answers to these questions determine the goals for developing the AITP. After establishing long-term outcome goals, coach and diver work backward to determine short-term process goals for the AITP. Where do we want to finish in next year's championship? What point total will it take to achieve that finish? What optional dives will it take to achieve the point total? What changes in fundamentals, physical conditioning, mental skills, consistency, and entry are needed to achieve this point total in the championship meet? When will tapering for the championship occur? To better understand how to develop an annual training plan, let's work step-by-step through a plan for a U.S. high school boy diver using the blank AITP template shown in figure 9.1. Because many U.S. high school divers compete in USA Diving, USA Diving competitions are included in the AITP.

Outcome Goals

For our annual training plan, we begin by prioritizing the competitions we want to peak for. Coach and diver meet and decide where the diver would like to place in each meet. Place of finish will vary from diver to diver depending on each diver's goals. Let's say that the boy diver we are considering for this AITP template wants to win his state high school championship. Consequently, we prioritize the following competitions and places of finish:

1. High school state championship—champion
2. High school sectional meet—champion
3. High school conference meet—champion

Performance Goals

The next step is to analyze the previous year's results for each competition to determine what point totals, degree of difficulty (DD), and new dives will be required to attain these goals. He would first look at last year's results and see how many points it took to win and also the types of optional dives (i.e., the total DD) needed to achieve the point total. As a rule of thumb, it is wise to assume that next year's total will need to be greater than the previous year's total. Consequently, extra points should be added when establishing a point total. The diver goal scores worksheet in figure 9.2 is used to determine the number of points needed for each dive in a diver's competition list to reach the overall goal scores.

After establishing point totals and the difficulty level of dives, the coach and diver should consider the consistency level required to attain the desired place of finish. For example, the diver hoping to win the state high school championship is unlikely to reach that goal if he can't consistently attain that score in practice. To track dive consistency before the championship phase, divers should use the dive performance chart in figure 9.3.

At this point, let's add some specific details for performance goals to our AITP:

- High school state championship: 450 points to win
- High school sectional meet: 420 points to win
- High school conference meet: 400 points to win
- The diver needs a DD total of 16.0 for optional dives.
- The diver needs to learn 107C, 305C, 5333D, and 5134D.
- Consistency level: 90 percent

Skill and Technical Goals

Next, the coach, along with the diver, determines the skills and techniques necessary for learning more difficult dives and improving consistency. **Skill** refers to the performance of an action or series of movements. **Technique** refers to how the action or series of movements are made. For example, to learn a more difficult skill, such as a forward somersaulting optional dive (e.g., progressing from a 105B to a 107C), the diver needs to learn the techniques of achieving the magic position and the 90-90-90 position, because both are critical for performing a more challenging forward optional dive. To progress from a 303B to a 305C, the diver needs to learn a proficient C position, small tuck, and hollow reverse somersault to perform the 305C a safe distance from the board. To learn a proficient 5333D, the diver has to improve twist initiation and square-out.

Skill, however, isn't about just physical movement. It also includes perceptual skills such as visual spotting. To progress from a 303B to a 305C, for example, the diver needs to improve spotting skill (the diver should also spot 303B but spotting for 305C is typically more difficult for divers), which in turn improves performance consistency.

ANNUAL INDIVIDUALIZED TRAINING PLAN (AITP) TEMPLATE

Annual Individualized Training Plan

For: _____

From: _____ To: _____

Outcome Goals	Performance Goals	Skill and Technical Goals
	Point scores:	Skills mastered:
	DD totals:	
	New dives:	Technique changes:
	Consistency level:	
	Individualize with athlete input.	Individualize with athlete input.

Month	Aug		Sept				Oct					Nov				Dec				Jan				
Week (Monday)	21	28	4	11	18	25	2	9	16	23	30	6	13	20	27	4	11	18	25	1	8	15	22	29
Competition priority 1 = peak; 5 = low																								
Event																								
Training phase																								
Strength and power																								
Flexibility																								
Test dates																								
Basic dives																								
Optional dives																								
New dives																								
Skills training																								
Technique training																								
Dryland training																								
Psychological skills																								
Meet simulation																								
Key: low (L), moderate (M), high (H), maintenance (Mt), off (O), engage (X)																								

Figure 9.1 An annual individualized training plan (AITP) template.

<table>
<tr><td colspan="2">Physical Goals</td><td colspan="2">Psychological Goals</td></tr>
<tr><td colspan="2">Increase strength and power:</td><td colspan="2">Mental skills for training:</td></tr>
<tr><td colspan="2">Increase flexibility:</td><td colspan="2">Mental skills for competition:</td></tr>
<tr><td colspan="2">Increase training volume & intensity:</td><td colspan="2"></td></tr>
<tr><td colspan="2">Individualize with athlete input.</td><td colspan="2">Individualize with athlete input.</td></tr>
</table>

Month	Feb				Mar				Apr					May				Jun				Jul					Aug	
Week (Monday)	5	12	19	26	5	12	19	26	2	9	16	23	30	7	14	21	28	4	11	18	25	2	9	16	23	30	6	13
Competition priority 1 = peak; 5 = low																												
Event																												
Training phase																												
Strength and power																												
Flexibility																												
Test dates																												
Basic dives																												
Optional dives																												
New dives																												
Skills training																												
Technique training																												
Dryland training																												
Psychological skills																												
Meet simulation																												
Key: low (L), moderate (M), high (H), maintenance (Mt), off (O), engage (X)																												

From J. Huber, 2016, *Springboard and Platform Diving* (Champaign, IL. Human Kinetics).

Diving Goal Scores Worksheet

Point Total for 1 Meter, 3 Meter, and 10 Meter

1. Decide on your highest desired place of finish for a particular dive level.
2. Look up last year's results, and find the dive total for that place of finish.
3. Add 10 to 20 points to that finish, and write the total in the space provided on your goal sheet in figure 9.4.

If competing voluntary dives in competition (voluntary dives are not performed in college and senior national and international events), follow the same procedures throughout the worksheet to determine your voluntary score by finding how many points were scored on voluntary dives in the preceding year.

For Dive Average for 1 Meter, 3 Meter, and 10 Meter

1. Divide the point total you wrote on your goal sheet by the total number of competition dives.
2. Write that number in the column for Dive Avg. on the goal-setting worksheet.
3. Round up (e.g., 66.66 would be 67 points).

For Individual Judge Score

1. Divide your dive average by the degree of difficult (DD)
2. Next, divide by 3.
3. Round up (e.g., 7.4 would be 7.5).
4. Write this number in the column Judge score on the goal-setting worksheet.

Example:

Dive total / number of dives = dive average

378 / 6 = 63

Dive average divided by DD divided by 3 = individual judge score

63 / 3 / 3 = 7

Figure 9.2 Diver goal scores worksheet.

DIVE PERFORMANCE CHART

Name: _____ Date: _____ Board: _____

Dive								Average
Forward								
Back								
Reverse								
Inward								
Twister								
Twister								
Subtotal								

Dive								Average
Forward								
Back								
Reverse								
Inward								
Twister								
Twister								
Subtotal								

Figure 9.3 Dive performance chart.

From J. Huber, 2016, *Springboard and Platform Diving* (Champaign, IL. Human Kinetics).

Physical Goals

Additionally, the goals of learning more difficult dives, gaining consistency, and improving skills and techniques are associated with the goals of increasing flexibility, strength, and power. For example, progressing to a 305C is facilitated by improving flexibility to increase the C position (hip flexors, low back, and shoulders) and by improving strength and power to increase the height off the springboard and the speed of the quick connect.

If this diver wants to become state champion, he will also have to increase his training volume and intensity from last season both on the board and on the dryland. Divers need to understand that their training level (volume and intensity) must be comparable to their goal level. In other words, as their level of goal attainment increases, so must their training demands. Making this increase part of their physical goals at the outset of the season helps them recognize, accept, and prepare for the training level they will endure during the upcoming season.

Let's add the skill, technical, and physical goals to our AITP:

- *Skills mastered*: Spotting, hollow reverse somersault, small tuck
- *Technique changes*: C position, twist connection and square-out, magic position, 90-90-90

▪ *Increase strength and power*: Squat increase by at least 20 percent, vertical jump by at least 2 inches (5 cm), and speed of hanging tuck-up by 20 percent.

▪ *Increase flexibility*: Hip flexors, low back, and shoulder reach.

▪ *Increase training volume and intensity*: at least 20 percent increase from previous year.

Notice the words *at least* in our strength and power goals. The goals are stated in terms that won't limit the amount of physical adaptation achieved during the season. It is certainly permissible for the athlete to increase his squat by more than 20 percent and the vertical jump by more than 2 inches (5 cm)! The diver goal setting worksheet in figure 9.4 will help coaches and athletes establish long term outcome goals and short term process practice goals.

Psychological Goals

Coach and diver must also consider psychological readiness for both practice and competition when completing the AITP. Our prospective state champion, for example, will need to learn how to handle the fear of learning more difficult dives, stay relaxed when spotting, and deal with the stress of championship competition. Chapters 10 and 11 outline effective mental skills and strategies for ensuring psychological readiness for practice and competition.

Let's add the psychological goals to our AITP:

▪ *Mental skills for training*: handle fear of learning new dives and relax during dive rotation and spotting.

▪ *Mental skills for competition*: relax during the approach and handle competitive stress. Since the diver wants to be state champion, let's also have him more fully develop his preperformance routine.

To this point, the AITP is incomplete. Much like a rough sketch on a canvas waiting for the artist to embellish it with depth, color, interpretation, and meaning, the AITP is waiting for the coach and athlete to add the finishing details for each seasonal phase and training cycle. The following sections take an in-depth look at the plan and offer some points of emphasis for individualizing each seasonal phase of the bottom portion of the AITP in figure 9.1. The completed AITP can be found at the end of this chapter in figure 9.5.

Individualizing the AITP

An annual training plan is most effective when tailored to the needs of the athlete. The coach and athlete must create a plan that fits with the goals, needs, weaknesses, and strengths of the athlete. For example, the outcome, technical, physical, and psychological goals for a beginning high school freshman diver with no diving experience will be vastly different from those of an experienced high school senior diver. Coaches must be cognizant of not only these types of athlete differences but also differences in athlete progression throughout the season. For example, during the season, some divers will advance more quickly than others, and some will master certain skills while other divers will not. An annual training plan is most effective in meeting the needs of a diver when it is individualized and evaluated and modified when necessary throughout the season.

Diver Goal–Setting Worksheet

Goals are important for guiding immediate and future actions, evaluating success, and sharpening mental focus. Goals give you a plan for what to do for each workout and for the season. As the season progresses, use your plan to evaluate your progress. By continually reminding yourself of where you are going and what you want to achieve and have achieved, your goals can be a source of inspiration and sustained motivation.

Long-Term Goals

Long-term goals are the things you want to achieve in the future. In this section consider what you would like to achieve during the championship part of the season.

Best meet finishes I want to reach this season:

Meets: _____ _____ _____ _____

Best place of finish:

1 meter _____ _____ _____ _____

3 meter _____ _____ _____ _____

10 meter _____ _____ _____ _____

	Total	Dive Avg.	Judge Score
Point total needed for highest-place 1-meter finish:	_____	_____	_____
Point total needed for highest-place 3-meter finish:	_____	_____	_____
Point total needed for highest-place 10-meter finish:	_____	_____	_____

New dives I want or need to learn to reach my goals this season:

1 meter _____

3 meter _____

10 meter _____

Goals I most want to accomplish before I retire from diving:

_____

_____

_____

Short-Term Goals

Short-term goals are the things you want achieve in practice to reach your long-term goals. Without short-term goals, long-term goals are simply unrealized fantasy goals. What you accomplish in practice determines whether you

(continued)

Figure 9.4 Diver goal setting worksheet.

will reach your long-term goals. Successful divers take responsibility for their diving. If you want to be successful, come to practice focused and committed to your specific goals. Before each practice, remind yourself of what you want to accomplish. At the end of each practice and each week, evaluate your progress and establish new goals for the upcoming week. Think of short-term goals as a road map for reaching long-term goals. The more specific your short-term goals are, the clearer the directions for reaching your final destination will be. Following are factors you need to consider. Please feel free to use the back of the paper for additional space.

Forward approach and hurdle:

Back press:

Takeoff, flight, and come-out:

Entry:

Consistency:

Practice expectations and attitude:

Practice and competition performance (e.g., staying motivated to train, handling competitive stress, staying relaxed):

Academics:

Nutrition:

Strength and flexibility:

Lifestyle:

Other:

    Body weight: Current: _____ Competition: _____

    Basal metabolic rate (BMR): _____ (Use online BMR calculator.)

    Total daily energy expenditure (TDEE): _____

    Total daily caloric intake (TDCI): _____

To determine TDEE and TDCI go to Super Tracker at the following USDA government website: https://www.supertracker.usda.gov.

Now that you have set your goals, sign your name and record the date. Your signature indicates that you are making a commitment to yourself to do whatever it takes to reach your goals. To remind yourself of your goals, post them where you will see them each day. Best of luck with your journey!

_____   _____
Signature   Date

Figure 9.4 *(continued)*

From J. Huber, 2016, *Springboard and Platform Diving* (Champaign, IL. Human Kinetics).

Guidelines for Determining Volume and Intensity

Recall the admonition presented earlier in this chapter: Keep in mind the time of season. For example, at the outset of the preseason, most divers are likely to be somewhat out of shape and therefore unprepared to handle a high volume and high intensity of training. **Volume** refers to the amount of training (work) an athlete does. **Intensity** refers to the amount of effort (both physical and psychological) an athlete is required to give during training (work). There is an inverse relationship between volume and intensity: the greater the intensity is, the less the volume should be. In other words, the harder the workload is, the less time that workload can be sustained.

Volume can be controlled by adjusting the number of repetitions (e.g., drills, dives, hanging pike-ups, squats) and the number of stations (e.g., at various points in the season, divers work on dryland training, technique, skills, basic dives, optional dives, and new dives) performed during each practice. Intensity can be controlled by adjusting practice parameters such as the allotted time to perform a certain number of repetitions (e.g., 30 dives in 45 minutes instead of 60 minutes), task difficulty (e.g., a 304C on a 3-meter platform instead of a 5-meter platform, a backward somersault on dryland with a weighted vest instead of just body weight), dive quality (e.g., performing dives for score), and degree of difficulty (e.g., four each of a 307C instead of a 305C).

Individualizing an AITP involves determining the workload divers will carry during each seasonal phase based on their individual goals. For example, during the early and midseason phases of training, divers should maintain a heavy workload. To attain a training effect, divers should be fatigued and sore at the end of the week during these phases. However, during the championship phase, divers should carry a lighter workload so that they are rested and ready to perform at their best at the end of the week when championship competitions are typically held. Into our plan let's now add volume and intensity.

Preseason: Volume begins low and then increases each week. Intensity begins low and then jumps to high with an emphasis on the accuracy of basic dives, skills, and drills (both in the water and on dryland) as well as adaptive strength and conditioning.

Early season: Volume for conditioning is reduced somewhat from high to moderate so that it can remain high for basic dives, skills, and drills. Intensity of training is high with an emphasis on speed and power in conditioning and the accuracy of basic dives, skills, and drills.

Midseason: Volume for basic dives, skills, and drills is reduced to moderate, while volume for optional dives increases from low to high until optional dives become the main focus of practice. Volume for conditioning remains moderate but with high intensity. Intensity increases from low to high when working on the accuracy of optional dives.

Championship season: Volume for conditioning moves from moderate to low and then to maintenance. Volume for basic dives, skills, and drills is reduced from moderate to low and then to maintenance. Volume for optional dives moves from high to moderate as the championship approaches. Intensity remains high for optional dives.

Postseason: Volume and intensity depend on individual goals and how much time the coach and diver decide to take off. The postseason can be a time to take a break, reduce training, focus solely on conditioning, combine conditioning with some skill work, or a combination of these.

Let's now look at each of the five seasonal phases and complete our AITP "painting."

Preseason

The **preseason** is the beginning of the season, a time when team rules are communicated and enforced, expectations such as work ethic and teammate support are set, goals are determined, the overall team persona and practice atmosphere are established, and a personal AITP is presented to each athlete. Following is a checklist for coaches of what needs to occur at the outset of the preseason. *Conduct a team meeting.* At this meeting, the divers set team goals that include not only outcome goals (e.g., everyone qualifies for state, everyone makes top 12 at conference) but also process goals (e.g., everyone shows up on time for practice, all missed practices must be made up, divers support each other in and outside the pool). The coach provides input on the team goals.

- *Clearly communicate and post team rules and penalties for not following the rules.* For a more in-depth discussion of team rules and enforcement, see *Applying Educational Psychology in Coaching Athletes* (Huber, 2013).
- *Post team goals.* Post them in the locker rooms and provide each athlete with a copy.
- *Emphasize high effort.* Remind divers of the importance of laying a solid foundation now, at the beginning of the season, rather than at the end of the season.
- *Conduct baseline testing.* Test strength, conditioning, flexibility, and skill level.
- *Begin strength and conditioning training.* Preseason is the perfect time to begin this type of training.
- *Divers complete diver goal setting worksheet.* Divers complete this and the diver goal scores worksheet.
- *Conduct individual meetings.* Coach and diver review the diver goal setting worksheet, complete the AITP, and discuss any factors (e.g., personal issues) potentially affecting the diver's training.
- *Begin with simple skills and drills.* Optional dives can wait.
- *Conduct team-building experiences.* Activities such as team meals, day at the park, team cookout, rock wall climbing, and volunteerism go a long way in building cooperation, camaraderie, trust, and enthusiasm.

Although a sense of urgency in training is important, a sense of urgency during the preseason phase of training should be about high levels of motivation, mental activation, expectations, and attention to detail rather than high levels of volume and intensity. In their zeal to achieve a phenomenally successful season, overly eager coaches and athletes sometimes do too much too soon—just as the U.S. Major League baseball players cited earlier in this chapter did at the outset of their preseason training—which can cause preseason injuries. Coaches must be sensitive to individual differences and athletes' physical, mental, and emotional responses to volume and intensity.

The preseason is composed of one or two mesocycles, depending on the diver's length of season. Recall that a mesocycle is approximately two to four weeks long, so the preseason can last anywhere from two to eight weeks. If you have a short season, which many high school divers have, the preseason might last only two weeks. Because the collegiate season is much longer than the high school season, I typically wanted the preseason to consist of two mesocycles each lasting three weeks. During the first mesocycle, divers quickly become sore and fatigued. After about two weeks, however, they begin to accommodate, at which point volume and intensity can be increased, especially heading into the second mesocycle. Volume and intensity depend on athlete recovery. If they are recovering quickly, then volume and intensity can be increased after two weeks. If they are recovering more slowly, then another week to adapt to training demands may be necessary.

Foremost, the preseason is the time to work on physical conditioning and the fundamentals of diving. It is not a problem if the divers are physically drained and sore during the week, because they are working only on simple skills and drills. The preseason is the time to make a commitment to laying a solid foundation of conditioning and technique. Many coaches can't resist the urge to have their divers immediately start performing competition dives. Resist that urge! Divers should work as long as possible on the skills and drills outlined in the preceding chapters. Although it might not seem as though they are working on the actual dives, they are indeed (although indirectly), and the longer the preseason can be extended to work on the fundamentals, the better.

Even though the championship season is in the future, the preseason isn't too early for divers to begin practicing mental skills, particularly divers who are new to the sport. An early start to mental training gives divers time to appreciate and embrace mental training, practice mental skills, and apply these skills to practice and competition performances. Some coaches and athletes make the mistake of waiting until the championship phase to engage in mental training. Mental skills, however, are like diving skills. They need to be practiced throughout the season so that they become habituated and incorporated into performance.

Following are points of emphasis during the preseason phase:

- Team rules, expectations, work ethic, and team and individual goals
- Physical conditioning
- Skills, drills, and basic dives
- Mental skills for practice

Duration: two to eight weeks

Strength and power: Adaptation and then moving toward maximal strength training. Pre- and posttests for strength should be performed at the beginning and end of the preseason phase.

Flexibility: Yes, with an emphasis on increasing flexibility

Basic dives: Yes

Optional dives: No

New dives: No

Skill training: Yes

Technique training: Yes

Dryland training: Yes, with a focus on drills, skills, and technique

Volume: Low and then increasing throughout the phase

Intensity: Moderate to high with an emphasis on movement accuracy (correctness)

Psychological skills: Introduction of mental skills for practice (see chapter 10)

Meet simulation: A few competitions using only drills, skills, and basic dives. It is good to stoke divers' competitive fires and remind them that training is a means to an end, the end being competition. It is also a nice form of deliberate play.

From experience, I have found that the preseason should last as long as possible within the AITP. This is because it is the phase of training in which so many critical foundational blocks are laid—not only for a successful preseason but also, more important, for a successful championship season.

Early Season

The **early season** follows the preseason, and its theme is *more of the same* because it continues the preseason emphasis on conditioning, drills, skills, and techniques. The early season phase of training, therefore, can be considered somewhat of an extension of the preseason. However, during the early season phase, a foundation is also being established for the new and more difficult dives that divers want to learn and master during the season so they can showcase them during the championship phase.

Establishing such a foundation involves identifying the new dives and then matching them with the corresponding techniques, skills, drills, and lead-up dives necessary for learning them. For example, if a diver competed a backward somersault last season but wants to compete a 203C this season, then the early season phase is a time to work on skills and drills such as the backward line-up, 201C, and 202A on springboard and 203C in the spotting belt.

During this phase coach and diver should remain patient and not look too far into the future. Sure, there may be some dual meets on the horizon, but these are more than likely not the priority meets. Many outstanding coaches have their divers perform a simple list of dives in dual meets in the early season and midseason so they can continue working on skills and drills in practice. This is the reason many divers' dual meet records for the 1 meter, 3 meter, and 10 meter are below their championship records. They perform their best at the end of the season.

The early season phase is approximately four to six weeks long. Toward the end of the phase and at the beginning of the midseason phase, divers should begin practicing their optional dives. This is a good time to introduce mental training for learning new dives, such as handling fear, maintaining mental focus, and managing energy level (e.g., breathing, relaxation), since the divers will be preparing to perform their new dives for the first time.

Following are the main emphases during the early season phase:

- Physical conditioning
- Drills, skills, basic dives, and lead-ups
- Refining technique
- Preparatory skills and drills for new dives
- Mental skills for practice and learning new dives

Duration: Four to six weeks

Strength and power: Maximal strength and then power. A posttest for strength should occur at the end of the phase.

Flexibility: Continue to increase flexibility.

Basic dives: Yes

Optional dives: Yes, but not until approximately the last week of the phase

New dives: Yes, if ready, but not until the last week of the phase

Skill training: Yes

Technique training: Yes

Dryland training: Yes

Volume: Moderate for conditioning, but high for basic dives and lead-up dives.

Intensity: High with an emphasis on movement accuracy for skills and techniques.

Psychological skills: Continue emphasizing mental skills for training; introduce mental skills for handling the fear of learning new dives, and so on.

Meet simulation: A few competitions using basic dives only

Midseason

The **midseason** phase follows the early season phase and emphasizes much of the same things except that now divers are performing their optional dives in practice. This phase lasts approximately six to eight weeks during which new optional dives are performed and gradually integrated into the diver's routine list of practice dives. Even though divers are practicing optional dives, there is still a mixing throughout the week of skills, drills, basic dives, and lead-ups. For example, on Monday, divers may practice skills and drills, and then on Tuesday work on their competition dives and new dives. Or, they might practice skills and drills in the morning and then practice their optional and new dives in the afternoon. The point is that the building blocks (i.e., the basic mechanics) of the sport are still being revisited, rehearsed, and reemphasized. Now is a good time to emphasize mental skills for competition.

Following are the main emphases during the midseason phase:

- Skills, drills, lead-ups
- Practicing optional (competition) dives
- Integrating new dives into daily workouts until they are no longer new dives
- Increasing the number of competition dive repetitions
- Emphasizing mental skills for competition

Duration: Six to eight weeks

Strength and power: A mesocycle of maximal strength followed by a mesocycle of speed and power. A posttest should occur at the end of the phase or shortly thereafter.

Flexibility: Maintenance and slight improvements if possible

Basic dives: Yes

Optional dives: Yes

New dives: Yes

Skill training: Yes

Technique training: Yes

Dryland training: Yes

Volume: Increase volume from low to high for optional dives throughout phase. Decrease volume from high to moderate to low for conditioning, basic dives, technique, skills, and dryland work.

Intensity: Begin working on optional dives while still working on basic dives, skills, drills, dryland exercises, and conditioning. Intensity is high because of the high physical demand on divers. This is a period of heavy training load.

Psychological skills: Emphasize mental skills for competition.

Meet simulation: Yes, using competition dives during the last few weeks of the phase

Over the winter holiday break, I would run an intensive training camp during which volume and intensity were kept high. Before camp, we were already into heavy training, but during winter camp, the number of competition dive repetitions (volume) and the quality of dive execution (intensity) were significantly increased. By the end of camp, divers were often fatigued and susceptible to sickness, which was fine because if they were going to break down and, say, get the flu, now was a good time because they had plenty of time before the beginning of the championship phase of the season to recover from whatever bug was rampaging through the university student body that winter. This training camp was one reason, I believe, that my athletes rarely got sick during championships.

Championship Season

The **championship season** follows the midseason and encompasses, of course, the championships. In our example of the high school diver, championships include the conference meet, sectional meet, and state championship. At this phase of the season, the hay is in the barn. In other words, the work has been done, the foundation has been laid, and everything is set in place, at least as much as is humanly possible. If the work hasn't been done, well, it's too late to do anything about it. That is why urgency at the beginning of the season is so critical. The championship phase begins about two weeks out from the championship. For our example, the championship we are aiming to peak for is the state meet. So the championship phase begins about two weeks before the state meet.

I use the word *about* because coach and diver have to be careful. The diver in our example wants to peak for the state championship; however, the diver must first *qualify* for the championship. Consequently the conference and sectional meets can't be overlooked.

As the championship nears, training is altered to prioritize good health and high-quality performance. During this phase it is easy for athletes to do something inappropriate or ill advised such as stay up too late, skip meals, fool around or incur an avoidable injury. I am not sure why this is so. Perhaps it is the result of the stress of the upcoming championship. Or perhaps it is because the decrease in training volume and intensity results in increased personal time or physical energy, and the athletes don't know how to constructively use their free time or direct their energy.

The championship phase is a time to revisit the basics. At the start of the championship week, for example, divers should work on the forward approach and the backward press. They should be reminded that everything comes back to setting up with good takeoffs, and that a good takeoff makes it much easier to hit a dive.

The championship phase also is a time to rehearse, to make practice much like competition, which can be accomplished in several ways. One way to rehearse is to practice dives in **list order,** the order in which they will be performed in competition. In other words, divers perform each competition dive once before repeating. Let's say a diver has the following competition list order: 105B, 203B, 303B, 403B, and 5233D. And let's say the diver is doing four repetitions of each dive. The diver will do a 105B, then a 203B, then a 303B, then a 403B, and then a 5233D. After doing each of these dives once, the diver starts over from the beginning. These dives should be performed for score and the scores logged onto the dive performance chart.

This type of rehearsal is in contrast to **block order,** in which the preceding diver would perform four 105Bs, then four 203Bs, four 303Bs, and so on. List order is a highly effective way of preparing for championships because it places demands on athletes that are similar to competition demands. When divers miss a dive, their first reaction is to want to repeat it—but there are no mulligans (repeats) in diving competitions. When practicing in list order, they must wait until they have performed their entire list of dives before having an opportunity to repeat the dive they missed. List order requires divers to mentally prepare and focus on hitting the first dive just as they have to do in competition.

Following are the main emphases during the championship phase:

- Injury avoidance and good health maintenance
- Mental skills for competition
- Practicing dives in list order
- Rehearsal
- Back to the basics—if only briefly

Duration: Approximately two to four weeks
Strength and power: Maintenance
Flexibility: Maintenance
Basic dives: Yes, but moderate
Optional dives: Yes
New dives: No
Skill training: Yes, but moving from moderate to low and then to maintenance
Technique training: Yes, but moving from moderate to low and then to maintenance
Dryland training: Yes, but moving from moderate to low and then to maintenance
Volume: High for optional dives but low to maintenance for other areas of training
Intensity: High for correct performance of all dives
Psychological skills: Emphasis on mental skills for competition
Meet simulation: Yes, using competition dives, dive performance chart, and championship-like rehearsal.

Postseason—Revisited

After a disastrous championship, a meet at which we had had high expectations, I met privately with Mike behind the bleachers. We were emotionally crushed. I would like to say that it was a terrible championship for Mike, but it wasn't even that good. What comes after terrible? Whatever it is, that is how bad the meet was for Mike. He finished dead last in two events, and his season of promise was over. But behind those bleachers, we talked earnestly and honestly, and with laser-like focus we began reformulating our plan of attack for next season. The end of that horrible season was really the beginning of what would become one of the most amazing transformative season I had the privilege of witnessing during 37 years of coaching.

As mentioned earlier in this chapter, every season really begins with the culmination of the preceding season. After the dust has settled from the last competitive battle and emotions have subsided enough to think rationally and reasonably, the postseason begins—a time for honest reflection, introspection, evaluation, clarification, and redirection. It is a time to examine successes and failures, evaluate goal attainment, establish new goals, and analyze and amend the AITP (e.g., with new techniques, drills, skills, and dives).

The postseason also is a time for rest and recovery. The duration of rest and recovery and the degree of training volume and intensity during the postseason depend to a large extent on the level of goal attainment established for the upcoming season. Divers dreaming of becoming champions may elect to use the postseason as a time for a brief hiatus of perhaps one week and then resume moderate or maintenance training. Breaks are important for both diver and coach, so periodically getting away from the pool even for a week is healthy and rejuvenating. Notice in our completed AITP in figure 9.5 that there are four break periods throughout the year. Keep in mind, however, that the longer the break is, the longer the adaptation phase must be. In other words, the more time divers take off, the more time they will need to get back into diving shape.

Following are the main emphases during the postseason phase:

- Reflection, introspection, evaluation, clarification, and redirection
- Short to medium break from training
- Strength and flexibility maintenance
- Light skill and drill training depending on the goals for the next season
- Cross training—a good diversion from diving and a good way to stay in shape

Duration: One to two weeks
Strength and power: Light to moderate with emphasis on maintenance
Flexibility: Emphasis on maintenance
Basic dives: Yes, if desired
Optional dives: No
New dives: No
Skill training: Yes, if desired
Technique training: Yes, if desired
Dryland training: Yes, if desired
Volume: Low or maintenance
Intensity: Low or maintenance
Psychological skills: Yes; it is always good to work on these outside the pool.
Meet simulation: No

Figure 9.5 shows our now fully completed AITP. Although completing the AITP takes time, it is well worth the effort. It saves time for coaches and athletes throughout the long season and contributes to athlete preparation, confidence, and peace of mind. It also significantly contributes to goal attainment and long-term achievement. It is a road map to success.

Keep in mind that the AITP in figure 9.5 is simply used as an example for how to complete an annual plan. AITPs will vary depending upon the individual diver's outcome goals, as well as individual differences in recovery needs, diving experience and proficiency, and so on. For example, some divers may be able to train through certain qualifying meets while other divers will have to peak for these meets. Consequently, their AITPs will look much different.

For a recap for developing an AITP, see the sidebar Twelve Steps for Completing an Annual Individualized Training Plan.

Twelve Steps for Completing an Annual Individualized Training Plan

1. Determine the priority competitions and desired places of finish.
2. Determine the point scores needed to attain the places of finish.
3. Determine the degree of difficulty needed for places of finish.
4. Determine new dives needed to attain necessary degree of difficulty.
5. Determine the consistency level needed to attain places of finish.
6. Determine skills and techniques that need to be changed and/or mastered.
7. Determine areas in which the diver needs to improve flexibility, strength, and power.
8. Determine the amount of increase in training volume and intensity for dryland and water workouts.
9. Determine the psychological skills that need to be learned or strengthened for practice.
10. Determine the psychological skills that need to be learned or strengthened for competition.
11. Individualize and periodize the training plan for each seasonal phase to meet the needs of each diver.
12. Evaluate the AITP at the end of the season, set new goals, and make changes to next year's AITP.

Annual Individualized Training Plan

For: _____

From: August 20   **To:** August 12

Outcome Goals	Performance Goals	Skill and Technical Goals
• Conference champion • Sectional champion • State champion	Point scores: 450 (state), 420 (sectional), 400 (conference DD totals: 16.0 New dives: 107C, 305C, 5333D, 5134D Consistency level: 90% Individualize with athlete input.	Skills mastered: spotting, hollow reverse somersault, small tuck Technique changes: C position, twist connection and square-out, magic position, 90-90-90 Individualize with athlete input.

Month	Aug		Sept				Oct					Nov				Dec					Jan			
Week (Monday)	20	27	3	10	17	24	1	8	15	22	29	5	12	19	26	3	10	17	24	31	7	14	21	28
Competition priority 1 = peak; 5 = low															5	5	5	5		5	5			
Event	Break														Intrasquad	Dual meet	Dual meet	Dual meet	Break	Dual meet	Dual meet	Dual meet		
Training phase	Postseason		Preseason						Early season						Midseason								Championship	
Strength and power	Mt	Mt	L	M	M	H	H	M	H	M	H	H	M	H	M	H	H	M	H	H	M	H	M	L
Flexibility	Mt	Mt	L	M	M	H	H	M	H	M	H	H	M	H	M	H	H	M	H	H	H	H	M	L
Test dates			X						X						X								X	
Basic dives	O	O	L	M	M	H	H	H	H	H	H	H	H	H	M	M	M	L	L	L	L	L	L	M
Optional dives	O	O	O	O	O	O	O	O	O	O	O	O	O	O	O	L	M	M	H	H	H	H	H	H
New dives	O	O	O	O	O	O	O	O	O	O	O	O	O	O	O	L	L	M	M	H	H	H	M	O
Skills training	O	O	L	L	M	M	H	H	H	H	H	H	H	H	M	M	M	M	M	L	L	L	L	M
Technique training	O	O	L	L	M	M	H	H	H	H	H	H	H	H	M	M	M	M	M	L	L	L	L	M
Dryland training	O	O	L	L	M	M	H	H	H	H	H	H	H	H	M	M	M	M	M	L	L	L	L	M
Psychological skills	O	Mt	X	X	X	X	X	X	X	X	X	X	X	X	X	X	X	X	X	Mt	X	X	X	X
Meet simulation			X						X						X							X	X	X

Key: low (L), moderate (M), high (H), maintenance (Mt), off (O), engage (X)

Figure 9.5 A sample portion of a completed annual individualized training plan.

<table>
<tr><td colspan="2">

Physical Goals

*I*ncrease strength and power:
increase squat by at least 20%, vertical jump by 2 in. (5 cm), and hanging tuck-up speed by 20%

Increase flexibility:
hip flexors, low back, shoulder reach

Increase training volume & intensity: 20%

Individualize with athlete input.

</td><td colspan="2">

Psychological Goals

Mental skills for training:
handle fear of learning new dives; relax during dive rotation and spotting

Mental skills for competition:
relax during approach; handle competitive stress; improve preperformance routine

Individualize with athlete input.

</td></tr>
</table>

Month	Feb				Mar				Apr					May				Jun				Jul					Aug	
Week (Monday)	4	11	18	25	4	11	18	25	1	8	15	22	29	6	13	20	27	3	10	17	24	1	8	15	22	29	5	12
Competition priority 1 = peak; 5 = low	3	2	1			2					1			5	4			3					2				1	
Event	Conference	Sectionals	State meet	Break										Intrasquad	Invitational			Regions				Zones					Jr nationals	Break
Training phase				Postseason	Preseason						Early season			Midseason				Championship										Postseason
Strength and power	L	Mt	O	Mt	Mt	L	M	M	H	H	M	H	H	M	H	H	M	M	M	M	H	M	M	H	M	L	O	Mt
Flexibility	L	Mt	Mt	Mt	Mt	L	M	M	H	H	M	H	H	M	H	H	M	M	L	M	H	M	Mt	H	M	L	Mt	Mt
Test dates					X						X			X														
Basic dives	M	M	L	O	O	L	M	M	H	H	H	M	M	M	L	L	L	L	M	M	H	M	M	H	M	M	L	O
Optional dives	M	M	L	O	O	O	O	O	O	O	O	O	O	L	M	M	H	H	H	H	M	M	H	H	H	M	L	O
New dives	O	O	O	O	O	O	O	O	O	O	O	O	L	L	M	H	H	M	L	L	O	O	O	O	O	O	O	O
Skills training	L	L	Mt	O	O	L	L	M	H	H	H	M	M	M	M	M	M	M	M	L	M	M	L	M	M	L	Mt	O
Technique training	L	L	Mt	O	O	L	L	M	H	H	H	M	M	M	M	M	M	M	M	L	M	M	L	M	M	L	Mt	O
Dryland training	L	L	Mt	O	O	L	L	M	H	H	H	M	M	M	M	M	M	M	M	L	M	M	L	M	M	L	Mt	O
Psychological skills	X	X	X	Mt	X	X	X	X	X	X	X	X	X	X	X	X	X	X	X	X	X	X	X	X	X	X	X	Mt
Meet simulation					X						X			X			X	X	X			X			X	X		

Key: low (L), moderate (M), high (H), maintenance (Mt), off (O), engage (X)

From J. Huber, 2016, *Springboard and Platform Diving* (Champaign, IL. Human Kinetics).

CHAPTER 10

Mental Training for Practice

Mental training is included in this book because mental challenges are the most formidable obstacles divers confront. They need to know how to overcome them if they are to achieve their goals. What good does it do divers if they know what to execute (the Xs and Os) and how to learn but they don't know what mental skills to acquire or how to mentally prepare for challenges such as fear, lagging motivation, and competitive pressure. At any meet, for example, it's not the diver who looks the best in warm-up who wins, advances to finals, or makes the team but, rather, the diver who best handles the stress and performs when it counts most in competition.

Having worked with hundreds of divers over the years, I have noted that their most pressing concern is how to be mentally prepared. Every sport has its mental demands, but none is more mentally demanding than diving. Consider some of the demands of our beautiful sport. Divers stand on the springboard or platform nearly naked with every spectator's eyes directed on them. One mental misstep and the dive can be a disaster. Moreover, if they make a mistake there is no place to hide. They can't blame it on a lineman, point guard, catcher, or teammate. If they make a mistake, it is their mistake, and it can feel like the whole world sees it. Beyond all of this, there is the looming threat of becoming disoriented in midair, hitting the board, landing flat on a water surface that can feel as hard as concrete, or injuring a shoulder or back. It is a crazy sport.

And yet, it is also a sublime sport, offering moments of bliss: surreal practices, unforgettable dive performances, and peak competition experiences. This chapter and the next discuss how coaches and athletes can create these moments of bliss in both practice and competition through effective mental training.

But first, a short story . . .

Grant, a boy around the age of 13, had been struggling for well over a year to learn a back 2 1/2 somersault off the 3-meter springboard. The last day of camp, I pulled him aside and said, "Grant, it's time to learn this dive." Without a word, Grant climbed the ladder, set the fulcrum, walked out to the end of the board, turned around, placed his feet on the end of the board, took a deep breath, and after a short pause, threw the dive. I will never forget the look of relief, joy, and pride on his face when he came up out of the water. It was the same look that I am sure was on my face as well. I gave him a high five and hug when he climbed out of the pool and, before I could ask him anything, he said, "Coach, I just kept telling myself: Eye of the storm. Eye of the storm. Eye of the storm."

During my weekly camp lecture, I talked about how to become the eye of the storm—the calm, cool, focused athlete amid all the "turbulence" when learning new dives and performing under stressful competitive situations. We discussed self-talk, mental imagery, having a mental game plan, and other techniques for handling the fear of learning new dives (a popular topic among camp attendees). As Grant ably demonstrated that last day at camp, even a small amount of mental training can make a big difference.

Some diving coaches and divers believe that some individuals are natural-born performers and competitors and others are not. They believe these traits are inherent and unalterable. A diver either possesses them or does not, and no amount of learning can alter these traits. Consequently, these athletes and coaches are uninterested in mental training. Nothing, however, could be further from the truth. Successful divers use specific mental skills that make them more mentally prepared than unsuccessful divers. They weren't born with these skills. They learned them just as they learned specific diving skills.

What are the mental skills that separate the successful diver from the unsuccessful diver, the diver who throws the backward 2 1/2 somersault from the diver who does not, the diver who performs well in competition from the diver who performs poorly? One skill Grant employed when he told himself "Eye of the storm" was self-talk—one of the five pillars of mental training.

Five Pillars of Mental Training

The five pillars of mental training, which are the foundation for the psychology of training and the psychology of competition are self-talk, mental imagery, energy management, cognitive restructuring, and self-monitoring. Self-talk, for example, keeps divers motivated for training, relaxed and confident, and focused for competition. *Keep in mind that these strategies are as important and effective for coaches as they are for divers*. It is just as important, for example, for coaches to be the eye of the storm during turbulent times as it is for divers. In fact, it may be even more important because it is difficult for divers to maintain their cool under fire when their coaches are losing it mentally. Divers and coaches feed off each other mentally. Let's take a look at these strategies.

Self-Talk

Self-talk includes the words divers utter to themselves out loud and their private thoughts. All athletes talk to themselves, even if they aren't always aware of it. These words and thoughts create emotions, and emotions generate physiological, cognitive, and motivational consequences that either enhance or impair performance. Positive self-talk is performance enhancing, and negative self-talk is performance impairing. Most athletes and coaches have had some amount of interaction with the Negative Nelly athlete who always talks doom and gloom to self and teammates. Negative self-talk is self-destructive and debilitating to personal performance, team cohesiveness, and training atmosphere.

What are some kinds of self-talk for developing a positive mental attitude, instilling self-confidence, and increasing motivated behavior? Landin and Herbert (1999) identified three types of self-talk that positively affect emotions and performance: task-specific statements relating to technique, encouragement and effort, and mood words.

Task-Specific Statements Relating to Technique

This category involves self-talk that reinforces specific techniques used during performance. For example, the diver getting ready to perform a reverse dive might say or think, "Relax in the approach, get to the end of the board, and keep the head neutral" as reminders for safely and correctly performing the dive.

Encouragement and Effort

This type of self-talk uses self-encouragement to persevere and try hard. For example, the diver who has just missed a dive in a meet might say or think, "Okay, forget about that one and get ready for your next dive. It is a good one, and you can nail it. Go get it!" At the NCAA national championship in the United States, Cassandra missed her first dive, a 6243D that is typically her best dive. Getting out of the water, she reminded herself that there were four more dives and that missing her first dive was a challenge, not an obstacle. She nailed her next four dives and was crowned national champion.

Mood Words

This type of self-talk employs words that favorably affect an athlete's mood or arousal level. For example, the diver looking to increase arousal might say or think "Aggressive!" In contrast, the diver looking to remain calm might say or think "Patience" depending on the type of performance or the stage in the performance routine.

Self-talk is more effective when the statements are (1) brief and phonetically simple to utter, (2) logically associated with the actual performance, and (3) appropriate and connected to the sequential timing of the performance (Landin & Herbert, 1999). For example, during the approach and hurdle phase for a 107, arousal needs to be relatively low, but on takeoff, arousal needs to be quite high. The diver might say or think "Patience" as she approaches the end of the board and then "Hard" as she throws into the somersault.

Interestingly, Grand and Goldberg (2011) suggest that negative thoughts serve a useful purpose. They suggest that negative thoughts can be perceived as the mind's way of warning athletes of potential pitfalls, injuries, or failures. It is as though the athlete's mind is unconsciously warning, "Look out; be careful; there might be a problem up ahead." These authors suggest that athletes should acknowledge negative self-talk rather than ignore it, and then move forward with positive talk that counters the negative. For example, during a forward approach, a diver might hear a voice say, "You are going to miss this hurdle." Before the hurdle, however, the diver responds with another voice that says, "No, you are going to get your arms up early and nail this hurdle." Do you think this type of scenario might be farfetched? A U.S. Olympic bronze medalist diver I know occasionally experienced such inner dialogue throughout his career.

Mental Imagery

Mental imagery is willful daydreaming—creating or recreating an experience in the mind that includes corresponding senses, such as visual, kinesthetic, auditory, and tactile, in the absence of real external stimuli. In other words, mental imagery is seeing, feeling, hearing, and sensing the execution of a dive without actually performing it. Mental imagery also involves incorporating and simulating the emotional states athletes experience during dive performance.

The two types of mental imagery are success imagery and coping imagery. **Success imagery** involves visualizing successful performances along with the positive emotions associated with them. **Coping imagery** involves picturing overcoming events such as mistakes (e.g., missing a dive in competition), unexpected occurrences (e.g., another diver hitting the board), and distractions (e.g., a spectator coughing or dropping a camera during the forward approach). Coping imagery is an effective strategy for preparing for the unexpected so that, if it actually occurs, it is expected. For example, divers can imagine a diver immediately ahead of them in the dive order hitting a dive for 10s in competition. Through repeated imagery, they learn how to cope with this situation. Having a coping strategy is extremely helpful in building mental toughness, confidence, and refocusing skills.

Mental imagery has a number of advantages for athletes (McCann, Haberl, & Bauman, 2006), including the following:

- Practicing and refining skills
- Correcting mistakes
- Enhancing decision-making skills
- Practicing and enhancing the use of psychological skills
- Increasing confidence
- Coping with adversity
- Refining concentration
- Strengthening motivation
- Managing emotions
- Preparing for competition

Energy Management

Athletic performance is partly about energy regulation: when to use it and when to save it. Consider a diver performing a reverse 2 1/2 somersault in the tuck position. The diver will have to throw harder for this dive than for a reverse 1 1/2 somersault, but the key is to avoid anticipating the dive, which is the process of separating the hurdle from the dive. The diver needs to perform the hurdle first and then throw hard for the dive. Some divers become impatient and expend too much energy in the hurdle and, consequently, jump over the end of the springboard and then can't throw hard for the dive. They use up their explosive burst of energy too soon.

But energy regulation isn't just about physical energy. It also includes mental and emotional energy. Consider divers who think all day about learning a new dive and by practice time are mentally and emotionally drained. A similar thing often happens at major competitions. Divers arrive several days before the competition, and by the time of their event, they are mentally worn out and emotionally flat. **Energy management**, then, is the process of conserving physical, mental, and emotional energy and expending that energy at the appropriate time for effective and successful diving performance. Energy conservation and expenditure requires athletes to recognize how much energy their thoughts and emotions consume, monitor and measure their energy intensity levels, learn techniques for changing their energy levels, and practice these techniques consistently.

Cognitive Restructuring

Our personal (private) thoughts powerfully affect our emotions and behavior. Some of these thoughts can be beneficial. The thought "I don't care where I finish; I just want to give my best effort in a meet," for example, produces the positive emotions of joyful excitement, eager anticipation, and bold aggressiveness. On the other hand, some thoughts can be debilitating. The thought "If I don't win, everyone will hate me," for example, leads to the emotions of fear, anxiety, foreboding, and tentativeness. Many (but not all) negative thoughts lead to dysfunctional and impairing emotions and behaviors.

Cognitive restructuring is the process of removing faulty thinking (i.e., irrational and counter-factual negative thoughts) and replacing it with sound, rational, logical thinking. For example, the irrational thought "If I don't win, everyone will hate me" can be addressed and eliminated through cognitive restructuring. Because many private thoughts are deeply engrained, habitual, and unconscious, the first step in cognitive restructuring is becoming aware of these thoughts. The next step is addressing them by challenging their rationality. The third step is substituting faulty thoughts with positive, rational, and performance-enhancing thoughts.

So, the diver in our example might answer the irrational thought by thinking: "That is nonsense. I am not loved or hated for winning or losing. Winning or losing has nothing to do with who I am as a person or how people relate to me both in and outside the pool. The reason I dive is because I enjoy it, not because I need to win." Cognitive restructuring is effective for combating mental obstacles such as the fear of new dives, competitive anxiety, and unmotivated behavior. Achieving one's goals begins with maintaining the right perspective.

Self-Monitoring

The preceding four pillars of mental training are worth little if they are not accompanied by the fifth pillar: self-monitoring. **Self-monitoring** is the conscious and ever-vigilant mental process of overseeing and managing the four processes of self-talk, mental imagery, energy management, and cognitive restructuring. These four pillars are effective only if they are monitored and maintained. For example, an athlete's positive self-talk can suddenly, unexpectedly, and unconsciously turn negative during critical practice and competition moments. This is particularly true for athletes who tend to think negatively in other areas of their lives outside the pool.

Following are two simple but effective guidelines for self-monitoring.

Ask the Question

Coaches and athletes should develop the habit of routinely asking this simple question: *How am I doing?* This means: *How am I feeling emotionally? How am I feeling physically? How is my thinking and self-talk? Am I following my game plan? Am I within my zone of optimal functioning?* Plain and simple: *Am I doing the things physically, mentally, and emotionally that I should be doing?*

Self-monitoring keeps divers in the zone and prevents what I call the 2,000-pound (900 kg) invisible gorilla from getting on their backs. Every diver has had a moment like this: the body freezes up, the mind goes numb, and the emotions spin wildly out of control. At this point it's nearly impossible to shake the beast. Game over. Consequently, the best strategy is prevention. Routinely practice self-monitoring during training and competition by asking the question.

Create a Mental Checklist

One effective way to self-monitor is to create a checklist. Write down those things that from experience you know you need to monitor, such as anger, anxiety, physical tension, thoughts, and behaviors. Once the list is created, commit it to memory so that they can use it as a mental checklist.

The day-to-day demands of training are physically, mentally, and emotionally rigorous. During training, divers must combat fear, fatigue, monotony, self-doubt, failure, and a host of other foes. But training is where it's at, where divers test themselves, where they prove themselves, where they meet the challenges that ultimately prepare them for achieving their competition goals. To meet these practice challenges, divers must be motivated to train. Following are some simple but proven tips for getting motivated for practice.

Getting Motivated for Practice

One factor that helped Grant learn his backward 2 1/2 somersault at camp that day was his motivation to learn it. Motivation is a key ingredient for success, whether it is in diving or other endeavors, and it is especially important when it comes to training. Training is where it all happens. Divers don't become successful in competition without first becoming successful in training. They can't hit a dive in competition that they never or seldom hit in practice. Sure, a blind squirrel gets a nut once in a while, but successful divers don't depend on luck. They get the job done in practice, and getting the job done in practice means getting motivated to train by using mental training skills.

Embrace Mental Training

Some divers (and some coaches) don't readily embrace and engage in mental training because of a lack of experience using mental training, a lack of knowledge about its significant positive impact on performance, or both. According to Massey (2013), three factors positively influence the increased use of mental training by athletes. The first is the support of a friend, teammate, or coach. The second is rewarding themselves for consistently engaging in mental training. And the third is using mental training as an alternative to engaging in negative activities that impair performance (e.g., engaging in breathing techniques and positive self-talk rather than worrying about negative outcomes in an upcoming competition).

Massey offers other useful suggestions for promoting the use of mental training, such as swapping out 15 minutes per day of social media for mental training, researching a mental training topic, reading a sport psychology book, setting a reminder on the phone to engage in mental training, and partnering with a mental training teammate. Coaches can encourage mental training by practicing it themselves and by setting aside practice time for activities such as lecturing on mental training, guiding divers through relaxation exercises, and including mental training in individual goal setting. As athletes engage in increasingly more mental training, they begin to see its benefits and embrace it as a valuable part of their overall training.

Set Goals

As mentioned earlier in the book, goal setting is critical for creating an annual individualized training plan. Goal setting is equally important for motivating athletes for practice by increasing motivation, directing behavior, and providing feedback.

Goals for Increasing Motivation

Years ago, we missed placing third as a team at the summer U.S. national championship by a mere 3 points. If we had placed third, we would have received a stunningly beautiful trophy in the shape of a pyramid. The base was the color of deep-water blue, and the body of the pyramid was clear with a suspended bronze figure of a diver in a pike position. I decided it would be good motivation for the team to set a goal of placing at least third at the next national championship so we could capture that gorgeous trophy. On the plane ride home, I wrote down everything I could think of to help us reach that goal. At our first team meeting, I asked the divers to adopt the goal and list everything they could do to accomplish it. I compiled a list of their suggestions and posted it. A mere eight months later, we competed at the winter U.S. national championship and not only reached our goal but exceeded it. We won the men's team title, placed second in the women's team race, and won the combined men's and women's team title. We went on to win 11 consecutive combined national team championships. Goal setting increases motivation for both athletes and teams.

Goals for Directing Behavior

Once divers know their destination, they can map out a route for getting there. There are three types of goals: outcome goals, process goals, and performance goals. **Outcome goals** are the things athletes want to achieve such as make finals in a meet, win a meet, or make varsity. Outcome goals are important because they let divers and coaches know how high to set the bar—how hard they will have to work to achieve the outcome goals. The problem with outcome goals is that they don't tell divers or coaches exactly what they need to *do*. This is where process goals become important.

Process goals are the specific things divers need to do to achieve their outcome goals. What does a diver with the goal of, say, winning a state championship have to do, specifically, to become state champion? As you might recall from our annual individualized training plan we developed in chapter 8, the diver had to learn specific new dives, skills, and techniques, increase strength and power, and so on.

Performance goals focus on performance improvements, such as exceeding a personal best score. Once they have established outcome goals, divers should focus on process and performance goals. By focusing on personal performance and active process goals, athletes are task involved rather than ego involved.

Outcome, process, and performance goals can be divided into short-term and long-term goals. **Short-term goals** are things to accomplish immediately or in the near future. **Long-term goals** are accomplishments to be achieved in the distant future. A novice freshman high school diver, for example, might want to set a short-term outcome goal of winning a dual meet. A long-term outcome goal would be to win the state championship as a junior or senior. For a short-term process goal, the freshman might set a goal to learn a 105C, but a long-term process goal to learn a 107C.

Goals for Providing Feedback

When divers are in the middle of training, they can have difficulty seeing their improvement. In fact it is sometimes easier to see a teammate's improvement than one's own. Goals, then, let divers and coaches know objectively how much they are progressing toward their goals. Goals can also act as a kick in the tail for coaches and divers who find they are not progressing toward their goals. For this reason, daily practice process goals go a long way in getting divers motivated to train.

Set a Goal of Mental Preparation

As a young junior diver, U.S. Olympic silver medalist Scott Donie was considered a talented diver but dreadful competitor. After several especially disappointing meets, Scott decided to set a goal to become a great competitor. He worked on his mental preparation throughout his career and, by the time he retired, he was known as one of the best competitors in the world on both platform and springboard. *Great competitors are made, not born.* The first step in becoming mentally prepared is making it a priority goal, as Scott did.

Set Inside- and Outside-Pool Goals

Goal commitment occurs both inside and outside the pool. Divers can't train intensively on a daily basis and reach their diving goals unless they are getting enough rest, eating the right food, staying current with classroom assignments, and so on. Eventually, problems outside the pool affect performance inside the pool. Drug and/or alcohol abuse, for example, will tear down even the most talented and promising diver or coach. Therefore, divers and coaches must develop inside-pool and outside-pool goals and commit to them.

Use the Three RE's

The **three RE's** of goal setting are *remind*, *review*, and *rewrite*. Because goals motivate, direct, and inform, divers should *remind* themselves of their goals before, during, and after practice. While stretching, recall the practice goals so that they are the focus of their efforts. After practice, *review* what was worked on and what needs to be accomplished at the next practice. People forget approximately 70 to 80 percent of newly presented information within 48 hours unless they somehow rehearse it or elaborate on it. Consequently, divers should take the time to review their practice so that they understand and remember the things they learned and are mentally prepared at the next practice. *Rewriting* process goals keeps them current and challenging for subsequent practices. Practicing the three RE's is equally important for coaches in helping their divers achieve their goals.

Establish Time-Bound Goals

Goals with no time limit for attainment are often never achieved. The adage *Never put off until tomorrow what you can do today* is worth heeding when it comes to goals. Without a time limit, there is generally no sense of urgency. Without a time limit, it is easy to think: "Why get committed for today's practice? I can always get it done tomorrow." Goals are sooner achieved when there is a deadline.

Match Behavior With Goals

Goals aren't the things divers write down on a piece of paper. They are the daily behaviors they exhibit. It's a cliché, but nonetheless true, that actions speak louder than words. Divers and coaches must ask themselves: *Do my actions reflect my goals? Is my behavior in line with my goals? Am I doing the things I want and should be doing?* Some divers' behaviors suggest that their goals are to avoid doing something new and uncomfortable, to do as little work as possible, to make practice a miserable experience, to balk the minute a hurdle feels bad, to give up and break if a dive doesn't feel perfect, to repeatedly make the same mistake, to wait until tomorrow to make a correction, or to be the last one in the water and the first one out.

It's easy to veer off track or fool yourself into believing that you are doing the right things. Be honest with yourself. Take time to mentally step outside yourself and observe your behavior. When off track, forcefully redirect yourself so that your behavior is goal driven.

Correlate Practice With Competition

What divers do in practice is most often what they will do in a meet. If they repeatedly do something in practice, they are most likely to do the same thing in competition. Draw a correlation between practice and competition. See the strong relationship between your actions and habits in practice and your performances in competition. Such a perception motivates you to get after things in practice. If you want to avoid going short of vertical on your entries in the meet, for example, then get vertical on your dives in practice. Set a goal of placing the same restrictions on yourself in practice as you do in meets. For example, you can't balk or break in a meet, so don't balk or break in practice. Rarely do divers do things in competition that they don't habitually do in practice.

Start Where You Left Off

Divers sometimes work hard and take a step forward at one practice only to take a step backward at the next. Unthinkingly, they come to the next practice and revert to their old habits. Near the end of practice, the coach might cajole them into again making the same correction they made at the last practice. The result after two days of practice is one step forward when it could have been two steps forward.

While stretching, think about your last practice and where you left off. Next, think about what you want to do on your first drills and dives for that day's practice so that you are mentally prepared to perform yesterday's correction. Starting where you left off allows you to repeat the new action, make it a more comfortable and automatic response, and begin working on another correction.

Mental review and preparation result in a step forward followed by another step forward at the subsequent practice. Now the result after two days of practice is two steps forward instead of one. Progressing toward your goals at twice your previous pace will increase your motivation to train.

Dive Outside Your Comfort Zone

Learning means change. And change means trying something new. But trying something new is generally awkward, disjointed, and uncomfortable. Those feelings, however, are the normal part of motor learning progression.

Think back to anything you learned the first time in diving. It wasn't nearly as smooth and comfortable then as it is now. So don't be afraid of the awkward, disjointed, and uncomfortable. Embrace them. Dive outside your comfort zone. If you are training in your comfort zone, you aren't changing (learning). *Elite athletes consistently train outside their comfort zones by setting challenging daily practice goals.* The more you train outside your comfort zone, the more comfortable you make competition. The more comfortable you make practice, the more uncomfortable you make competition.

Staying Motivated for Practice

Being occasionally inspired to train is easy. Every diver can train hard at random times during the season. The challenge for all divers is to sustain that motivation and train hard on a consistent basis. Without the ability to stay motivated, divers won't reach their long-term outcome goals. Following are some simple but effective suggestions for staying motivated.

Motivation and the Five Pillars of Mental Training

Recall that self-talk is a technique for providing encouragement, increasing effort, establishing mood, and elevating arousal. As a diver, you can use the technique for staying motivated. Self-statements such as "Come on; you can do it"; "Today is the day I reach my goal for ripping reverses"; "Forget about what happened in the classroom today and get in a good mood to dive and be coached"; "Forget that last dive; fire up and nail the next one"; and "I can't wait for the next practice" provide encouragement, increase effort, set mood state, elevate arousal for practice, and most important, maintain motivation.

Because mental imagery strengthens motivation, divers should practice both coping and success imagery. As a young diver, I pictured myself atop the award stand at the state meet years before it actually happened. That success imagery kept me motivated, particularly during cold outdoor winter practices.

Managing physical, mental, and emotional energy levels help divers stay motivated for training. Postponing studying and then stressing out about impending exams, not getting enough sleep, being overly anxious about learning new dives, ignoring unresolved problems outside the pool, skipping meals, and eating poorly are all factors that drain physical, mental, and emotional batteries and decrease motivation. Avoid and eliminate factors that expend energy and decrease motivation for practice.

Perhaps the simplest and most effective way of staying motivated is restructuring faulty thinking. For example, instead of thinking "Shoot, I have to practice today," it is more motivating to think: "Practice is something I *get* to do, not something I *have* to do. Practice is a privilege, not a right." Remember that practice is a wonderful but short-lived opportunity. It won't last forever, so make the most of it. And, of course, vigilant self-monitoring ensures that you are using the other pillars for staying motivated for practice. The more you use self-monitoring, the more it becomes a mental habit.

Create a Motivational Environment

To sustain motivation, divers—and coaches—should surround themselves with things that inspire them and keep their passion alive and growing. Let the world outside the pool be a constant reminder of the glorious world inside the pool and future hoped-for accomplishments. Activities such as posting goals, displaying posters and inspirational quotes, reading inspirational books, watching inspirational movies, viewing past championships, and watching performances of great divers sustain motivation.

Make Practice Fun

Staying motivated for practice is difficult when practice isn't fun. Approach practice with a sense of joy, humor, and delight. Motivation and long-term success are better achieved when having fun while working hard rather than simply working hard. Practice can be a game. The list of games to play is limited only by the imagination. For example, you can challenge a teammate to a dive-off, rehearse hitting a dive to win the championship, or see how many times you can correctly repeat a drill. Making practice fun also includes maintaining a sense of humor, seeing the lighter side of things, telling a good joke or laughing at one. Working hard and having fun are highly compatible, not mutually exclusive. Set a goal to approach practice with a smile on your face, joy in your heart, and appreciation for the opportunity to practice.

Keep Practice Precious

Some divers believe that behaviors such as missing one or two practices a week, skipping certain drills and dives each practice, or arriving late to practice and leaving early are inconsequential. Yet, if they added up all the missed training opportunities at the end of the month, they would be surprised to find that they took perhaps three or four "vacation days" from training. If told that they missed that much training time, they more than likely wouldn't believe it. But they did. And what they really missed were valuable opportunities for making changes in their diving, opportunities that can never be regained.

Improvements often come when least expected. Sometimes the mental lightbulb illuminates because a coach happens to say the same thing in a different way. But divers never know when these moments will occur. It requires practice performing that particular drill or dive for it to happen. For this reason, think twice before deciding to skip a practice, drill, or dive. Staying motivated involves keeping practice precious.

Understand the Purpose

Divers benefit more from doing something such as a lead-up or line-up if they understand why they are doing it and how it fits into the grand scheme of things.

Too often, divers don't associate a certain drill with a specific dive. They may practice the drill one way, but perform the action a different way when doing the actual dive. When they understand why they are doing a particular drill, they stay motivated to master it and perform the correct movement during dive performance.

It doesn't do the diver much good if the coach understands why a diver is practicing a particular drill but the diver doesn't. If you don't understand something, ask your coach for a more detailed explanation. That's part of your coach's job as coach and part of your responsibility as a diver. If you are a coach, create a climate in which divers are encouraged to ask questions and then correct any misunderstanding so that they clearly understand the purpose for what they are practicing.

Find Objective Sources of Feedback

Sometimes it seems as if there are two types of divers: those who think they are diving better in practice than they really are, and those who think they are diving worse in practice than they really are. Diving quality can be easily misjudged because it is difficult to objectively evaluate goal attainment progress, especially in a sport such as diving in which athletes can't consult a stopwatch or some other objective measurement tool. Therefore, divers need to find objective sources of feedback, especially during long or arduous training cycles, to determine their level of practice performance. Sources of objective feedback include honest coach assessments, digital replay analyses, dual meet scores, and performance charting.

As mentioned in chapter 9, performance charting tracks dive consistency and involves scoring practice dives and logging those scores on a chart. Like a stopwatch, a performance chart is an objective record that allows divers and coaches to compare current performances to past performances. These charts also can be used to discover potential performances hidden within the numbers. For example, a diver can perform four of each dive and then take the highest score for each dive and add up the scores to see the total score she is capable of achieving when she becomes more consistent. Divers shouldn't limit performance evaluation to just dive execution. Measuring vertical jumps, sit-ups, pike-ups, leg strength, flexibility, and body mass index can provide motivating feedback telling divers that they are working hard, accomplishing much for their efforts, and moving closer to their goals.

Remember That Human Progress Isn't Constant

Every diver would like to experience a constant rate of increased diving performance with each practice. Unfortunately, human beings don't progress at a constant linear rate. There will be days when nothing seems to work, especially during challenging or long training cycles when performance might plateau or even regress. These experiences can cause discouragement, which can act as a barrier to new learning and lead to further regression. Therefore, athletes must remember that improvement is sometimes preceded by performance plateaus or regressions.

Why is this? Perhaps it is because of overtraining, staleness, fatigue, decreased motivation, learning curve, or some other factor. But whatever the reason, athletes and coaches need to perceive a decrease in performance as the beginning of a learning period that ultimately leads to improved performance. This perception blocks discouragement, increases motivation to train, and encourages self-examination and self-questioning as athletes ask themselves, *What can I do during this training cycle to improve?*

Consider the saying *It's only at night that we can see the stars.* Only in our darkest hour do we clearly see and understand what it is we want, need, and must do. When you begin to plateau or regress in practice, instead of seeing it as a time of frustration and discouragement, see it for what it really is: a time for staying motivated, reassessing performance, making changes, and becoming better.

Give 100 Pennies

When I was a small child, there was a machine where you placed four U.S. quarters (the equivalent of 100 pennies) in the coin slot and then operated a claw-like device to pick up a toy, drop it in a chute, and take your newfound prize home. The machine wouldn't allow you to receive your prize until you first put in four quarters (i.e., 100 pennies). Reaching a goal is much the same. You can't attain your goal without giving 100 pennies—100 percent effort. Ninety pennies won't do. Ninety-five won't do. Even 99 pennies won't be enough. You have to give 100 pennies—100 percent effort—to get the prize. Moreover, there is no difference between 90 pennies and 50 pennies. Neither one is enough to capture the prize.

Athletes (and coaches) who give less than 100 percent effort delude themselves into thinking they are on track and moving toward their goals. They also miss the real prize of giving 100 percent, which is the experience of making practice challenging, worthwhile, meaningful, productive, satisfying, and motivating. Mental and physical fatigue set in for any diver working hard on a regular basis. And on some days 100 percent effort just isn't possible. But that should be the rare exception, not the standard rule. If you experience mental and physical fatigue, don't see them as signs to quit (although on rare occasions that can be prudent) or to avoid practice. See them as simply personal challenges and part of the process of becoming a great diver.

Unfortunately, some divers wait for something great to happen with their diving before they commit to giving 100 percent effort in practice. What they don't understand is that the converse is true. They must first give 100 percent effort before they can reach their potential. Perhaps these divers are afraid to give the effort out of fear that they won't reach their goals and then all their work will be for nothing. *Divers never lose out when they give 100 percent.* The worst they can obtain are valuable prizes such as incredible self-satisfaction, heightened self-esteem, a sense of pride, increased self-discipline, and improved physical condition.

Don't Spin Your Wheels

As a high school diver, I wanted to conquer the world. Sometimes, however, my zealousness mentally sidetracked me with negative thoughts. One day my coach said, "Stop spinning your wheels." At first I didn't understand what he meant, but the more I thought about it, the more I understood it. Like a car stuck on a muddy road, I was spinning my mental wheels and not getting anywhere. I wasted energy on stupid and irrelevant thoughts and emotions that kept me stuck in one place. To move forward, I needed to focus my mental energy on productive, goal-directed thoughts. Avoid spinning your wheels by positively channeling mental energy to maintain motivation and forward progress toward your goals. Mental garbage (negative thoughts) should be left curbside for the trash collector to carry away.

Set Daily Process Goals

Research on expertise indicates that elite performers in all fields, not just diving, engage in deliberate practice. Part of what entails deliberate practice is setting daily process goals for all aspects of practice. Rather than practicing aimlessly, these performers have specific process goals that motivate and direct their *every* action. Enough has been said about goals to appreciate their motivational value, but some divers and coaches still make the mistake of not taking the time to set daily goals.

Take time before each practice—it doesn't take long—to map out practice goals for every activity: stretching, simple drills, line-ups, lead-ups, and so on. Sweat the small stuff, because the small stuff matters. For example, although she was already an acclaimed diver, two-time U.S. Olympian Christina Loukas set a goal of becoming more flexible and altered her stretching routine. Her increased flexibility allowed her to collapse more quickly into a pike and improve all of her optional dives in the pike position

Handling Fear

By far the most requested lecture topic at my summer diving academy was handling fear, particularly the fear of learning new dives. Handling fear is part of every sport to some degree, but perhaps to a much greater degree in the sport of diving. A person has to be a little crazy, a little off-kilter mentally, to take up the sport in the first place. Consider the reverse dive. A diver walks forward and then throws his body backward toward a piece of solid aluminum (the springboard). Any rational human being would say: "No way. That's nuts. I might hurt myself." Now consider the reverse dive off a 10-meter platform. Let's see . . . you climb atop essentially a three-story building, hurtle yourself into space backward toward a solid piece of concrete, and then hit the water at approximately 33 miles per hour (53 km/h). That's a traffic accident essentially, isn't it—two objects hitting each other at a high speed?

Yet, as scary as all this might seem, many people decide to take up the sport, perhaps for the shear challenge of it. After all, it is a beautiful endeavor. I never climbed Mount Everest, but I imagine the feeling of reaching the summit must be as sublime as meeting the challenge of performing a reverse dive or a reverse 2 1/2 somersault for the very first time. After all these years, I still remember the days and circumstances in which I performed my first reverse dive, my first reverse 2 1/2 somersault, and my first optional dive on a 10-meter platform.

It's ironic that the most difficult part of our sport is also the most rewarding: confronting and overcoming fear. But climbing that mountain—conquering fear—isn't easy. As the saying goes, *If it were easy, everyone would do it.* As a former diver, I have experienced the fear of learning new dives and also the ability to handle this fear. And as a coach, I have taught literally hundreds of divers to overcome the fear of learning new dives. This section offers some simple but incredibly effective techniques for handling fear.

Fear and the Five Pillars of Mental Training

Sometimes, all it takes to move past one's fear is a little nudge, a little something extra to bolster confidence and provide a boost up the mountain. The five pillars can provide that boost.

Self-Talk

Recall the story at the beginning of this chapter about Grant. Repeatedly saying the phrase *"Eye of the storm"* gave him the edge he needed to manage his fear and throw the new dive. He found the phrase positive, motivating, and directing.

Mental Imagery

Mental imagery is also an effective tool for managing fear, especially when learning new dives. Maintaining positive mental imagery and repeatedly seeing in their mind's eye how they want to successfully perform a new dive provides that little nudge divers need to overcome their fear. Unfortunately, some divers let their fears get the best of their mental imagery. They imagine failure instead of success, crashing instead of safe vertical entries, disorientation instead of focus and concentration. When this occurs, forcefully alter your imagery.

Energy Management

Simply controlling breathing and arousal level helps many divers keep their heads in the game and gives them an edge for managing their fears. Keep in mind that whatever is biological is also psychological. The two intimately interact. Consequently, keeping physically calm makes it easier to maintain mental clarity and emotional calmness.

Because the two pillars of cognitive restructuring and self-monitoring are so effective for handling fear, the following two sections examine them in greater detail.

Cognitive Restructuring

As all elite divers will attest, keeping perspective is crucial for handling fear and finding ultimate success. Following are some tactics for cognitive restructuring.

Keep Things in Perspective

Fear can be debilitating and even paralyzing at times, making learning new dives and training effectively impossible. One mistake some divers make is blowing things out of proportion. They see crashing on a dive as the equivalent of being run over by a 2-ton dump truck and, consequently, their fear becomes unmanageable. In reality, our sport is quite safe. Many gymnasts, for example, transfer to diving because they have sustained serious injuries such as broken ankles, wrists, and elbows. In diving, these types of injuries almost never occur. Diving is much more forgiving on the body than other sports are. Even after the worst of smacks on the water, divers are up and moving around and feeling fine physically after just a few minutes. Divers who perceive wiping out as the worst physical punishment imaginable need to restructure their thinking so that they see it for what it really is: a temporary unpleasant minor inconvenience.

Reinvent Yourself

I remember Gary Miller because on the first day of water polo tryouts my freshman year of high school, I was sure he would be the first one cut from the team. Don't get me wrong—I wasn't sure about my place on the team either. In fact, I was pretty sure I would be cut too. I was just glad it would be Gary before it would be me. I didn't want to be the poor guy cut first from the team. Gary was meek, timid, and undemonstrative. A butterfly could knock the kid over. But I was dead wrong about Gary.

Gary did make the cut—as did I. Sure, it wasn't varsity and it wasn't B team, but C team looked a lot more attractive to me and to Gary than *no* team. However, after two years of water polo, I deciphered the handwriting on the wall. I wasn't going to be tall enough, stout enough, or swift enough to become a good water polo player. Besides, all along I wanted to be a diver; it's just that our swimming coach made everyone go out for swimming and water polo, even if they wanted diving. And Gary, well, that crazy dreamer decided to become a water polo goalie.

What a nutcase. Did he know how hard a young boy in high school can throw a water polo ball or how high in the air a water polo ball can ricochet off a goalie's face? We were actually coached to throw our first shot on goal in competition into the face of an opposing team's goalie so he would flinch on our next shots. But sometime during our formative high school years of traversing from adolescence to adulthood, of discovering who we are and, more important, who we can become, Gary reinvented himself. By his senior year, Gary had become a force to be reckoned with—a focused, fearless, and formidable all conference varsity goalie welcoming the most menacing of shots.

Nothing has to stay the same or for that matter can stay the same. Hills erode, rivers meander, seasons change. Ugly hairy caterpillars shed their chrysalises to become stunningly majestic monarch butterflies. And people change. Just because you are who you are now doesn't mean that is who you must be in the future. As a coach for 37 years, I had the gratifying privilege of witnessing countless divers reinvent themselves. A high school camper scared to death of learning a 305C on the 3-meter springboard becomes Big Ten conference platform champion (a major U.S. college competition) two years later, throwing 107B, 407C, and 5253B on the 10 meter. A high school diver afraid of simply standing backward on the 10 meter (his age group coach said he didn't have the guts to be a collegiate diver) smokes a 207C cold turkey on the 10 meter his junior year of college. People change.

Often, our fiercest adversary is ourselves because of our self-imposed limitations. Through cognitive restructuring, however, it is possible for divers and coaches to transform themselves from caterpillars into butterflies. By confronting and refuting irrational and often unconscious limiting self-beliefs, we reinvent ourselves and create new self-images. The scared athlete becomes the emboldened diver. The gutless diver becomes the brave platform diver. The meek and mild athlete becomes the fierce and unstoppable force. The no-name coach becomes the acclaimed coach. Reinventing ourselves is possible because within us all is a wellspring of transformative power waiting to be tapped.

Laugh Instead of Cry

Our physical actions have a powerful influence on our perceptions. Believe it or not, after crashing, divers have a choice: to laugh or to cry. Crying unconsciously creates a perception that missing a dive is a traumatic experience to be feared and avoided. Laughing, however, creates a perception that crashing is no big deal. It is just a part of the diving game.

There was a young junior diver who was petrified of crashing. In fact, he quit diving for three years because of his fear. When he started high school, however, he decided to go out for the diving team. The first day of practice, somebody crashed on a dive. To his amazement, everyone started laughing, even the diver who crashed. The young boy received a lesson on perspective that day. After being immersed in the program's mental culture, the boy developed a new mantra: *I'll cross that bridge when I come to it*. He ceased worrying about learning a new dive. When it came time to learn a new dive, he stepped up, counted to three, and chucked the dive. On the few occasions when he did crash, he laughed instead of cried.

If you think that laughing after a crash is impossible, you're wrong. Laughter is a unique human response that often occurs as a coping strategy during difficult times. Think of **gallows humor**: humor that makes fun of life-threatening, disastrous, or terrifying situations. (What did the condemned prisoner say as he was being led to the electric chair? "Are you sure that thing is safe?") Laughter bolsters human resolve through times of illness, captivity, confusion, and *fear*.

See Fear as a Challenge

One of the most compelling and irresistible allures of diving is the unique situation of diver versus dive. Learning a new dive can induce fear, but overcoming that fear and conquering the dive is what makes diving such a rewarding experience. See fear, then, as a good thing, a challenge to be embraced and mastered. Learn to love fear. Go ahead, ride the bucking bronco, harpoon the whale, reel in the marlin, slay the two-headed dragon, tame the beast.

And while you are at it, take the dives you have learned but continue to fear and master them as well. Stop treating certain dives as special dives you put in pretty little boxes and open up only on special occasions. Instead of practicing those dives occasionally when you feel good, or the weather is right, or your coach gets on you about the dive, do the dives every practice. In fact, do them more often than the dives you like doing. You will be surprised at how soon your special dives become your best dives. You see, you made them special in the first place because you treated them differently from your other dives.

Remember It's a Matter of When, Not If

Nothing is forever. Even fear. As a diver, you should perceive fear as something temporary, something surmountable, something that with persistence will be conquered. It is not a matter of *if* you will do the dive, only a matter of *when*. Trust in this truism and let it fortify your spirit, hopes, ambitions, and confidence. You are more talented than you yet realize, more capable than you once were, and more determined with each day. The passage of time does indeed bring change and resolution. With each new sunrise there is hope, the possibility of success, and the conquering of fear. Hope, determination, and optimism are three powerful emotions for overcoming fear and achieving success.

Self-Monitoring

The first four pillars for mental training are never completely learned and habituated unless they are consistently practiced. And consistent practice involves self-monitoring. Without self-monitoring, many divers fail to consistently engage the four pillars or, worse, unconsciously use them to their own detriment. For example, during school time a diver might unwittingly engage in negative self-talk (causing rumination) and negative imagery (of crashing) before learning a new dive at practice later that day. By practice time, the diver is physically, mentally, and emotionally drained and overtaken by fear.

Self-Monitor Fear

Keep tabs on your fear level. Some moderate level of fear, of course, is natural, and you should remind yourself of that fact. With self-monitoring, you can immediately detect when your fear level begins to increase beyond a moderate level and quickly engage the four pillars to moderate fear before the 2,000-pound invisible gorilla takes control. One area to monitor is working memory.

Fill the Space

Cognitive psychology suggests that the human mind is like a computer that contains a space called working memory. **Working memory** is the place where we temporarily hold our conscious thoughts, and we are genetically engineered to fill this space. If we don't consciously put something in it, it seems to fill itself. Even when we sleep, the space is filled—with dreams! So monitor and purposely fill this space with the right stuff.

Thoughts create emotions, and emotions create consequences for performance. For example, the thought *I might smack on the water* can generate the emotions of fear and apprehension, which result in the consequences of physical tension, mental confusion, and an inability to execute the dive. Therefore, monitor your working memory and forcefully pack it with thoughts such as *I can do this dive, I am ready and capable, This dive scares me but I know I can handle the fear and do it,* and *Eye of the storm.*

Go the First Time

For divers new to the sport, it is more important that they learn *how* to learn new dives than *what* new dives they learn. Too often, young divers are given unlimited time and balks and are permitted to spin their mental wheels before finally attempting a new dive. By the time they go, their minds are mush, their legs are wobbly, and their concentration is shot. They don't wait for the coach's call, and the result is a crashed dive and a fear of future attempts.

When divers step up to learn new dives, they should have the greatest possible chance for success. They can increase their chances for success by stepping on the board and going the first time. The less time they wait, the more relaxed and focused they will be and the more likely they will be to perform the dive successfully. If they balk or wait too long, the coach should have them move on to a different dive or drill. By moving on, they avoid wasting valuable practice time and they establish a different mindset for learning future dives (*I better go the first time or I'll have to move on and won't get to learn the dive*).

Coaches can support this strategy by counting out loud *1-2-3-Go*. If the diver doesn't go, he must step back, reset himself, and try one more time. If he doesn't go the second time, then he must move on to another dive or drill. Going the first time is particularly important for learning platform dives, which require that divers stay relaxed and focused so they can pick up visual cues, respond to the coach's call for coming out of the dive, and remember to stay tight on entry into the water.

Never Give Up

Where there is a will there is a way. Dick Wilson offered a $100 reward (equivalent to about $450 today) to any coach who could teach Krista, his young daughter, a reverse dive on the 1 meter springboard. Her parents and several coaches had tried everything to get her to do the dive, but nothing worked. She could do a reverse dive in the spotting belt on the trampoline and in the spotting belt over the water. But take her out of the belt, and she just couldn't get her body to move. This went on for so long that many divers would have given up hope. But she didn't. Eventually, she did indeed learn the dive and went on to win several NCAA and U.S. national titles and become a member of a U.S. World Championship team.

Many divers can relate to Krista's saga. They may struggle with a forward double, back twister, reverse 2 1/2, or some other dive. Fear is unbiased. It attacks every diver at one time or another—even national champions like Krista. So, it is important that divers not see themselves as isolated from the "brave" divers. And, most important, they should never give up. If divers persevere in looking for ways to overcome their fears, they eventually do overcome them.

One week at my summer diving academy, nine divers needed to learn a reverse dive. The first day one diver learned the reverse dive. That night I talked with them about Krista and about never giving up. The next day one more diver learned the reverse dive. By the end of that second day, however, the other divers had become discouraged. I again reminded them to never give up. On Wednesday, two more divers learned the reverse dive. By Friday all but one diver had accomplished the reverse dive, and that diver learned the reverse dive the following week.

Another summer I worked with an academy diver who could not learn a back twister in the twisting belt no matter how hard she tried. Every time she tried twisting to the left, she turned her head to the right. When she tried twisting to the right, she turned her head to the left. This went on for almost two weeks. She was upset and in tears. I told her to keep trying and never give up, but honestly, I had run out of ideas. Near the end of camp, she came up to me with a huge smile and said, "I learned a back twister!" I was happy for her and congratulated her, but immediately asked, "What did you do to learn it?" Her reply was that when she started to twist, she turned her head in the correct direction and bit her shoulder! Sometimes, in the worst of situations, divers find the answers they most need to succeed. The path may be roundabout, but divers who never give up will reach their destinations. Hope starts the dream, but determination achieves it.

Control the Situation

English philosopher James Allen (2006) wrote, "In all human affairs there are efforts and there are results. And the strength of the effort is the measure of the result. Chance is not" (p. 41). Divers need to decide whether they control the situation or the situation controls them. It's that simple. Those who decide the situation controls them sit helplessly back, watch events unfold without their input, and let fear control them. Those who decide that they control the situation put effort into creating a plan and taking action. And the result of that effort is that they eventually control fear.

Have a Plan

A young diver developed a fear of doing a forward double somersault. He had tried it when he was younger and ill-prepared and smacked on his first few attempts. Instead of giving up, however, he devised a plan. He would do 15 forward 1 1/2s each day and see if he could eventually flip one over into a double. Although this plan was rudimentary, it nonetheless was a plan—and it worked! After about a week of practice, lo and behold, he flipped one over into a double. Many divers deal with fear by ignoring it, by not thinking about it, by pretending it isn't there. Ignoring it simply postpones the inevitable and compounds the problem. Ignoring it breeds the 2,000-pound invisible gorilla that climbs on their back and won't get off no matter how sternly they asked it to leave.

Divers need to take the offensive and attack the beast. To paraphrase Sir Francis Bacon, *The mold of a diver's fortune is in his or her own hands.* Most divers are surprised at how quickly they can combat fear once they attack it rather than retreat from it. A plan, even a rudimentary plan like doing 15 forward 1 1/2s each day, is effective because it encourages proactive action and instills a sense of personal control. A plan of attack can include regressing to a simpler lead-up to gain confidence, trying a different lead-up that provides for greater transfer of learning, getting in a spotting belt to learn the new dive, traveling to another facility to use a spotting belt if one isn't available at the home pool, and of course, using the five pillars of mental training.

Increasing Confidence

Confidence is the belief that you possess the ability to meet the challenge ahead. Bandura (1993) referred to this type of confidence as **self-efficacy**. Athletes with high confidence (self-efficacy) believe in themselves and trust their performances. They think, behave, and feel differently than athletes with low confidence do. Athletes with low confidence exhibit behaviors such as lack of persistence when confronting obstacles, lack of effort, unwillingness to take risks, and tendency towards hesitancy and tentativeness. Their thoughts tend to be negative (*I can't hit this dive*), judgmental (*I am a loser*), and pessimistic (*I will never learn this dive*). And their feelings include negative emotions such as anxiety, dread, tension, depressed mood, guilt, shame, and embarrassment. In contrast, athletes with high confidence exhibit behaviors of persistence, high effort, risk taking (i.e., accepting challenging and difficult tasks), and determination. Their thoughts are positive and optimistic, and their feelings include positive emotions such as excitement, anticipation, eagerness, and pride. Following are some simple strategies for dramatically increasing diver confidence.

Confidence and the Five Pillars of Mental Training

Once again, the five pillars of mental training empower the diver—in this case to increase a feeling of confidence.

Self-Talk

Self-talk is a powerful tool for enhancing confidence and feelings of competency (Zinsser, Bunker, & Williams, 2001). When athletes push the self-talk button ("You are good and can do it," "Hang in there," "You've got it—keep going"), they self-motivate, maintain psychological momentum, and build confidence. Unfortunately, self-talk can also have the opposite effect. I have heard divers come up after a dive and say things such as "I suck," "What an idiot," and "I can't do this." Negative self-talk chips away at a diver's confidence.

Of course, being self-critical is necessary to some degree. Contentment breeds stagnation. We can't improve if we never critique ourselves. But there is a right way and a wrong way to critique. The right way instills confidence. The wrong way creates a defeatist attitude. Successful divers engage in forceful but positive self-talk. When they must criticize, they do so using positive self-talk. For example, they might say, "That dive sucked [not 'I suck']. I know I can do it better next time by getting my arms through sooner in the hurdle" (a positive and directive statement).

You can use self-talk to build confidence by reminding yourself of past successes and all you have achieved to this point in your career. Take the time to praise yourself when you do something good. Let the voice inside your head be your best friend, your biggest booster, your confidante, your teammate, your ally. Let it be a voice of praise, reason, support, encouragement, and confidence.

Mental Imagery

At the 2004 Olympic trials, 2000 Olympic gold medalist Laura Wilkinson knew she had to hit her second-to-last dive on the 10-meter platform to make the team. The dive (207C) was fairly new and inconsistent for her, and she wasn't as confident on it as she was on her other dives. So, before executing the dive, she visualized a similar scene from the 2000 Olympic Games, when she had to hit her last dive (405B) to win. She was unconfident about the dive because several months before the Games she had broken her foot doing a lead-up for the dive. The bone had not completely healed. Her foot ached. She was scared of the dive. She was unsure. But she nailed it anyway and won the gold medal. Mentally replaying that scene at the 2004 trials filled her with the confidence she needed to perform her 207C. She told herself, "If I could do it then, I can do it now." And she did. She buried the dive and made her second U.S. Olympic team.

When he was very young, a dance teacher taught legendary Olympic gold medalist Greg Louganis to use imagery to prepare for performing. Greg believes that his habitual use of imagery from such a young age is one factor that helped his performances and his confidence. If you are a diver and feel your confidence waning, take the time to replay past successes and accomplishments in your mind's eye. Imagine not only the performance but also the feelings of excitement, pride, and confidence you felt before, during, and after those performances. Then imagine your current dives, seeing and feeling yourself perform smoothly, gracefully, accurately, and successfully. If you have trouble imagining your dives, here are six simple tips.

■ *Prepare the learning environment*. Begin practicing mental imagery in a warm room with the lights out and no interruptions. Trust me on this one. One summer we had a problem with the thermostat in the classroom, and trying to get the campers to relax and visualize in a freezing room was mission impossible.

■ *Practice mental imagery.* Mental imagery is a skill developed through practice. So practice it on a daily basis as you would your forward approach. Practice it before and during training so there will be distractions, just as there will be at competitions. Incorporate it into your daily mental training and your preperformance routine. Don't wait until the competition to practice mental imagery. If you do, it will be too little, too late, and the 2,000-pound invisible gorilla will be squarely on your back. Mental imagery is a powerful mental strategy, but it becomes so only with practice.

■ *Analyze video.* To reach elite status, successful divers watch hours of video of great divers until those images are burned into their brains. Olympic gold medalist Mark Lenzi said that he was so critical of himself that he couldn't imagine himself diving. Instead, he watched hours of video of Greg Louganis diving and then imagined Greg's dives. Junior divers should watch videos of elite divers so that they can visualize the correct movements of each dive component.

■ *Incorporate specific emotions.* There is a discernable difference between performing in practice and performing in competition, particularly the-whole-enchilada championship competition. Consequently, incorporate into your imagery emotions you know or suspect will be associated with competition. Anxiety? Maybe. Nervousness? Sure. Negative emotions? Possibly. Doubt? Perhaps. Mental imagery is a way to rehearse dealing with these emotions innumerable times before competition. Elite divers report putting themselves in certain scenario so many times mentally that when the moment arrived, they were ready. Also, incorporate emotions into mental imagery in preparation for learning new dives or tackling new and challenging skills such as spotting.

■ *Imagine internally and externally.* Some divers prefer visualizing their performances externally (as if watching themselves on television), whereas others prefer to visualize internally (from inside their bodies). Although an internal perspective for diving might allow for greater kinesthetic imagery, both perspectives are beneficial, so consider using both.

■ *Finish mental imagery on a positive note.* Never finish practice with a bad dive. Similarly, never finish mental imagery with a negative image. Some divers have trouble imagining themselves performing well. Finish a mental imagery "workout" with a good dive, even if you have to rewind, imagine only parts of the dive, or replay the dive until you see yourself performing it correctly.

Some divers respond poorly to mental imagery. They prefer to consider a variety of scenarios and effective responses to these scenarios. Darian, for example, would consider five scenarios before each dive: (1) landing on the right side of the board, (2) landing on the left side of the board, (3) landing over the end of the board, (4) landing back of the end of the board, and (5) landing on the end of the board. Greg Louganis incorporated similar scenarios into his imagery.

Energy Management

Confident athletes are never rushed. They are physically loose and almost serene, even in critical competitive moments. Unconfident athletes, in contrast, are hurried. They rush through the warm-up (often skipping parts of their normal routine) and move quickly with tense muscles, stiff movements, and taut facial expressions. Physical actions have a pronounced effect on self-perception and confidence. Confidence leads to energy management, but energy management breeds confidence. The two interact symbiotically. Abdominal breathing; an upright, relaxed posture; smooth, easy steps; an evenly paced warm-up; and moderate rather than rapid speech are examples of physical actions that reflect energy management, indicate the presence of confidence, and simultaneously build confidence.

Cognitive Restructuring

There are moments for every athlete when confidence wanes. You do a lousy dive in competition. How do you regain confidence for your next dive? You get lost in a twister. How do you restore confidence so that you believe that next time you will do the right number of twists? You miss a visual spot and crash on a dive. How do you increase confidence to try the dive again? There are many reasons to lose confidence in these scenarios but there are also many reasons to maintain confidence. Cognitive restructuring involves having a forceful conversation with yourself. It puts the situation into perspective by providing reasons for future success, and it maintains or recaptures confidence.

Consider the experience of getting lost in a twisting dive. Now, getting lost can be the result of a technical issue that requires retraining and regressing to a lead-up. However, in some cases it may simply be a fluke. A diver who has gotten lost in a twisting dive can approach the next one by thinking: "The lead-up looks great. I've never gotten lost before, and it's time to get back on the horse—to get back up on the board and throw the dive."

Cognitive restructuring is a means of restoring confidence by correcting false thinking and replacing irrational thoughts with rational ones: "Getting lost was just a fluke, so don't buy into the thought that I can't do this dive. I have done this dive a hundred times without ever getting lost. My lead-up is good. My coach says I am ready to do this dive. I won't let the dive control me. I control the dive. There is no reason to believe I can't do this dive. I am ready to do it. I *can* do it. I *will* do it!"

Self-Monitoring

By now you know that playing the inner (mental) game of diving involves vigilant self-monitoring and consistent use of the four pillars of mental training. Self-monitoring maintains confidence and regains confidence. At the first sign of waning confidence, divers should engage the four other mental skills.

Establish a Confidence Baseline

How confident should a diver be to perform well, especially in critical moments? How confident are you now and how confident will you be during those critical moments? Establish a confidence baseline by completing an online sport confidence inventory questionnaire or by simply evaluating honestly your confidence level and then compare your idealized image of a highly confident athlete to your self-assessment. Use the strategies in this chapter to increase your confidence and thereby reduce the difference between your perceived self-confidence and your idealized self-confidence.

Test Yourself in Practice

One of the best strategies for increasing confidence is to test yourself in practice. Challenge yourself to perform in practice as you want to perform in competition. Let's be honest. If you can't do it in practice, you won't do it in the meet. On the other hand, if you can do it consistently in practice, chances are exceedingly great you will do it in competition. By passing these practice tests, you prove to yourself that you have the ability and self-efficacy to handle the "final exam," the future competitive challenge.

One practice test is to performance chart your dives to see how close or far away you are from achieving your outcome goal. If, for example, your goal is to win the state championship and you are consistently reaching your target score in practice, it is easier to feel confident heading into the state meet. Concentrating on your target score keeps you focused on the process, rather than winning and losing, and realistic about your ability to perform. If you are scoring, say, 100 points below your target score, you need to either lower your outcome goal or raise your practice effort.

Another test is to challenge yourself to consistently hit your dives. After hitting a dive, some divers like to transition to a new dive so they feel good about the dive. When you hit a dive, challenge yourself to hit it again to prove it wasn't luck. If you miss the next dive, then work on your concentration and continue testing yourself in practice until you hit the dive consistently. Consistency is important for diving success.

Yet another test is to see if you can hit your first dive. Elite divers make every dive count. You have to hit your first attempt in competition, so hit it the first time in practice. Another test is to hit a dive cold turkey (without any preparatory work such as lead-ups and practice hurdles). Stretch, mentally and physically rehearse, and then step up and perform the dive. If you can hit the dive under these stringent circumstances, you will feel confident about hitting the dive in the meet.

Another test involves hitting your dives under unfavorable practice circumstances. Perceive circumstances like cold and windy weather, poor lighting, noisy environment, and long waits in line as challenges to dive well, rather than as excuses to dive poorly.

Create a Best Dives Compilation

An effective strategy for increasing confidence is to create a best dives compilation—a digital collection of all your best dives put back-to-back. These are your greatest hits, and you get to watch them repeatedly until your stellar performances are burned into your brain. A best dives compilation is proof of your ability and reminds you of just how good you really are. As divers see the value of digitally documenting their best dives and expanding their compilation, they become increasingly more diligent about collecting best dives. If you don't have a replay system, get one. If you don't have a best dives compilation, create one. All elite divers have one.

Experience Success

Nothing builds confidence like experiencing success. Success doesn't necessarily mean winning. Remember that the most important goals are the process goals, the things divers want to do. So, experiencing success can mean accomplishing simple incremental process goals, such as getting vertical on a line-up, swimming sooner on an entry, eliminating balking in practice, and squaring out of a twister.

Coaches should carefully script practices so that each athlete is working on challenging but attainable tasks. Asking divers to perform drills and dives they aren't physically, emotionally, or mentally prepared to perform will certainly produce failure and diminish confidence. One of the greatest shortcomings for many coaches is impatience. In our eagerness to help our divers, we impatiently rush through the learning process and create failure experiences. The slow route is the most expeditious route. The tortoise eventually beats the hare.

Act Confident

Physical actions have a powerful influence on self-perception, thoughts, and emotions. So, sometimes the best way to begin feeling confident is to start acting confident. Observe confident athletes (observe confident coaches if you are a coach) in diving and in other sports, and select the mannerisms, mental outlooks, and emotions that you admire. Then imitate them. Many teams get better simply because they have a great diver on their team whom the divers admire and emulate. But take it one step further. Sure, imitate what you see, but become your own confident person with your own style that reflects your self-confidence and unique personality.

Over time, some athletes become entrenched in old habits—behaviors, thoughts, and feelings that reflect low confidence. Because old habits die hard, it is important to monitor your behaviors, thoughts, and emotions. Ask yourself, "Am I acting, thinking, and feeling like a confident athlete (or coach)?" If the answer is no, then retrain yourself to act with confidence, even if you have to fake it at first.

Communicate the Right Message

Coaches influence athlete confidence through their interactions with athletes. Sometimes this influence is direct and overt, such as when they praise an athlete. Sometimes this influence is indirect and covert, such as when their actions demonstrate a genuine faith in the athlete's ability. Coaches can increase athlete confidence by communicating high expectations, providing positive corrective feedback, and offering specific explanations for success and failure. Many divers become successful simply because at some point in their careers a coach sent the message *I believe in you and am confident you will succeed*.

Avoid Undermining Confidence

Unfortunately, coaches sometimes unintentionally send the wrong message and thereby undermine athlete confidence. To avoid undermining athlete confidence, coaches should adhere to the following guidelines (McCann, et al., 2006), which summarize many of the concepts discussed in this section.

- Design practices that provide the optimal level of confidence-building challenge (i.e., neither too difficult nor too easy).
- Provide divers with simulations of the competitive environment.

▪ Focus on the process, not just the outcome, and measure success by the amount of improvement.

▪ Allow for mistakes.

▪ Don't punish mistakes.

▪ Focus on what is done correctly as well as what is done incorrectly.

▪ Encourage athlete self-talk that is motivational and instructional and leads to positive emotions and productive focus.

▪ Make coach communication motivational and instructional rather than negative and judgmental.

▪ Perceive setbacks and errors as temporary, rather than permanent, and part of the learning process.

▪ Discourage athlete overconfidence or cockiness, which leads to a failure to prepare.

▪ Help athletes perceive coaching corrections as constructive feedback rather than character criticism.

▪ Avoid drastically changing preperformance routines at the last minute.

▪ Provide a comprehensive annual training plan.

▪ Provide for adequate athlete recovery.

Increasing Concentration

Concentration is the ability to maintain a focus over time on the right things at the right times. Concentration is important, especially when learning a new dive, performing a difficult dive, or performing in critical competition moments. When learning a new dive, divers who come out before their coach's call and land flat on their backs are exhibiting a lack of concentration. At the Canada Cup meet in Montreal some years ago, a diver lost concentration, came out early, landed feet-first, and then whipped flat to his back on a 307C on the 3-meter springboard. Angrily, he got back on the board and nailed his next attempt at the dive. Concentration is essential for consistent performance in practice and competition. What are the characteristics of concentration, and how is it maintained?

The three characteristics of concentration are strength, controllability and flexibility, and endurance. **Strength** is the ability to direct attention to the correct point, keep it there, and ignore distractions. **Controllability and flexibility** is the ability to swiftly shift focus at the right times during performance. **Endurance** is the ability to maintain focus during the entire performance, especially when fatigue or stress, or both, set in.

Strengthen Concentration

Successful diving is to a great extent about focusing on the right things at the right times and ignoring distractions. Divers who can block out the noise and concentrate under pressure separate themselves from the pack. They are the special ones. All divers, then, should find ways to test, challenge, and thereby strengthen their concentration so that they can become top dog, leader of the pack. Divers can take the things they find annoying and distracting and embrace them and incorporate them into their practice. For example, Olympic silver medalist Scott Donie said that what prepared him for competition was to take all the things he once thought of as negatives and turn them into positives. Things such as gusts of wind, landing over the end of the board on an approach, or someone shouting during his dive weren't distractions to him; they were good things that made him concentrate even more than usual. He would tell himself: "Bring on the wind. Give me the biggest gust you've got. Toes over the end of the board? No problem. Watch me nail this dive."

What things tend to break your concentration? Zero in on them and include them in your training. Have someone shout during your approach or dive. Instead of balking, go on that bad hurdle. Learn to ignore distractions. Concentration is like a muscle. The more you exercise it, the stronger it gets. Conversely, the more you avoid challenging it, the weaker it becomes.

Strengthen Controllability and Flexibility

It's easy to hit a dive when everything is perfect in a hurdle. But a perfect hurdle isn't what you always get. At my first international competition as a coach, I watched this unfamiliar diver come up from an entry with a shorn head and face planted down in the water. He slowly made his way to the gutter. He never said anything; he simply looked up at his coach, nodded, and then got out of the pool. I thought, "Well, who is this guy? He doesn't seem to look much like an accomplished diver. Well, I guess I'll watch one of his dives and then leave." After watching his first dive, I decided to watch his second, and then his third, and then his fourth. Eventually I parked myself on the bleacher and didn't move until his practice was over. For an hour the great Russian diver Dmitri Ivanovich Sautin never missed a dive. At one point, he landed far back on the end of the board for a 307C and I thought, "Okay, now he's going to finally miss a dive." He crushed it. Not for a second did he lose concentration because of an imperfect hurdle.

Some divers see performance imperfections as a reason to lose concentration and miss the dive. Others see imperfections as simply a time to maintain concentration, shift focus, make adjustments, and nail the dive. How do you perceive imperfections? Welcome situations in which you have to shift your concentration to make adjustments to your dive. Strengthen the control and flexibility of your concentration. Separate yourself from the other divers.

Strengthen Endurance

Embrace fatigue and stress. Concentration endurance can be increased by embracing fatigue and stress in practice. Don't use fatigue or stress as an excuse to lose concentration. Fatigue and stress of training are similar to the stress of competition. If you can concentrate when you are tired and stressed out at the end of a long training session, you will concentrate and perform well in a stressful competition. See fatigue and stress as forces forging you into a battle-hardened warrior capable of maintaining concentration in the heat of combat.

Train the eyes. After a U.S. national championship event, one of my divers told me that just before he started his forward approach, he unexpectedly found himself staring at a spectator in the stands. He lost his concentration and, needless to say, the dive was less than spectacular. The eyes will look somewhere during performance, so it is important to learn where to look and then train the eyes to look at these spots at the appropriate times during execution. These visual performance cues were identified in chapter 5.

Understand the Dimensions of Attention

Nideffer (1989) suggested that there are two dimensions of **attentional focus:** broad/narrow (a wide-angle focus versus a specific focal point) and internal/external (focused inwardly versus focused outwardly on the environment). Perhaps the best way to explain Nideffer's model is to describe how elite-level divers shift their focus as they concentrate during dive preparation and performance.

Before dive performance, elite divers have a fairly internal-narrow focus. They focus on their physical state (internal) such as controlling their breathing and staying moderately relaxed. They focus on imagery of the dive and a few simple reminders (narrow) as they rehearse the dive on deck. Once on the board, their focus doesn't alter much. They are still fairly internal, focusing on their breathing and self-talk, and they are fairly narrow, focusing on a few simple reminders (e.g., "Get on the tip of the board. Get my arms through early"). As they set the fulcrum and establish their stance before the approach, however, their focus becomes more external, focusing now not on themselves but on the board. Their focus is still narrow because they focus on placing their last step in the right place or they simply focus on the tip of the board. Once they leave the board, their focus becomes broader as they look for their spots farther out in the water during dive rotation. During the come-out, their focus is once again internal and narrow as they focus on being tight in their bodies and ripping the dive.

Recognize Past-Present-Future Attention

I have observed many nonelite divers experience a bad takeoff and then go extremely far past vertical on entry. When asked why they went over, they usually report something like, "I had a bad takeoff" or "All I could think about was the bad takeoff." Even though they had a poor takeoff, they still were able to make the dive (and even go over on the dive) and still could have finished the dive well had they not concentrated on the past —the bad takeoff—but, rather, on the future—the entry into the water.

To Nideffer's two dimensions, then, add the dimension of time—past, present, and future (Huber, 2013). Anticipation is the key to elite-level execution. For example, when elite divers experience a poor takeoff, they hold their concentration on the present ("Pick up my spots") and then shift to the future to anticipate the entry ("Forget about the start. Get ready for the entry. What do I need to do to land vertically in the water?"). In contrast, nonelite divers (Huber, 1997) lose concentration on the present and fail to shift concentration to the future to anticipate the entry because they get stuck concentrating on the past ("Oh no, that was a terrible start").

Control Arousal Level

All performers use specific cues during performance to enhance execution, which Easterbrook (1957) referred to as **cue utilization**. Two diving cues, for example, are the tip of the board during the forward approach and external spots during somersaulting. Easterbrook suggested that if arousal becomes too high, a process called **perceptual narrowing** occurs, in which the performer's concentration deteriorates and attentional focus becomes too restricted, causing the athlete to miss performance cues. For example, an experienced and well-trained diver who never misses a spot in practice suddenly becomes overly nervous and misses those spots in the championship finals. Or, a diver with a consistent hurdle fails to look at the end of the board and lands 5 inches (12.7 cm) back on a reverse optional dive.

Things go easily awry when arousal level extends beyond a diver's zone of optimal functioning. Concentration and focus dramatically decrease, and performance takes a dive (Sorry, couldn't resist that one). Consequently, the best method for maintaining concentration is to manage arousal level. Like Grant, the young boy mentioned at the outset of this chapter, be the eye of the storm and strive to remain calm and composed during turbulent moments to maintain optimal concentration and identify relevant performance cues.

For more information on developing motivation, confidence, and mental focus and resilience, read Cogan's (2012) and Cogan's & Halbert's (2012) guides for divers. As a USOC sport psychologist, Cogan has worked extensively with U.S. Olympic divers.

CHAPTER 11

Mental Training for Competition

There are two essential objectives coaches need to teach and divers need to learn: (1) how to dive well and (2) how to dive well in competition. Any diver who has ever competed can verify that these two objectives are vastly different. That dive you smoked in practice yesterday wasn't there for you in the meet today. You were in the groove in warm-up, but where was that groove in the meet? Typically, when a group of divers is asked how many have "won" the warm-up but faltered in the competition, every hand is raised. Divers don't receive medals for warm-up performances, only competition performances.

Good diving requires learning specific diving skills. Similarly, good competing requires learning specific mental skills. These skills can be taught by coaches and learned by divers. The following sections offer some surprisingly simple but highly effective strategies for performing well in competition. Keep in mind that these strategies, although mostly addressed to athletes, are also applicable to coaches, because both must be the eye of the storm come competition time.

But first, a short story . . .

Caleb had trained hard all season. Throughout the early segment of the season, he had performed like a champ, and at the conference championship, he won both the 1-meter and 3-meter springboard events. Now, here he was at the season-ending championship ready to fulfill his dream of becoming U.S. national champion. At least he thought he was ready. As he was drying off with his chamois after finishing a spectacular warm-up, he heard the announcer say: "Last dive. The boards are closed. Please get ready for the start of competition." As though a light switch had been flipped, Caleb was instantly overcome with fear and anxiety. His muscles knotted up and he could barely move. His breathing became rapid, and his thoughts confused. It was a condition he couldn't shake, and unfortunately, his competition performance was a disaster. Instead of fulfilling his dream, Caleb finished in last place.

What good does it do for coaches to teach competitive divers how to dive well in practice if their divers can't perform well in competition, especially at critical moments such as a national championship? And what good does it do for competitive divers to learn how to dive well in practice (and warm-up) if they can't showcase their hard work in competition? Both, of course, are necessary. Divers can't dive well in competition if they never dive well in practice. Good practice dives must precede good competition dives. But one of the saddest stories in our sport is the one about the diver who trains hard all year, looks like a superstar in warm-ups, and then crumbles in the meet. Mental skills won't guarantee winning a medal, but a lack of mental skills will guarantee losing one (McCann et al., 2006).

Early Championship Preparation

Mental preparation for competition doesn't begin the day of the meet. It begins the first day of practice at the beginning of the season. Everything done during practice should have a twofold purpose: to learn to dive well in practice and to learn to dive well in competition. Hopefully, a solid foundation of work has been laid throughout the season, and as the championship nears, divers are getting ready to rev the engine, pop the clutch, and put the pedal to the metal. With the championship just a few weeks away, there are some effective ways to fine-tune the engine in preparation for the big race.

Five Pillars of Mental Training

The five pillars of mental training were important for practice and are no less important now for championship competition. Let's take a look at how they can be utilized to prepare mentally for the pressure of competition.

Self-Talk—Listen to Your Inner Voice

Self-talk and self-statements are powerful sources of comfort, support, motivation, and confidence—sources divers want to continue tapping into as they prepare for championships. It is ironic that something as tiny and private as self-talk can have such an enormous and observable impact on diving performance. Remember, however, that self-talk and self-statements don't carry much weight if they haven't been used and haven't been backed up throughout the season. If you haven't laid a foundation of hard work, you might fool others but you can't fool yourself no matter how much inner dialogue you engage in. The statement "I have worked hard and am ready to dive well" is weak and meaningless if in fact you haven't worked hard. Deep down you know that you aren't ready to dive well On the other hand, if you have worked hard and are ready to dive well, listen to your inner voice and let it bolsters your confidence.

Mental Imagery—See Your Championship Performance

Like self-talk, mental imagery is something you engage in throughout the season but especially now leading up to the championship. Take time to visualize; see the championship performance you dream of having. Post pictures of the championship diving well and imagine performing your dives in that pool. See yourself stretching, warming up, and competing in the pool. See yourself doing the things you want to do in the championship pool, the things you have committed to doing all year long in practice. And imagine how you want to act and feel: confident, resolute, determined, focused. Continue watching your best dives compilation. Etch those images into your brain.

Additionally, practice competition coping imagery. Recall from chapter 10 that coping imagery involves visualizing overcoming obstacles, mistakes, distractions, and so on. Visualize overcoming potential competition scenarios that could occur. Practice competition coping imagery both away from the pool and at the pool. Before dive execution in practice, imagine a scenario such as missing your previous dive, having your competitor nail a dive right before you dive, or needing to hit your last dive to win the championship. Then perform your dive. Coping with imagined competition scenarios during diving practice augments the practice experience, teaches refocusing, increases mental toughness, makes the unexpected expected, and prepares you to confidently and calmly cope with challenging competition situations.

Energy Management—Recognize the Time of Season

Early season is the time to train with a sense of urgency and to establish a foundation for future success. As the championship approaches, however, there is less urgency to train and more urgency to conserve physical, mental, and emotional energy for the championship. Sadly, some divers and coaches conserve energy throughout the season and then make a big push at the end of the season in the hope of gaining the confidence they didn't earn during the season. However, excessive work at the end of the season tears down the body, making athletes susceptible to injury and illness before the championship. Recognize the time of season and conserve energy for when it counts—at the championship.

Cognitive Restructuring—Answer the What-Ifs

Athletes are human beings and, therefore, capable of complex cognition. They think about things and often ask themselves questions, especially when they become nervous and anxious. They have that working memory space that needs to be filled with some type of information. Before the championship, self-doubts, negative thoughts, and unwanted and unwarranted worries can rear their ugly heads and creep into that space. These types of thoughts are natural; many high-performing elite athletes report have similar thoughts. The difference between elite athletes and nonelite athletes is that elite athletes rapidly respond to the what-ifs.

When the worry monster attacks, instantly battle back by answering the what-ifs. "What if I'm not good enough to dive well in this meet?" Answer: "Nonsense. That is just my nervousness interrupting my thinking. I worked my tail off all year, and I am ready to do the things I worked on. I am committed to them and will get them done." "What if I don't win?" Answer: "Well, what if I don't? I didn't win last year, and I didn't get executed, dragged through the streets, disemboweled, or have my fingernails pulled out. My friends still loved me and life continued on as usual. What I really want to do are the things I have worked on and then let the chips fall where they may. I only have control of the things I can do. Winning is secondary. Effort and performance goals are primary."

It's not unnatural or weird to have such inner dialogues; so don't worry that you might be losing it mentally if you engage in such talk. Remember, however, that you can fool many people—but not yourself. How, for example, do you answer self-doubt about the adequacy of your preparation when you have neither committed to your goals nor done the preparatory work to achieve them? The answer is brutally simple—you don't.

Self-monitoring—Now More Than Ever

It is not uncommon for the looming championship to affect thoughts, emotions, and behaviors, so it is important now more than ever to continue self-monitoring and utilizing of the other four pillars to remain mentally rock solid heading into the championship.

Use Secondary Meets as Rehearsals

Coaches and divers need to remember that sometimes to win the war you have to lose a few battles. The battles are the secondary meets (e.g., dual meets, invitational meets). The war is the championship. Use secondary meets as mental training boot camp for the championship. Customize your preperformance routine, identify individual emotions, select performance goals, and sharpen mental skills during secondary meets so that you are mentally battle-ready for the championship. Many divers underuse secondary meets perhaps because these meets seem unimportant, far removed, and irrelevant to the championship. Perhaps they think: "Well, this is just a simple dual meet. I won't worry about mental skills and preparation until the championship."

During his collegiate career, Olympic gold medalist David Boudia followed his mental routine as stringently in a dual meet as he did in a championship meet. Like David, rehearse everything in dual meets so that when you arrive at the championship your mental routine is personalized, comfortable, and automatic. Don't worry about your results in secondary meets. Sometimes you have to lose a few battles to win the war.

Establish an IZOF

Lawrence used a high level of anger to perform well in competition, but Marc found that a moderate level of anger worked best for him. In sharp contrast, Amy found that even a small amount of anger hindered her competition performance. She needed to be more upbeat. According to Hanin (2000), each athlete has an individual zone of optimal functioning (IZOF). In other words, each athlete has specific emotions and ranges of emotions for optimal performance. Use early season dual meets to experiment and identify the emotions and ranges of emotions that work best for you so that you are mentally and emotionally prepared for the championship. The appendix offers an Individualized Emotion Profile Worksheet (adapted with permission from Hanin, 2000) for identifying individual zones of optimal functioning. For more information on emotions and athlete performance, see *Applying Educational Psychology in Coaching Athletes* (Huber, 2013).

Establish a Mental Readiness Baseline

Athletes differ in competitive mental readiness. Some are more mentally ready to handle competitive stress than others are. Some athletes can handle certain competitive situations better than they can handle other types of competitive situations. For example, some athletes can recover more quickly from a missed dive in competition than others can. Take inventory of your mental strengths and weaknesses during and following secondary meets. Establish your mental readiness baseline, and then work on maximizing your strengths and minimizing or eliminating your weaknesses throughout the season.

One way to take inventory is through deep introspection and objective analysis of your thoughts, emotions, physical state, and performances during past meets. Another way to take inventory and assess mental readiness is to use diagnostic paper-and-pencil tools such as the Test of Performance Strategies (TOPS) by Thomas, Murphy, and Hardy (1999); MeBTough (Mack & Ragan, 2008); and USA Diving—Sport Psychology Program (Carr, 2005).

Also important is determining state and trait anxiety tendencies. **State anxiety** refers to a person's response (level of anxiety) to a specific situation. **Trait anxiety** refers to a person's general response tendency (level of anxiety) when exposed to stressors. Athletes differ in their normal levels of anxiety. Research suggests that athletes with high trait anxiety typically tend to experience high state anxiety in competitive sport situations (Martens, Vealey, & Burton, 1990). In other words, athletes who tend to be highly anxious outside the diving pool setting also tend to be highly anxious in competitive situations. Athletes whose state anxiety levels are outside their optimal zones can use strategies (e.g., meditation, relaxation exercises) for reducing them (Huber, 2013).

Keep a Journal

As you win and lose the battles throughout the season, you learn much about yourself and what works best for you as a competitor. Keep a journal of your insights. Write down your thoughts after meets and practices, noting what worked well for you and what didn't work well. And don't limit your comments to simply technical aspects of your diving. Include things such as emotions, thoughts, self-talk, physiological state, warm-up routines, and personal interactions that you experienced before, during, and after meets and practices.

In college our bus arrived late for a dual meet, so late, in fact, that I had time for only two warm-up dives. I scored a personal best in the meet. On the bus ride home, I asked myself how I could dive so well with so little warm-up and why, when I did have a lengthy warm-up, I didn't dive well. I then pondered the usefulness and purpose of a warm-up. It was an awakening that made me a much better competitor (we will discuss the championship warm-up in great detail later in this chapter). Putting pen to paper forces athletes (and coaches) to review and clarify experiences, evaluate behaviors and outcomes, formulate new perspectives, and, ultimately, gain valuable insight on becoming a mentally prepared competitor.

Simulate the Championship

Too often, competitive divers and diving coaches become so preoccupied with training that they forget about competition. They forget that training is a means to an end, and that the end is performing well in the championship. Everything done during the season should physically, mentally, and emotionally prepare divers for the championship. This preparation becomes even more significant in the weeks leading up to the championship. The work's finished and now it's time to focus exclusively on the end—the championship. Following are some effective strategies for simulating the championship.

Practice Dives in List Order

During the season, divers should experiment to see what order of dives is most effective for them in competition. Once this **list order** is determined, you should stick with it and practice the dives in this order leading up to the championship. If performing, say, four dives each in practice, then run through your list four times. If you miss a dive, you have to refocus and hit the next dive in your list; you have to wait until the next list of dives to get another shot at hitting the dive you just missed. Practicing in list order forces you to concentrate like you will want to in the competition. Some seasons I had some divers practice list order several months before the championship.

Simulate the Competition Session

Divers can mentally simulate their upcoming championship session and give greater meaning to their current practice by perceiving each practice dive as if it is the actual championship dive. Let's say you are doing five each of your competition dives in practice. First you perform two each in block order of all your dives and perceive them as your warm-up dives. Next, perform three times in list order all your dives. The first list is perceived as the prelims, the second list as the semifinals, and the third list as the finals. To enhance the simulation, take more time between dives for the "prelim" list since there are more competitors in prelims than there are for semifinals and finals.

This is a simple but effective simulation because you now perceive a routine practice as a championship competition session and everyday practice dives as critical competition dives. Through this perception, practice takes on a whole new meaning and you gain valuable championship rehearsal experience. Perception shapes meaning and meaning shapes experience.

Simulate the Week

Before the U.S. Olympic trials, I scripted each practice, warm-up, and competition session for each day of the entire week of trials. We followed that script for three weeks preceding trials. By the time Christina Loukas arrived at trials, she was so mentally dialed in that everything was automatic. Although she had never won a senior national championship before trials, she won the trials—so handily, in fact, that she could have skipped her last dive and still won.

Even though divers might be competing at the end of the week, the championship really starts at the beginning of the week at least physically and mentally. Things are just different that week, as they should be given the fact that it is the culmination of the season and the week of the big dance. Divers are rested but antsy, focused but forward thinking, excited but nervous. Simulating the entire week helps divers feel on track, automatic, and focused like Christina heading into the championship.

Play Competition Games

There are many games divers can play to prepare for the championship. These games make practice entertaining while simultaneously preparing for competition. Games include challenging another diver to a dive-off, announcing dives in your head, announcing dives on a loudspeaker, creating imaginary scenarios (e.g., hit this dive and I make the cut), and performance charting. All of these games get the competitive juices flowing, provide mental rehearsal, and establish a mind-set for the championship.

Make Good Transitions

When transitioning from one drill to another or from one dive to another, get in the habit of hitting the first attempt. Good transitions demand high concentration and discipline, the same requirements necessary for making transitions from one round to the next in championship competition.

You Can Afford a Day Off

One week before the NCAA championships his senior year, Mark Lenzi sprained his knee and couldn't train. He was concerned that his inability to train would hamper his performance at the championship. After some thought, however, he determined that he had worked hard all year and could afford a few days off. A few missed practices weren't going to make a difference. In fact, the rest might do him some good. He went on to win the 1-meter springboard, break the 3-meter scoring record, and place second on the platform.

It's a shame when divers train hard all year and then let some mishap psych them out of believing that they can dive well in the meet. Meet preparation doesn't have to be perfect. In fact, it may never perfectly match your expectations. But that doesn't mean you can't or won't dive well. You don't even have to feel good to dive well. At a U.S. national championship, Kristin Kane had a fever, headache, and nausea before the start of the 1-meter springboard finals. We debated over whether to scratch her from the event. She decided to compete. Our trainer drove to the drugstore to pick up a prescription the team doctor had called in, and by the time he returned, Kristin had been crowned national champion.

Have a Plan

Many divers train hard all year but arrive at the championship clueless and directionless. Aside from knowing that they want to dive well, they have no plan. I have observed divers forget to register for their events, fail to complete and turn in their dive sheets, arrive at the wrong time (or day!) for their event, incorrectly complete their dive sheets, and miss scheduled warm-ups. Feeling prepared and confident can be difficult when confronted with unfamiliar situations and filled with a sense of uncertainty. Fortunately, the opposite is equally true. With a well-thought-out and detailed plan, it is easy to feel prepared and confident, avoid the unexpected, and deal with competitive pressure.

Take the time to learn what to expect at a meet and to have a plan of action. A plan directs your actions and keeps you from wandering aimlessly around the pool deck. It keeps you focused on the only thing you have control over—your own actions. Get to know the procedures, routine, and protocol of the meet. With this information, construct a plan of action, enter it in your journal, and incorporate it into your mental rehearsal. Don't, however, make your plan so rigid that you believe all is lost if something goes awry. Remain flexible and ready to adjust your plan. You wanted oatmeal for breakfast but all they had was cereal? Okay, then cereal it is.

Pack Your Bag Early

At a team meeting, a highly successful diver described her plan for packing before a competition. She talked for 10 uninterrupted minutes—no kidding.

Divers should begin packing their bags several days in advance of the departure for the championship. Packing may seem like an insignificant event, but it isn't. Arriving at a meet and not having what you need makes it easy to feel that something is missing from your preparation. Having your own pillow so you don't get a crick in your neck, bringing your favorite suits, packing your chamois and toothpaste—all these and more are important for feeling prepared, confident, and in control for the championship.

When I was a diver, a certain indoor pool was popular for hosting NCAA and U.S. national championships. I never performed well there, and on reflection realized that one of the reasons was that I was always cold because of the cold water and drafty conditions. When packing for the next national championship at that pool, I included shoes and socks, extra towels, a heavy robe, and a sweatshirt. Besides feeling warmer during the competition, I also felt prepared and confident, which gave me a mental edge that helped me perform well enough to final. Little things make a big difference. Items to consider packing include a pillow, toiletry supplies, suits and chamois (you would be surprised), nutritious snacks, personal music, headphones, a recharger, an adapter (if going overseas), school work, textbooks, inspirational book, sunglasses, eyeglasses, extra contact lenses, laptop, cell phone, best dives compilation, journal, medications, vitamins, and athletic tape.

Acknowledge the Presence of Pressure

Some divers make the mistake of dealing with competitive pressure by ignoring it or pretending it won't be there. But it will be there, and ignoring it won't make it magically disappear. In fact, it exacerbates the pressure. Accept beforehand that some competition pressure will be a normal part of the championship experience and create a plan for dealing with it. Part of your plan should include predicting competition anxiety level.

Predict Competition Anxiety

Research indicates that athletes can fairly accurately predict how they will feel immediately before a competition (Raglin & Hanin, 2000). Assess beforehand the level of anxiety you are likely to experience, and then implement preventive and coping strategies for maintaining an optimal level during competition (see Huber, 2013). The more critical the competition is, the higher the anxiety level is likely to be. Prior assessment and preventive and coping strategies maintain individualized zones of optimal functioning for both athlete and coach.

Get a Good Night's Sleep

Many divers report difficulty sleeping the night before the championship. You have trained all season for the championship, and it is almost at hand. Understandably, you are filled with expectations, hopes, nervousness, and anticipation. But getting a good night's sleep is important for performing at your best. The following list offers some suggestions for getting adequate sleep.

Suggestions for Sleeping the Night Before the Championship

- Stick to your normal bedtime routine.
- Bring your pillow from home.

- Make sure the room is comfortable (good room temperature, fresh air, blinds closed).
- Read an inspirational book.
- Listen to a relaxation recording.
- Avoid eating a late meal.
- Avoid bright lights.
- Take a warm shower.
- Spend some time stretching.
- Review the next day's schedule (e.g., breakfast time, warm-up time, competition time).
- Read your journal.
- Watch your best dives compilation.
- Visualize your dives.
- Lay out your clothes for the next day.
- Prepack a backpack for the next day: suits, chamois, snacks, credential, music, towel.
- Set a wake-up alarm and maybe a backup alarm if necessary.
- Set the alarm early enough so you don't have to rush when you get up.
- Turn off your cell phone.
- Discuss roommate etiquette if you are sharing a room with another diver.
- Take care of any unfinished business (e.g., return a phone call).

Expect Success

A favorable expectation for success promotes enhancing emotions such as confidence, certainty, and motivation. In contrast, an unfavorable expectation causes disengagement in further effort and feelings of self-doubt and inadequacy (Carver, 1996). You have trained hard all season, made the most of each practice, and prepared for the championship. Why not expect success? Why not expect to dive well? You can create an expectancy of success by engaging in activities such as using positive self-talk (e.g., "I am a much better diver than I was this time last season."), posting signs ("Expect the best!"), reviewing objective data (e.g., performance charts, past meet results, best dives compilation), trusting your coach's comments, maintaining a positive attitude, and mentally replaying past successes.

Develop Defensive Psychological Coping Strategies

Defensive psychological coping strategies are psychological defenses that distort the perception of the competitive situation (Smith, 1996). By lessening the seriousness and gravity of the competition, divers appraise the competitive situation as less threatening and thereby experience less anxiety. For example, before any major competition, a collegiate diver always had a reason she would probably not perform well in the upcoming competition. Her arm hurt. She wasn't feeling well. She had personal problems. But she almost always performed well. Her excuses acted as a defensive psychological coping strategy, because they provided her with a mental alibi, a reason for not performing well, which made the approaching competition less formidable and allowed her to relax and experience less anxiety. It was as though she were telling herself and others: "Listen, this is probably not going to be my day to shine; I've got some issues, so don't expect much from me." She did indeed shine and went on to become a U.S. national champion and Olympian.

Practice Dealing With the Unexpected

You can never completely prepare for every unexpected situation in the sport of diving, but you can come close! Prepare for the unexpected by putting yourself in practice situations that mimic championship scenarios such as missing a dive and rebounding on the next dive, having to hit your next dive to win the championship, and performing your dive after the preceding diver nailed a dive. The scenarios are limited only by your imagination. Another strategy for dealing with the unexpected is to visualize scenarios and how you are going to respond to them. For example, some Olympic divers visualize getting a bad takeoff, making an adjustment, and performing the dive well anyway.

Resolve Inner Conflict

Some problems don't resolve themselves, and ignoring them doesn't make them disappear. In fact, ignoring them makes them even more problematic. Before major competitions, resolve problems that produce inner conflict by engaging in honest and open discussions, problem solving, preplanning, and responsibility taking. There is enough to focus on concerning the upcoming championship without having to angst over such things as relationship problems with significant others, unfinished school assignments, missed exams, unpaid bills, and so on.

One problem typically cited as a source of inner conflict is parental involvement, or rather, over-involvement, during competitions. To avoid this problem, coaches can distribute guidelines for how parents can appropriately support their children at diving meets. Parents generally appreciate such guidelines, because they often don't know how to best support their child at competitions. Following is an example.

Parent Guidelines for Competitions

1. Do not act like a coach and give advice to your child about what he or she needs to be doing better in diving. That is the job of the coach.

2. Give your child his or her space at meets. If your child does not want to do something, then leave it at that and do not push the issue. For example, you may want to go to dinner, but your child may need time alone, time to relax, and/or time to rest.

3. Set specific times for getting together and specific amounts of time that you will spend together. For example, you may both decide to go out to dinner, but your child may want a brief dinner so there is time later in the evening to relax. To accommodate him or her, don't select a fancy restaurant where it may take hours to get served, eat, and pay the bill.

4. Allow your child to follow his or her normal meet preparation and routine. This means that your child knows best what he or she wants to do. Therefore, refrain from acting like Father knows best or Mother knows best.

5. Wait to be asked before giving your child advice. Remember, though, that giving advice is different from lecturing.

6. Be a good listener. Most of the time, that is all your child wants and all you can really offer.

7. Before the season starts, ask your child how you can be most supportive at competitions, and spend some time drawing up additional guidelines for competitions.

8. Your child is ready to dive well at the championship meets, and it is important that you be a source of positive support and not a source of distraction and negative influence.

Express Emotions

In the U.S. national championship men's 3-meter springboard finals, four consecutive divers where performing the same dive. The first diver did his dive for 7.5s and 8s. The second diver did his for 8s and 8.5s. And the third diver did his for 8.5s and 9s. As you might guess, all eyes were now focused on the fourth diver, and everyone was wondering whether he was going to perform the best dive of all. Then the fourth diver did something unexpected. Before he performed his dive, he let out a noticeable sigh and announced to the crowd in a relieved voice, "It's not getting any better than that last dive!" The crowd laughed, and the diver looked not only relieved but also more relaxed. Then he nailed his dive for 8s and 8.5s.

Expressing emotion has a **cathartic effect** that allows you to feel better physically and mentally and connect with healthy emotions. Often, the best thing you can do to relieve tension and stress is to express your emotions ("Coach, I am feeling really nervous about the championship"). By sharing your feelings, you not only experience catharsis but also connect with someone who can help formulate a plan for managing your nervousness, worries, anxiety, doubt, and so on.

Avoid Distractions—Control the Controllables

We are only human, and sometimes we let ourselves get caught up in things we have no business putting our noses into, mainly because they are none of our concern, unworthy of our attention, or simply out of our control. As the championship approaches, it is easy to become distracted by small mishaps such as a teammate's random or unthinking comment or a chamois accidently taken by another diver. Focusing on uncontrollable, or irrelevant, or unimportant distractions only drains physical and emotional energy, reduces mental focus, and disrupts emotional balance. Release the things you have no control over and focus instead on the controllables, the things worth your time and energy and under your control.

Championship Warm-Up

The warm-up is a sliver of time compared to the multitude of minutes of a season. But brief as it might be, its impact on competition performance is immense. The warm-up comprises those critical few minutes before the big show when dress rehearsal is coming to a close and the curtain is about to rise. What divers and coaches do during this prelude sets the stage for the performance that is about to unfold. It is easy at this moment to unexpectedly do something stupid, out of character, or unplanned, such as become suddenly hypercritical, focus on other divers' performances, veer from the planned warm-up routine, entertain negative thoughts, or become rushed.

This section offers some simple but effective techniques, tips, and suggestions for using those consequential moments during warm-up to physically, mentally, and emotionally prepare for the championship performance.

The Warm-Up and the Five Pillars of Mental Training

The warm-up is a critical time to in which to continue using the five pillars to bolster your confidence, direct your physical actions, guide your thinking, and control your emotions. Perhaps the most important pillar is energy management. Following are some techniques for energy management (McCann et al., 2006).

Energy Management When too Energized

- Check your breathing.
- Take abdominal breaths.
- Listen to calm or low-intensity music.
- Monitor your consumption of caffeine and sugar.
- If you feel the need to urinate more—do it.
- If you feel the need to yawn—do it.
- Use your energy for light preperformance physical activity.
- Move away from high-energy people.
- Move away from chaotic surroundings.

Energy Management When too Flat

- Check your breathing.
- Take abdominal breaths.
- Listen to faster, more intense music.
- Have a little caffeine or sugar.
- If you feel the need to urinate more—do it.
- If you feel the need to yawn—do it.
- Become a bit more physically active.
- Move toward high-energy people.
- Move toward busier surroundings.
- Recall your outcome goals.

How important is energy management? At the World University Games in Bangkok, Thailand, a U.S. diver realized that she was emotionally flat from having been at the competition for over two weeks, so she and her coach used reenergizing techniques. Her coach pointed out that her competitors probably felt the same way, and that if she could reenergize, it would give her an edge. And it did. She had a breakout performance, earned the silver medal, and more important, learned that she could compete with the best divers in the world.

Many athletes use **apical breathing,** another term for chest breathing. During chest breathing the abdominal muscles are constricted, which restricts air movement to the lower lungs so that only the upper part of the lungs are used. This results in an inefficient exchange of oxygen. The following abdominal breathing exercise increases breathing efficiency and relaxation (energy management). It is best done before and after practice to recover from challenging workouts and to become an abdominal breather (McCann et al., 2006).

Abdominal Breathing Exercise

- Place the palm of the left hand flat on the abdomen about 2 inches (5 cm) above the navel.
- Place the palm of the right hand directly over the left hand.
- Exhale the air from the abdomen through the mouth by lightly pressing the hands inward and forcing air out to assist in exhaling. If you do this correctly, you should feel the abdomen and hands moving inward.
- After completely exhaling all air out of the lungs, inhale through the nose. Focus on the hands and abdomen moving outward as the lungs completely refill.
- Repeat steps 3 and 4 until you are comfortable with this alteration-of-breathing style.

Hurrying Up Versus Slowing Down

It is understandably easy to get in a hurry when you arrive at the championship. After all, this is the event you and your coach have prepared for all season. It is show time and you are chomping at the bit to get the show going. Unfortunately, you can't affect time. If the meets starts in two hours, the meets starts in two hours. There is nothing you can do about it. But you can do something that will negatively affect your diving: hurry. In your haste, you unconsciously speed up everything you do—you walk faster, shorten your stretching period, skip some or all of your warm-up routine, breathe faster, talk faster, and even think faster. This is referred to as the **hurry-up effect**.

Diving performance has a specific timing, which is connected to the rhythm of the board. Impatience and hurrying on the pool deck often manifest on the board. You rush your approach, hurdle, and takeoff and get out of synch with the board's rhythm. The hurry-up effect also wastes valuable physical, mental, and emotional energy. Divers who hurry up often report feeling drained by competition time. Coaches can unwittingly contribute to the hurry-up effect by becoming excited, impatient, and rushed, extolling their divers, for example, to hurry up and get through stretching and get on the boards.

When you arrive at the meet site, take notice (self-monitoring) of the pace of your physical and mental behaviors. Maintain your normal pace and follow your routine. If you find yourself hurrying up, talk to yourself, slow yourself down. Follow your usual stretching routine and warm-up. Remain relaxed and committed to the game plan you established before the meet.

Maintain Appropriate Body Language

You can often (but not always) sense divers' and coaches' physical, mental, and emotional states by their walk, head position, shoulder movements, facial expressions, and other telltale signs referred to as **body language**. Divers and coaches experiencing resoluteness and determination have a certain commanding body language that says that they are in the zone. Conversely, athletes experiencing uncertainty and fear have an unmistakable countenance that says that they are out of the zone.

Monitor your body language. Often, changing your body language sends an intuitive appraisal message to yourself and others that positively alters your physical, mental, and emotional states. For example, Lisa was an extremely talented athlete who eventually learned the difficult dives she needed for the 3-meter springboard and high-level competition. However, even though she performed them easily, she remained uncertain and fearful, and these emotions were interfering with her ability to execute at a high level. When she walked down the board, she had an expression on her face suggesting that she was about to be thrown out of an airplane without a parachute. I asked her to practice replacing this expression with one that communicated determination, confidence, resoluteness, and a pinch of anger thrown in for good measure. The change made a difference. Soon afterward, Lisa reached her lifelong goal of becoming one of the top U.S. collegiate divers in not one, but two events.

Changing body language is surprisingly simple. Athletes can easily comprehend and quickly imitate body language that communicates resoluteness and determination, as Lisa did. What message are you sending yourself and others with your body language? Divers and coaches who are energetic, upbeat, and smiling and have relaxed shoulders, bright eyes, and an unhurried walk convey the message that they are enthusiastic, charged, motivated, alert, confident, and purposeful. In contrast, those who wear a look of worry or disgust, move frantically, yell, walk with slumped shoulders, or sit most of the time convey that they are bored, unmotivated, uncaring, panicked, uncertain, and distressed.

The three strategies for changing body language are observational learning, body language analysis, and mental imagery. **Observational learning** is the process of watching successful divers and coaches and then imitating their body language. **Body language analysis** involves recording yourself and then analyzing your body language. On more than one occasion, while watching digital replays of my divers, I observed myself in the background on the pool deck exhibiting embarrassingly poor coaching behavior—which immediately made me alter my body language and attitude. **Mental imagery** involves visualizing yourself behaving the way you want to behave when you are diving or coaching. Visualize the body language you want to portray to yourself and others. Before highly stressful competitions, I found it helpful to visualize how I wanted to act and feel at the competition pool when interacting with my athletes and other coaches.

Filter Emotional Messages

One summer I attended a U.S. national championship in the best shape of my diving career. The day before the 3-meter springboard competition, a nationally noted diving coach stopped to talk with me. I thought it unusual because he had never talked to me in the past. After the competition was over and I had returned home, our conversation stuck in my mind. At the time of our conversation, I didn't notice anything. But upon reflection, I recalled finishing the conversation feeling bad about my diving. I am not saying the coach deliberately tried to psych me out; I will take the blame for that. However, I think there was an emotional message being sent, and I made the mistake of receiving it.

All kinds of things get said at a championship, and although I believe in the goodness of people, not everything that is said is good. Statements can be accompanied by emotional messages that divers need to filter out. For example, the emotion can by pity: "Too bad you didn't make finals, but you did a good job anyway." (Emotional message: You don't have the ability to perform any better.) It can be jealousy: "Nice job today. Boy, the competition wasn't very good." (Emotional message: You aren't really that good; the competition was just weak.) Of course, the emotion can be positive and supportive. It can be the emotion of certainty and belief: "You didn't make finals. You need to train harder." (Emotional message: I believe in you; I know you can do better.)

Tune out irrelevant emotional messages sent by people who may have an agenda or harbor emotions such as jealousy and envy, and tune in to the positive and supportive emotional messages sent by people who genuinely care about you and have your best interests at heart.

Save It for the Meet

Congratulations! The gold medal for winning the warm-up goes to . . . . You have never heard these words, and you never will. No diver has ever been bestowed a medal for a performance in the warm-up, because you can't win the meet in the warm-up. No matter how well you dive in the warm-up, nothing counts until the meet. But how many times have you or a diver you know gotten pumped up and had a killer warm-up only to physically, mentally, and emotionally deflate and dive flat in the meet?

It's tempting to want to dive all out in the warm-up, to look sharp, to do the things you want to do, to gain confidence, to feel comfortable, and maybe even to feel relaxed, satisfied, and content. But is this how you really want to feel heading into competition? Sure, in practices days before the competition there are many reasons to dive well: rehearse your performances, impress any judges who happen to be watching, and maybe even psych out a few competitors. But the warm-up is an entirely different beast.

Research on emotions and motor performance (Hanin, 2000) indicates that feeling relaxed, satisfied, and content heading into competition, for many athletes, impairs performance. Think of how you have felt after a phenomenal practice. Such a practice is often followed by a physical, mental, and emotional letdown or relaxation. Consequently, see warm-up as save-up time, a time to get ready to dive well, not a time to dive well. In a personal conversation with four-time Olympic gold medalist Greg Louganis, he was emphatic about not wanting to hit a dive in warm-up. He would break, split his legs, or tuck up before hitting the water so he could save it for the meet.

Stick to Your Plan

Do you have a plan if you don't adhere to it? Not really. A plan not followed is no plan at all. So stick to your plan by monitoring yourself. Ask yourself, "Am I doing what I am supposed to be doing right now?" If not, then forcefully redirect yourself through self-talk. Often, the battle being fought isn't on the springboard or platform. It's in your mind.

I have observed divers who I know trained hard all season and deserved to perform well at the championship lose it during the warm-up. They simply let go of their plan, their diving, their coach's comments, their focus, their commitment to themselves. The championship is your party, your dance, your moment—so party on, take your dance, and seize your moment. Don't let anyone distract or dissuade you from the moment you have worked for, dreamed of, and planned for. In truth, no one can make you discard your game plan except you. So, in those precious warm-up moments, stick to your plan.

Maintain a Preperformance Routine

A **preperformance routine** involves the things athletes habitually do before every performance to physically, mentally, and emotionally ready themselves. Every great athlete in every sport has a preperformance routine, and so should you. Following is an example of a standard preperformance routine for competition.

- Find a semisecluded spot at the pool.
- Avoid watching the competition—unless in the past you have found it helpful.
- Wear headphones and listen to personal music.
- Do something to occupy your time, especially if it is a long competition.
- Rehearse the physical movements of the dive periodically throughout the contest.
- Walk over early and listen to your coach's comments.
- Model dive movements as the coach observes and points out performance cues.
- Walk over early to the springboard or platform.
- Rehearse the physical movements of the dive several times or more.
- Visualize the dive.
- Engage in positive, motivating, and directional self-talk.
- Monitor your breathing and relaxation.
- Get on the board early, set the fulcrum, drop your chamois on the pool deck, and assume your stance.
- Move your head and shoulders—gently relaxing them.
- Utter a brief statement or cue words either mentally or softly out loud.
- Take a short breath and then take your first step.
- Talk to your coach after your dive.
- Focus on next dive and repeat preperformance routine.

For a preperformance routine to be effective, especially at championships, it has to be customized by the diver and routinely used in practice and secondary meets.

The Championship

The warm-up is over. You have employed your five pillars of mental training, managed your energy, filter emotional messages, followed your plan, and saved your dives for the meet. Now what? Following are some effective mental strategies for performing well at the big dance.

Offset Warm-Up Decrement

Research indicates that no matter how adept a performer becomes at a skill, there is always a decrease in the level of performance after a period of inactivity (Adams, 1961). This decrease is referred to as **warm-up decrement**. Between the warm-up and the start of the meet, and between competition dives, especially in a long contest, there is a period of inactivity and a resulting decrease in the level of performance. No matter how proficient divers become, some measurable decrease still occurs. The more skilled you become, the smaller the decrease is. Nevertheless, there is still a decrease in performance.

This decrease, however, is easily offset by mental imagery and physical rehearsal. It is commonplace during national and international competitions to observe elite divers physically rehearsing their dive motions and closing their eyes to visualize the motions before climbing the ladder. At the World University Games in Sheffield, England, I observed Chinese diver Gao Min rehearse each of her practice dives perhaps a dozen times before stepping on the springboard. No wonder she was the most consistent diver in the world, winning the world championship, world cup, and Olympic Games—not once, but twice. Offset warm-up decrement, then, by imitating elite divers. Incorporate both mental imagery and physical rehearsal into your preperformance routine.

Get on the Board Early

Don't be one of those divers who waits until his or her name is announced to get on the board. Getting on the board late creates a hurry-up effect, added pressure, and self-consciousness. Make getting on the board early part of your preperformance routine. On the other hand, on some occasions, for whatever reason, you have to get on the board late. It happens. You misread the dive order, you had to go to the bathroom, or you just goofed up. In this scenario, keep calm, make your way to the diving board without hurrying, regroup, and rerun your performance routine. I have observed divers in this scenario run on the pool deck (and sometimes slip and fall), frantically get on the board as though their pants were on fire, hurriedly set the fulcrum, race to the end of the board in their approach, and then bomb the dive. It is your dance, so take your time and make the most of the moment. The judges, announcer, and fans can wait. You are the one who trained all season for the meet, not them.

Practice the Seven Rs

There are likely to be bumps in the road on the way to performing well in competition. It is important to remain calm, regroup, and maintain composure when encountering these bumps. The most obvious bump in the road for any diver is missing a dive. Let's be honest. Before the contest begins, you know you will fall short of perfection (straight 10s from all judges on all dives). There will be misses to some degree. How far short of perfection you fall is the question. If you miss a dive but are able to rally on the next dive, you are likely to not fall that far from your performance goals. Regrouping is like plugging a small leak before the hole gets bigger. But if you agonize over a missed dive and carry that emotion and focus with you to the next round, you are likely to miss the next dive as well, and now that small leak has become irreparable and the dam is about to break.

A big part of performing well in competition, then, involves weathering the storm of mistakes. Consider the baseball pitcher who throws a poorly placed ball that the batter knocks into the stadium parking lot. What does he do next—fold his tent, pack his bags, and throw more bad pitches? Or does he regroup and ready himself for the next pitch? It is a long game—nine innings or even more if the game goes into extra innings—and anything can happen and pretty much has in the celebrated game of baseball. The sport of diving is no different. Just as there is more than one inning in baseball, there is more than one round in diving. You can rebound from mistakes by using the seven Rs: responsibility, recognize, respond, release, regroup, refocus, and ready.

Responsibility refers to taking personal responsibility for the miss and also for moving on. *Recognize* means being aware of the situation and proactively dealing with it. *Respond* means taking positive actions after the miss. *Release* involves letting go of negative emotions and putting the dive in the past, which for many divers is no easy task. *Regroup* has to do with retracing your performance preparation steps and getting redialed in—again, no easy task. *Refocus* is about zeroing in on the next dive and your performance cues. *Ready* involves initiating your preperformance routine and getting ready physically, mentally, and emotionally for the next dive just as you did for the previous dive.

Practice the seven Rs in workouts each day. You can't rally from a missed dive in a meet if you have never practiced rebounding from one in a workout. Get in the habit of interpreting a missed dive as a challenge, as an opportunity to show your mettle, your resiliency, your ability to bounce back like an indefatigable rubber ball.

Never Give Up

You may ask, Why bother practicing the Seven Rs? What difference does it make? If I miss a dive, I'm toast. The meet's over, kaput, sayonara, adios. Not really. The great ones adjust. They deal with adversity, respond to setbacks, and remain the eye of the storm. Never give up. You never know what will happen during a contest. Don't make the mistake of mentally eliminating yourself from the contest after a missed dive. Don't erroneously assume that your competitors aren't going to miss and, therefore, the contest is essentially over, even though several rounds of diving remain. Dive determinedly to the end of the contest. If you are going to get beat, so be it, but make your competitors beat you; make them have to dive their best to the conclusion of the contest. Remember, every diver has to do an entire list of dives, and no list is perfect. Besides, one of the greatest characteristics you can learn from diving is perseverance.

Don't Try Too Hard

At the championship or after a missed dive, it is easy to try too hard. It is only human nature to want to give more effort to reach long-term championship goals or to try harder on the next dive to make up for the preceding missed dive. But trying too hard creates a **pressing effect,** in which muscles necessary for performance are overly tensed and unnecessary muscles are activated, causing these muscles to oppose each other. For example, tightening the neck and trapezium muscles tenses the shoulders and impedes the arm swing in the hurdle. Pressing also disturbs rhythm and timing, additionally altering performance. Trying too hard in the hurdle, for example, often causes divers to stomp the springboard. You can only do what you do in practice, so stay within your normal performance range.

Focus on the Process

An unknown diver found herself in first place with two remaining preliminary rounds at her first U.S. national championship. Suddenly, she started thinking about how wonderful it was going to be to dive in her very first finals. She made the rookie mistake of focusing on the outcome instead of the process and badly missed her next dive. Fortunately, she hit her last dive to squeak into the last qualifying spot. In the finals that night, she vowed to concentrate on the process for each dive to the end of the contest. After her last dive, she was mentally consumed with how she had performed. It came as a surprise and an afterthought when someone walked up to her and said, "Congratulations! You won!"

I don't know if this is true, but I have been told that the majority of mountain climbing accidents occur close to the top of the mountain, perhaps because climbers begin focusing on the outcome of reaching the summit rather than the process of climbing. Similarly, divers who focus on the outcome of the competition rather than the process of diving experience diving "accidents." Focusing on the outcome instead of the process diverts attention from the task at hand and creates superfluous thoughts such as "I am going to make finals!"

Divers have no control over external factors. They have control only over one thing—their diving. Before a junior U.S. national championship, I asked a diver, "What do you want to do at the championship?" He looked surprised at the question and after a pause responded, "Win?" Up until that moment, he had never considered what he wanted to *do* at the championship. I asked him again, "No, what do you want to *do*?" He replied, "Dive well?" I again asked, "No, what do you want to *do*?" Now he was really confused. He answered, "Hit all my dives?" Again, I asked, "What do you want to *do*?" By now he was getting warmer. He said, "Get a good hurdle?" Again the question mark, but he was getting closer to the correct answer. This time I asked, "What do you want to *do* to get a good hurdle?" He had the answer now: "Get my arms up early in my first swing." I responded with a smile, "That is what you want to *do* at the championship."

You can't guarantee winning, but you can always guarantee something as simple and attainable as getting your arms up early in the first swing of your hurdle. And achieving that goal just might lead to winning the championship. Following are simple process goals that elite divers focus on during championship performances. This section could appropriately be placed in the previous section, Championship Warm-Up, because focusing on and achieving process goals is much easier in competition when you focus on and achieve them in the preceding warm-up. The converse is also true.

Get to the end of the board. Landing on the end of the board makes every dive easier to perform. Landing back on the end of the board makes every dive more difficult. Want to have a successful championship? Focus on getting to the end of the board.

Be aggressive. You are much more likely to hit a dive if you are aggressive. Holding back guarantees that you won't perform up to your greatest potential.

If you are aggressive and miss the dive, at least you can tell yourself that you gave it your best effort and have no regrets. What do you tell yourself after you meekly attempt a dive and miss it?

Get vertical or past vertical on entries. Dives short of vertical are considered deficient dives by judges, and unlike dives past vertical in which you can perform a pike save or scoop knee save, there are no completely effective saves for dives short of vertical. Decide before your performance that you are going to get to the tip of the board, be aggressive, and get vertical.

Maintain your preperformance routine. Your preperformance routine is your lifeline, your automatic pilot, your cruise control. It readies you for performance and, once engaged, automatically initiates the performance you have practiced hundreds of times. Make sure to activate it in both the warm-up and the competition.

Execute your performance cues. Focus on those one or two simple performance cues that make all the difference in performance. For example, if it is beneficial to get your arms up early in the first swing in your hurdle, then focus on it. Control the things you have control over.

Focus on you and your diving. Sad, it's it? Some divers train hard all season and then get to the championship and completely lose focus because they can't take their eyes off their competitors. Attentional capacity is limited. You have only so much of it, and the more you focus on your competitors, the less you can focus on you and your diving. If you want to be a spectator, buy a ticket, sit in the stands, and watch all the competitors. If you want to be a participant, ignore the other divers, take your dance, and do your thing. By the way, your thing is pretty darn good, but you might forget or overlook that tidbit of information if you squander most of your attention on your competitors. The same goes for coaches. I have observed coaches missing some of their athletes' dives because they were too busy watching the competitors.

Focus on your coach's comments. Your coach knows your diving better than anyone else; has your best interests at heart; and has the experience, knowledge, and wisdom to guide you through the meet. Trust and rely on that advice. Before an Olympic trials finals, my diver and I were discussing what she should do for her warm-up. At one point she blurted, "Just tell me what to do." She was an experienced diver, but she trusted my advice. At that critical moment, she knew that all she had to do was focus on her coach's comments.

Engage in appropriate self-talk. It was one of those critical moments when hitting the next few dives would determine success or failure in reaching a lifelong goal of making finals at the U.S. national championship. Climbing the ladder, the diver was nervous and unconfident. Suddenly, a reassuring voice in his head repeated what he had told himself all summer, "You have trained hard and are ready to dive well." As he set the fulcrum, he was suddenly filled with confidence and a sense that he was about to perform the best dive of his career. And he did. Focus on your self-talk. It is powerful.

Monitor your game plan. Stick to your guns, man the battleship, and follow your plan of attack. This is no time to waffle, waver, or weaken. You prepared for this moment and created the perfect plan, so damn the torpedoes and full speed ahead—no looking back, no regrets, and no last-minute doubts. If your plan fails, it fails. But it won't. It surely will fail, however, if you vacillate and abandon ship. Monitor and adhere to your game plan. After all, what else should or can you do?

Maintain appropriate emotional balance. There are ups and downs in performance during every championship. Keep an even keel. Don't let your highs get too high or your lows too low. Be the eye of the storm. Practice good mental skills that help you maintain emotional balance and keep you within your zone of optimal functioning.

Do Your Dives One at a Time

Doing your dives one at a time may seem simplistic or even naïve, but elite divers know how important this becomes during the heat of battle. It means concentrating on the moment and the current dive, not the last dive you wish you had performed better, not the "problem" dive or scary dive you struggle with in practice that is coming up in three rounds, and certainly not the dive your competitor is performing. Concentrate on the task at hand to get the most out of each opportunity. If you miss a dive, put it behind you. Don't let the last dive negatively affect the next dive. If you have a special dive coming up in three rounds, then cross that bridge when you come to it. You can't do it until you have done the preceding dives. Be patient, stay in the moment, and do your dives one at a time.

Don't Make Your Dives Too Precious

A diver went to the championship in the best diving shape of his career. During the competition, he dived to not miss. And he didn't. He didn't miss a single dive. Unfortunately, he also didn't hit a single dive. His lackluster performance was the most disappointing experience of his career. From that point forward, he vowed never again to make his dives too precious. He vowed to be aggressive and dive to hit his dives.

There is a big difference between diving to not miss and diving to hit your dives. Diving to not miss guarantees mediocrity and eliminates the fun and spirit of competition. As the Olympic creed says, it "is not the triumph, but the struggle." You can't give your best effort (struggle) by holding back and diving to not miss. So, carpe diem. Seize the day. Seize the dive. Seize the championship. You can't steal second with your foot on first base. Now is the time, not later, to take the chance. You have nothing to lose, only something to gain. You will never be disappointed at the conclusion of the championship in which you gave your best effort and not played it safe. I love the Special Olympics athlete oath, "Let me win, but if I cannot win, let me be brave in the attempt." U.S. Olympic gold medalist figure skater Sarah Hughes (2006) nicely summarized the essence of carpe diem in competition.

> I am not a risk taker by nature. But when I stopped and thought about the Olympic moments that I remembered, they were not the ones where people played it safe and just did what they could. The greatest moments were when people put themselves on the line and then pulled it off. I wanted one of those amazing, unbelievable, edge-of-the-seat Olympic moments. That's the thing with the Olympics. We make our own destinies. You have to be willing to change the whole game plan for that shot at the glory of that moment.

Don't Miss the Moment—Have Fun

Sure, the championship is important, but how important? If you had terminal cancer and were given two months to live, which happens to people every day, would this meet seem less stressful and less significant? You bet. Don't miss the moment, whether you are a diver or a coach. Life is precious and all too fleeting. Don't let the wrong perspective keep you from enjoying the championship experience. Maintain a perspective that keeps competition fun. Perhaps the best way to have fun is to maintain a sense of humor.

Humor provides levity to a seriously perceived situation, keeps things in perspective, and most important, maintains a sense of joy, excitement, and fun. After all, isn't that why coaches and divers engage in the sport in the first place, to have fun? If it isn't fun, it isn't worth doing. Fun, of course, is defined differently by athletes. Fun might involve laughter but could also involve serene satisfaction from focusing on and achieving process goals. It definitely doesn't involve getting uptight, yelling at coaches and teammates, or dreading competition. Embrace the championship and the energy, excitement, uniqueness, magic, and fun that come with it.

Maintain an Elevated Self-Image

Self-image correlates with a standard of excellence. Athletes with a high self-image maintain a high standard of excellence. The converse is also true. This standard of excellence becomes a habit that manifests in all areas of their lives. Divers with a heightened self-image demand much from themselves in diving practice, dryland training, conditioning, classroom learning, employment, and personal relationships. Maintain an elevated self-image during championship competition. Remind yourself of how hard you have trained, how much you have improved, how prepared you are for the competition, and how you have distinguished yourself from your competitors. But don't put your ego on the line.

Don't Connect Performance to Self-Worth

Are you a better person if you dive well? Will your parents and friends love you more if you dive well? How well you dive or what place you take in the championship has nothing to do with how good a person you are or how much love you will receive, even though some divers erroneously think this. Don't put your ego on the line. You have enough pressure to deal with in the championship without adding additional pressure by connecting performance to self-worth. No matter how you perform, you are still a good person and your parents and friends (if they are true friends) will still love you. As part of his preperformance routine for maintaining perspective when thousands of eyes and cameras were on him, Olympic champion Greg Louganis reminded himself that no matter how he performed, his mother would still love him.

Have a Cornerman

Cornerman is a term used in combat sports for a coach or trainer who assists a fighter during a bout. The cornerman stands outside the combat area next to the fighter's corner and is responsible for providing instruction, applying ice, reducing swelling, stopping any bleeding, and on occasion, throwing in the towel. During diving competition, a diving coach serves as cornerman (or cornerwoman), someone in the diver's corner during the heat of combat providing advice, offering encouragement, bolstering confidence, reducing stress, acting as a calming presence, and stopping emotional bleeding.

A cornerman provides something extra that can often make the difference between divers reaching their competition goals and falling short of them, especially during critical championship moments. Divers and coaches collaborating during these moments find an edge over their competition. This diver–cornerman rapport, however, is only effective if a close working relationship has been established throughout the season and coach and diver have consistently engaged in mental training so both are the eye of the storm like Grant, the young diver.

Eye of the Storm

So, we have come full circle and find ourselves back to young Grant and the eye of the storm. How often have you heard someone say, "Just weather the storm and everything will be all right"? Diving success to a great extent depends on remaining the eye of that storm, the calm, coolheaded, and focused diver or coach during the maelstrom of competition, the challenge of learning new dives, and the numerous other stressors related to our sport. But becoming the eye of the storm doesn't happen by accident. It is a mind-set developed by practicing mental skills as diligently as practicing diving skills, and it is equally important for divers and coaches. As mentioned earlier in this chapter, it is difficult for divers to be the eye of the storm when their coaches are not. The calm, coolheaded, and focused diver relies on the cornerman or cornerwoman coach. With consistent mental training, divers and coaches can both be the eye of the storm.

After the Championship

The championship experience can be an insightful turning point in an athlete's career if used wisely. For example, after a disastrous U.S. national championship qualifying meet in which he finished near the bottom of the pile, a diver had a heart-to-heart conversation with his coach. They talked for a good 40 minutes before the diver finally opened up and admitted that he had choked and was mentally ill-prepared. Together they formulated a mental training plan for the subsequent semester. As the coach was leaving at the conclusion of their conversation, he looked back at the diver and thought, "He is going to have an amazing second semester." And he did. He returned home; worked on his mental skills; and became conference champion, conference diver of the championship, and NCAA All American on the 1- and 3-meter springboards.

Delay Evaluation and Decision Making

Attributing reasons for success and failure are important after a championship. However, these attributions can be clouded by emotions. Things said in the heat of the moment and evaluations and decisions made after an abysmal championship are often negatively skewed by emotion. Wait for emotions to subside before making evaluations and decisions. Only then can athlete and coach think clearly, talk freely, and make accurate evaluations and wise decisions based on objective feedback and rational thought. This cooling off period might last a few minutes, an hour, a day or two, or even longer. Delay evaluation and decision making, no matter how long it takes, until cooler heads prevail.

Learn From Your Mistakes

Greg Louganis said something I have never forgotten: "I never had a bad experience." Here was a diver who clearly had what many would consider bad experiences such as hitting his head on the board at the Olympic Games (and needing stitches), hitting his head on the platform at the world championship (and falling unconscious 10 meters and being rescued from the water), and enduring personal experiences well chronicled in his book (Louganis & Marcus, 2006). What he meant was that every life experience was also a valuable learning experience that helped him grow as an athlete and a person. He was adamant in his belief that athletes should cut away the emotion from each experience and harvest the information.

A promising young diver revealed to me that during the warm-up before the U.S. junior national championship preliminary 3-meter springboard event, she felt fine, but she completely lost her composure when the announcer called her name for her first dive. When I asked her what she had done to prepare mentally for the competition, she replied, "Nothing." Then I asked her a question that surprised her: "Have you asked yourself what you would do differently if you could do it all over again?" Her answer was no.

Some divers—and some parents—misperceive certain meets as the end-all ultimate competition of a young diver's career. However, there are many more competitions ahead of them, and they will gain the opportunity to do it all over again. Consequently, it is important to perceive each competition as a valuable learning experience, a stepping-stone toward improved performance. When the meet is over, cut away the emotion and harvest the information. Notice the things done well, particularly the things you have been working on in practice that you accomplished in the meet. And pat yourself on the back. But notice, too, the things you need to work on in practice to change. Vow to be a better diver both technically and mentally at the next meet because of your previous meet experience. It's okay to make a mistake, but when you repeatedly make the same mistake, something has to change. Einstein said that the definition of insanity is doing the same thing over and over and expecting different results. Learning is change, and change is the engine that drives improvement. Learn from your mistakes and make changes. As Spanish philosopher George Santayana wrote, "Those who cannot remember the past are condemned to repeat it."

Keep the Ball Rolling

On occasion, divers can be their own worst enemies. They can have one bad meet and talk themselves into believing that their diving is terrible (when in fact it is better than ever). Then the self-fulfilling prophecy occurs: they believe what they tell themselves, and their diving declines. One meet, however, can be an inaccurate and misleading measurement of overall improvement. For example, you might have your personal best score but place lower because it was a highly competitive meet. Or, you might be diving the best ever in practice, but simply have an off day in the meet.

Don't hold yourself back. Consider the snowball that gets bigger and bigger as it rolls down the mountain, and keep the ball rolling. You are working hard and things are getting better. Build on each meet so that you grow mentally stronger and tougher with each opportunity. When you do have a disastrous meet, turn the negative into a positive. Learn from it. In many ways, a disappointing meet is the most illuminating, educational, and motivational. Then put it behind you and point toward the next meet. Don't let one lousy meet mentally erase all your hard-earned progress.

Create a New Plan

"What we call the beginning is often the end. And to make an end is to make a beginning. The end is where we start from" (T.S. Eliot, 1942).The end of a championship is the time to make a beginning. Use emotions, such as dissatisfaction, determination, passion, hopefulness, excitement, anticipation, and resoluteness to establish future expectations and goals and to create a new annual individualized training plan.

One of the beautiful challenges and opportunities of sport is starting anew. Even champions must start anew, because there is no guarantee of future success in sport. You are either moving forward or backward. There is no such thing as staying in the same place. If you are complacent and satisfied with simply staying the same, you are losing ground to your competitors who are diligently working hard to improve. As U.S. Olympic gold medalist Bernie Wrightson (1970) aptly put it: "I know now that he who is content with what he's done in the past seems to make the most comfortable doormat for those on their way to the top for the first time. I often asked myself—What are Champions for? Well—they are for beating" (p.14).

Write in Your Journal

To make a new beginning at the end of your season, write in your journal while your feelings, thoughts, recollections, and reactions about the championship are fresh in your mind. Hopefully, you have written in your journal throughout the season. Reflect on your past and current entries to begin formulating a plan for the off-season and upcoming season. If your plan for the season succeeded, formulate a plan for an even more successful upcoming season. If your plan for the season failed, rise like a phoenix from the ashes to begin a new season, always persevering, learning from your experiences, challenging yourself, and striving to reach your greatest potential. Best of luck on your journey.

Appendix

Individualized Emotion Diver Profile Worksheet

Name_____ Date_____

This is an individualized assessment to identify emotions and range of emotions that are helpful or harmful for your competition performance. Steps in developing emotion profiles are as follows: (1) identify your most memorable successful and poor competition performances; (2) identify positive and negative emotions that were helpful to your successful performances; (3) identify positive and negative emotions that were harmful to your poor performances; (4) rate your emotional intensity before and during successful and poor performances; (5) establish your optimal and dysfunctional intensity zones for each emotion; (6) monitor your emotions in practices and competitions.

Step 1: Identify your most memorable successful and poor competition performances.

A. List three of your most memorable successful performances (indicate the date, place, and results).

    1. _____

    2. _____

    3. _____

Provide any important details about these performances.

_____

_____

_____

_____

B. List three of your most memorable poor performances (indicate the date, place, and results).

    1. _____

    2. _____

    3. _____

Provide any important details about these performances.

_____

_____

_____

_____

Step 2: Identify positive and negative emotions that were helpful to your successful performances.

A. Review the following list of positive (pleasant) emotions and circle as many as five that describe the emotions you felt before and during your successful performances. If you don't find a word that describes an emotion that is important to you, add it at the end of the list.

Helpful Positive Emotions (P+)

Active, dynamic, energetic, vigorous, relaxed, comfortable, easy, calm, peaceful, unhurried, quiet, cheerful, merry, confident, certain, sure, delighted, overjoyed, exhilarated, determined, set, settled, resolute, excited, thrilled, brave, bold, daring, dashing, glad, pleased, satisfied, contented, inspired, motivated, stimulated, lighthearted, carefree, nice, pleasant, agreeable, quick, rapid, fast, alert

Your own emotion: _____

B. Review the following list of negative (unpleasant) emotions and circle as many as five that describe the emotions you felt before and during your successful performances. If you don't find a word that describes an emotion that is important to you, add it to the end of the list.

Helpful Negative Emotions (N+)

Afraid, fearful, scared, panicky, angry, aggressive, furious, violent, annoyed, afraid, distressed, anxious, apprehensive, concerned, alarmed, disturbed, worried, depressed, discouraged, dispirited, dissatisfied, doubtful, uncertain, indecisive, irresolute, helpless, unsafe, insecure, inactive, sluggish, lazy, intense, fierce, jittery, nervous, uneasy, restless, sorry, unhappy, regretful, sad, cheerless, tense, strained, tight, weary, exhausted, worn out

Your own emotion: _____

Step 3: Identify positive and negative emotions that were harmful to your poor performances.

A. Review the following list of positive (pleasant) emotions and circle as many as five that describe the emotions you felt before and during your poor performances. If you don't find a word that describes an emotion that is important to you, add it to the end of the list.

Harmful Positive Emotions (P−)

Active, dynamic, energetic, vigorous, relaxed, comfortable, easy, calm, peaceful, unhurried, quiet, cheerful, merry, confident, certain, sure, delighted, overjoyed, exhilarated, determined, set, settled, resolute, excited, thrilled, brave, bold, daring, dashing, glad, pleased, satisfied, contented, inspired, motivated, stimulated, lighthearted, carefree, nice, pleasant, agreeable, quick, rapid, fast, alert

Your own emotion: _____

B. Review the following list of negative (unpleasant) emotions and circle as many as five that describe the emotions you felt before and during your poor performances. If you don't find a word that describes an emotion that is important to you, add it to the end of the list.

Harmful Negative Emotions (N –)

Afraid, fearful, scared, panicky, angry, aggressive, furious, violent, annoyed, afraid, distressed, anxious, apprehensive, concerned, alarmed, disturbed, worried, depressed, discouraged, dispirited, dissatisfied, doubtful, uncertain, , indecisive, irresolute, helpless, unsafe, insecure, inactive, sluggish, lazy, intense, fierce, jittery, nervous, uneasy, restless, sorry, unhappy, regretful, sad, cheerless, tense, strained, tight, weary, exhausted, worn out

Your own emotion: _____

Step 4: Rate your emotional intensity before and during successful and poor performances.

A. Write the words you chose in step 2, A and B, as helpful positive and negative emotions that you felt before and during successful performances. Think about the intensity of your emotions. Using the following scale (1-10), circle one number that indicates the degree of intensity for each emotion you experienced. Also, rate your expected performance outcome and your actual achieved performance outcome, as well as how recovered you felt before this competition, and how recovered you needed to be for this competition.

Intensity scale of emotions:

1	(very, very little)
2	(very little)
3	(little)
4-5	(moderate)
6-7	(much)
8-9	(very much)
10	(very, very much)

Helpful positive emotions (P+)	Intensity of emotions
1.	1 2 3 4 5 6 7 8 9 10
2.	1 2 3 4 5 6 7 8 9 10
3.	1 2 3 4 5 6 7 8 9 10
4.	1 2 3 4 5 6 7 8 9 10
5.	1 2 3 4 5 6 7 8 9 10
Helpful negative emotions (N+)	**Intensity of emotions**
1.	1 2 3 4 5 6 7 8 9 10
2.	1 2 3 4 5 6 7 8 9 10
3.	1 2 3 4 5 6 7 8 9 10
4.	1 2 3 4 5 6 7 8 9 10
5.	1 2 3 4 5 6 7 8 9 10

Performance outcome: result expected	1 2 3 4 5 6 7 8 9 10
Performance outcome: result achieved	1 2 3 4 5 6 7 8 9 10
Performance process: quality expected	1 2 3 4 5 6 7 8 9 10
Performance process: quality achieved	1 2 3 4 5 6 7 8 9 10
Recovery obtained before competition	1 2 3 4 5 6 7 8 9 10
Recovery required before competition	1 2 3 4 5 6 7 8 9 10

B. Write the words you chose in step 3, A and B, as harmful positive and negative emotions that you felt before and during poor performances. Think about the intensity of your emotions. Again, using the following scale (1-10), circle one number that indicates the degree of intensity for each emotion you felt. Also, rate your expected performance outcome and your actual achieved performance outcome, as well as how recovered you felt before this competition, and how recovered you needed to be for this competition.

Harmful positive emotions (P–)	Intensity of emotions
1.	1 2 3 4 5 6 7 8 9 10
2.	1 2 3 4 5 6 7 8 9 10
3.	1 2 3 4 5 6 7 8 9 10
4.	1 2 3 4 5 6 7 8 9 10
5.	1 2 3 4 5 6 7 8 9 10

Harmful negative emotions (N–)	Intensity of emotions
1.	1 2 3 4 5 6 7 8 9 10
2.	1 2 3 4 5 6 7 8 9 10
3.	1 2 3 4 5 6 7 8 9 10
4.	1 2 3 4 5 6 7 8 9 10
5.	1 2 3 4 5 6 7 8 9 10

Performance outcome: result expected	1 2 3 4 5 6 7 8 9 10
Performance outcome: result achieved	1 2 3 4 5 6 7 8 9 10
Performance process: quality expected	1 2 3 4 5 6 7 8 9 10
Performance process: quality achieved	1 2 3 4 5 6 7 8 9 10
Recovery obtained before competition	1 2 3 4 5 6 7 8 9 10
Recovery required before competition	1 2 3 4 5 6 7 8 9 10

You now have two emotion profiles, one for successful performance (optimal intensity) and one for poor performance (dysfunctional intensity). Examine both profiles carefully and note the largest differences in emotion intensity.

Step 5: Establish your optimal and dysfunctional emotion intensity zones for each emotion.

A. Look again at your emotion profile for successful performances (step 4A), and write down again the helpful positives and negative emotions you listed. Think about how you felt before and during several successful competitions and about the intensity of each of the emotions you selected. Use the same scale (1-10), but try to mark a range, or a zone, of intensity for each of the emotions to indicate how much of it is helpful for you before and while you compete. Circle two numbers for each emotion, one for the minimal amount of the emotion that is helpful and one for the maximal amount that is helpful.

Helpful positive emotions (P+)	Intensity of emotions
1.	1 2 3 4 5 6 7 8 9 10
2.	1 2 3 4 5 6 7 8 9 10
3.	1 2 3 4 5 6 7 8 9 10
4.	1 2 3 4 5 6 7 8 9 10
5.	1 2 3 4 5 6 7 8 9 10
Helpful negative emotions (N+)	**Intensity of emotions**
1.	1 2 3 4 5 6 7 8 9 10
2.	1 2 3 4 5 6 7 8 9 10
3.	1 2 3 4 5 6 7 8 9 10
4.	1 2 3 4 5 6 7 8 9 10
5.	1 2 3 4 5 6 7 8 9 10

B. Look again at your emotion profile for poor performances (step 4B), and write down again the harmful positives and negative emotions you listed. Think about how you felt before and during several poor performances and about the intensity of each of the emotions you selected. Use the same scale (1-10), but try to mark a range, or a zone, of intensity for each of the emotions to indicate how much of it is harmful for you before and while you compete. Circle two numbers for each emotion, one for the minimal amount of the emotion that is harmful, and one for the maximal amount that is harmful.

Harmful positive emotions (P–)	Intensity of emotions
1.	1 2 3 4 5 6 7 8 9 10
2.	1 2 3 4 5 6 7 8 9 10
3.	1 2 3 4 5 6 7 8 9 10
4.	1 2 3 4 5 6 7 8 9 10
5.	1 2 3 4 5 6 7 8 9 10

Harmful negative emotions (N–)	Intensity of emotions
1.	1 2 3 4 5 6 7 8 9 10
2.	1 2 3 4 5 6 7 8 9 10
3.	1 2 3 4 5 6 7 8 9 10
4.	1 2 3 4 5 6 7 8 9 10
5.	1 2 3 4 5 6 7 8 9 10

Step 6: Monitor your emotions in practices and competitions.

Your emotion profiles for successful performances (optimal zones) and unsuccessful performances (dysfunctional zones) can help you predict your performance based on your current or anticipated emotions. For instance, if you are experiencing most of the emotions in the profile close to, or within, the optimal zones before a competition, then the probability of a successful performance is high.

Emotion profiles, similar to the profiles described in step 5, A and B, can be developed for the assessment of emotional dynamics before, during, and after performance. These emotion profiles are useful for monitoring performance-related emotional states in practices and for evaluating the effectiveness of intervention and recovery procedures. In developing these profiles, it is useful to identify typical emotion intensity in specific situations as well as a working range of emotion intensity. Because a dual meet is different from, say, a championship meet, you want to develop specific profiles for specific competitions (e.g., state championship, national championship, Olympic trials).

Use the following self-rating individualized emotion diver profile as a diagnostic tool for identifying, assessing, and evaluating your emotions and emotion intensity levels in practice and competition. The steps in developing the emotion profile are the same as outlined in this worksheet.

Adapted, by permission, from Y.L. Hanin, 2000, *Emotions in sport* (Champaign, IL: Human Kinetics), 303-312.

From J. Huber, 2016, *Springboard and Platform Diving* (Champaign, IL. Human Kinetics).

Individualized Emotion Diver Profile

Name _____ Date _____

(Before/During/After) Competition _____

Circle a number to indicate the intensity of each emotion. Intensity scale of emotions:

    1   (very, very little)
    2   (very little)
    3   (little)
  4-5 (moderate)
  6-7 (much)
  8-9 (very much)
   10 (very, very much)

Helpful positive emotions (P+)	Intensity of emotions
1.	1 2 3 4 5 6 7 8 9 10
2.	1 2 3 4 5 6 7 8 9 10
3.	1 2 3 4 5 6 7 8 9 10
4.	1 2 3 4 5 6 7 8 9 10
5.	1 2 3 4 5 6 7 8 9 10

Helpful negative emotions (N+)	Intensity of emotions
1.	1 2 3 4 5 6 7 8 9 10
2.	1 2 3 4 5 6 7 8 9 10
3.	1 2 3 4 5 6 7 8 9 10
4.	1 2 3 4 5 6 7 8 9 10
5.	1 2 3 4 5 6 7 8 9 10

Harmful positive emotions (P–)	Intensity of emotions
1.	1 2 3 4 5 6 7 8 9 10
2.	1 2 3 4 5 6 7 8 9 10
3.	1 2 3 4 5 6 7 8 9 10
4.	1 2 3 4 5 6 7 8 9 10
5.	1 2 3 4 5 6 7 8 9 10

Harmful negative emotions (N–)	Intensity of emotions
1.	1 2 3 4 5 6 7 8 9 10
2.	1 2 3 4 5 6 7 8 9 10
3.	1 2 3 4 5 6 7 8 9 10
4.	1 2 3 4 5 6 7 8 9 10
5.	1 2 3 4 5 6 7 8 9 10
Performance outcome: result expected	1 2 3 4 5 6 7 8 9 10
Performance outcome: result achieved	1 2 3 4 5 6 7 8 9 10
Performance process: quality expected	1 2 3 4 5 6 7 8 9 10
Performance process: quality achieved	1 2 3 4 5 6 7 8 9 10
Recovery obtained before competition	1 2 3 4 5 6 7 8 9 10
Recovery required before competition	1 2 3 4 5 6 7 8 9 10

Adapted, by permission, from Y.L. Hanin, 2000, *Emotions in sport* (Champaign, IL: Human Kinetics), 303-312.

From J. Huber, 2016, *Springboard and Platform Diving* (Champaign, IL. Human Kinetics).

References

Adams, J.A. (1961). The second facet of forgetting: A review of warm-up decrement. *Psychological Bulletin, 58,* 257-273.

Adams, J.A. (1971). A closed-loop theory of motor learning. *Journal of Motor Behavior, 3,* 111-150.

Allen, J.(2006). *As a man thinketh.* New York: Tarcher/Penguin.

Bandura, A. (1993). Perceived self-efficacy in cognitive development and functioning. *Educational Psychologist, 28,* 117-148.

Bloom, B.S. (1976). *Human characteristics and school learning.* New York: McGraw-Hill.

Bloom, B.S. (1985). *Developing talent in young people.* New York: Ballantine.

Bloom, B.S. (1987). A response to Slavin's mastery learning reconsidered. *Review of Educational Research, 57,* 507-508.

Bompa, T.O. (1994). *Theory and methodology of training: The key to athletic performance.* Dubuque, IA: Kendall/Hunt.

Carr, C. (2005). *USA Diving—Sport Psychology Program: Post-competition evaluation form (athletes).* Indianapolis, IN: Self-publication.

Carroll, J.B. (1963). A model of school learning. *Teachers College Record, 64,* 723-733.

Carver, C.S. (1996). Cognitive interference and the structure of behavior. In I.G. Sarason, G.R. Pierce, & B.R. Sarason (Eds.), *Cognitive interference: Theories, methods, and findings* (pp. 25-45). Mahwah, NJ: Erlbaum.

Christina, R.W., & Corcos, D.M. (1988). Coaches guide to teaching sport skills. Champaign, IL: Human Kinetics.

Cogan, K. (2012). *Mental toughness in diving: A guide for developing motivation, confidence, and mental focus.* Colorado Springs, CO: United States Olympic Committee, Sport Performance Department.

Cogan, K., & Halbert, C. (2012). *Focus for peak performance. 14 Days of Focus: Developing mental resilience and strength to peak in diving.* Colorado Springs, CO: United States Olympic Committee, Sport Performance Department.

Côté, J., Baker, J., & Abernethy, B. (2003). From play to practice: A developmental framework for the acquisition of expertise in team sport. In J. Starkes & K.A. Ericsson (Eds.), *Expert performance in sports: Advances in research on sport expertise* (pp. 89-110). Champaign, IL: Human Kinetics.

Coyle, D. (2009). *The talent code: Greatness isn't born. It's grown. Here's how.* New York: Bantam Dell.

Csikszentmihalyi, M. (1990). *Flow: The psychology of optimal sport experience.* New York: Harper & Row.

Csikszentmihalyi, M., Rathunde, K., & Whalen, S. (1993). *Talented teenagers: The roots of success & failure.* Cambridge, UK: Cambridge University Press.

Dansereau, D.F. (1985). Learning strategy research. In J.W. Segal, S.F. Chipman, & R. Glaser (Eds.), *Thinking and learning skills* (pp.1, 209-240). Hillsdale, NJ: Erlbaum.

Easterbrook, J.A. (1959). The effect of emotion on cue utilization and the organization of behavior. *Psychological Review, 66*, 183-201.

Eliot, T.S. (1971). Little gidding. In T.S. Eliot (Ed.), *Four Quartets*, (pp. 49-55). Orlando, FL: Harcourt.

Ericsson, K.A. (1996). *The road to excellence: The acquisition of expert performance in the arts and sciences, sports and games.* Mahwah, NJ: Erlbaum.

Ericsson, K.A., Krampe, R.T., & Tesch-Romer, C. (1993). The role of deliberate practice in the acquisition of expert performance. *Psychological Review, 100* (3), 363-406.

Etnier, J., & Landers, D.M. (1996). The influence of procedural variables on the efficacy of mental practice. *The Sport Psychologist, 10*, 48-57.

Feltz, D.L., & Landers, D.M. (1983). The effects of mental practice on motor skill learning and performance: A meta analysis. *Journal of Sport Psychology, 5*, 1-8.

Gabriel, J.L. (2007). Handspotting basic dives and somersaults on poolside: Building a high response accuracy. In R.M. Malina, & J.L. Gabriel, J.L. (Eds.), *USA diving coach development reference manual* (pp. 603-616). Indianapolis, IN: USA Diving Publications.

Gibbons, T., McConnell, A., Forster, T., Tuffey-Riewald, S., & Peterson, K. (2003). *Reflections on success: U.S. Olympians describe the success factors and obstacles that most influenced their Olympic development.* Results of the Talent Identification and Development Questionnaire to U.S. Olympians. Colorado Springs, CO: USOC.

Gibson, J. (2012). *Sport nutrition for diving: A practical guide for athletes and coaches.* Colorado Springs, CO: United States Olympic Committee, Sport Performance Department.

Gladwell, M. (2008). *Outliers: The story of success.* New York: Little, Brown.

Grand, D., & Goldberg, A.S. (2011). *This is your brain on sports: Beating blocks, slumps and performance anxiety for good!* Indianapolis, IN: Dog Ear.

Green, S., & McAlpine, G. (2011). *The way of baseball: Finding stillness at 95 mph.* New York: Simon & Schuster.

Grossnickel, D.R., & Sesko, F.P. (1990). *Preventive discipline for effective teaching and learning.* Reston, VA: National Association of Secondary School Principals.

Hanin, Y.L. (2000). *Emotion in sport.* Champaign, IL: Human Kinetics.

Huber, J.J. (1997). Differences in problem representation and procedural knowledge between elite and nonelite springboard divers. *The Sport Psychologist, 11* (2), 142-159.

Huber, J.J. (2001). *Dryland training for diving.* DVD. Ames, IA: Championship Books and Video Productions.

Huber, J.J. (2007). *Becoming a champion diver: Skills and drills for success.* DVD. Ames, IA: Championship Books and Video Productions.

Huber, J.J. (2013). *Applying educational psychology in coaching athletes.* Champaign, IL: Human Kinetics.

Hughes, S. (2006, January 23). Going for broke. *Newsweek*, p. 47.

Jackson, S.A. (1996). Toward a conceptual understanding of the flow experience in elite athletes. *Research Quarterly for Exercise and Sport, 67*, (1), 76-90.

Janelle, C.M., Barba, D.A., Frehlich, S.G., Tennant, L.K., & Cauraugh, J.H. (1997). Maximizing performance feedback effectiveness through videotape replay and a self-controlled learning environment. *Research Quarterly for Exercise and Sport, 68*, 269-279.

Kernodle, M.W., & Carlton, L.G. (1992). Information feedback and the learning of multiple-degree-of-freedom activities. *Journal of Motor Behavior, 24*, 187-196.

Landin, D., & Hebert, E.P. (1999). The influence of self-talk on the performance of skilled female tennis players. *Journal of Applied Sport Psychology, 11*, 263-282.

Lavery, J.J. (1962). Retention of simple motor skills as a function of the number of trials by which KR is delayed. *Perceptual and Motor Skills, 15*, 231-237.

Lee, D.L., & Belfiore, P.J. (1997). Enhancing classroom performance: A review of reinforcement schedules. *Journal of Behavioral Education, 7* (2), 205-217.

Louganis, G., & Marcus, E. (2006). *Breaking the surface*. Naperville, IL: Sourcebooks.

Mack, M.G., & Ragan, B.G. (2008). Development of the Mental, Emotional, and Bodily Toughness (MeBTough) Inventory in collegiate athletes and nonathletes. *Journal of Athletic Training, 43*, 125-132.

Marland, M. (1975). *The craft of the classroom: A survival guide to classroom management at the secondary school*. London: Heinemann Educational Books.

Martens, R., Vealey, R.S., & Burton, D. (1990). *Competitive anxiety in sport*. Champaign, IL: Human Kinetics.

Massey, M.V. (2013). *Behavior change in applied sport psychology: The use of processes of change in psychological training for athletes*. Unpublished doctoral dissertation, University of Wisconsin, Milwaukee.

McCann, S., Haberl, P., Peterson, K., & Bauman, J. (2006). *Sport psychology: Coaches' guide to mental training manual*. Colorado Springs, CO: United States Olympic Committee.

Miller, D.I. (2001). *Biomechanics of competitive diving*. Indianapolis, IN: USA Diving.

Nideffer, R.M. (1989). Anxiety, attention, and performance in sports: Theoretical and practical considerations. In D. Hackfort & C.D. Spielberger (Eds.), *Anxiety in sports: An international perspective* (pp. 117-136). New York: Hemisphere.

O'Brien, R.F. (1992). Ron O'Brien's d*iving for gold*. Champaign, IL: Human Kinetics.

O'Brien, R.F. (2003). *Springboard and platform diving*. Champaign, IL: Human Kinetics.

Raglin, J.S., & Hanin, Y.L. (2000). Competitive anxiety. In Y.L. Hanin (Ed.), *Emotions in sport* (pp. 93-111). Champaign, IL: Human Kinetics.

Rothstein, A.L., & Arnold, R.K. (1976). Bridging the gap: Application of videotape feedback and bowling. *Motor Skills: Theory into Practice, 1*, 35-62.

Sands, W.A., McNeal, J.R., & Schultz, B.B. (1999). Kinetic and temporal patterns of three types of vertical jump among elite international divers. *Sports Medicine, Training and Rehabilitation, 9* (2), 107-127.

Scanlan, T.K., Stein, G.L., & Ravizza, K. (1989). An in-depth study of former elite figure skaters: II: Sources of enjoyment. *Journal of Sport and Exercise Psychology, 11*, 65-83.

Schmidt, R.A., Lange, C., & Young, D.E. (1990). Optimizing summary knowledge of results for skill learning. *Human Movement Science, 9*, 325-348.

Schmidt, R.A., & Lee, T.E. (2011). *Motor control and learning: A behavioral emphasis*. Champaign, IL: Human Kinetics.

Schmidt, R.A., & Lee, T.E. (2014). *Motor learning and performance: From principles to application*. Champaign, IL: Human Kinetics.

Schmidt, R.A., & Wrisberg, C.A. (2008). *Motor learning and performance: A situation-based learning approach*. Champaign, IL: Human Kinetics.

Schwartz, R. (2012). *Program constructor*. Colorado Springs, CO: United States Olympic Committee, Sport Performance Department.

Simon, H.A., & Chase, W.G. (1973). Skill in chess. *American Scientist, 61*, 394-403.

Smith, R.E. (1996). Performance anxiety: Cognitive interference, and concentration enhancement strategies in sports. In I.G. Sarason, G.R. Pierce, & B.R. Sarason (Eds.), *Cognitive interference: Theories, methods, and findings* (pp. 261-283). Mahwah, NJ: Erlbaum.

Swinnen, S.P. (1990). Interpolated activities during the knowledge-of-results delay and post-knowledge-of-results interval: Effects on performance and learning. *Journal of Experimental Psychology: Learning, Memory, and Cognition, 16*, 692-705.

Thomas, P.R., Murphy, S.M., & Hardy, L (1999). Test of Performance Strategies: Development and preliminary validation of a comprehensive measure of athletes' psychological skills. *Journal of Sports Science, 17*, 697-711.

USOC Sport Psychology Staff. (2006). *Coaches' guide: Sport psychology mental training manual*. Colorado Springs, CO: U.S. Olympic Committee.

Wightman, D.C., & Lintern, G. (1985). Part-task training strategies for tracking and manual control. *Human Factors, 27*, 267-283.

Wrightson, B. (1970). An Olympic championship: What does it prove? *Swimming World Magazine, vol. 11*, No. 6, June, p.14.

Wulf, G., Lee, T.D., & Schmidt, R.A. (1994). Reducing knowledge of results about relative versus absolute timing: Differential effects on learning. *Journal of Motor Behavior, 26*, 362-369.

Zinsser, N., Bunker, L., & Williams, J.M. (2001). Cognitive techniques for building confidence and enhancing performance. In J.M. Williams (Ed.), *Applied sport psychology: Personal growth to peak performance* (4th ed., pp. 284-311). Mountain View, CA: Mayfield.

Index

PLEASE NOTE: Page numbers followed by an italicized *f* indicate that a picture will be found on that page.

About the Author

Jeffrey Huber, PhD, was a collegiate diving coach for 37 years, the last 24 years as head diving coach at Indiana University. During his career he developed USA and NCAA national champions, Big Ten Collegiate Conference champions, international champions, dozens of NCAA All Americans, and a number of USA Olympians. As USA team coach, he accompanied his divers to every international competition in the world, including the Pan American Games, World University Games, FINA Grand Prix events, World Championships, World Cups, and three Olympic Games: Sydney (2000), Athens (2004), and Beijing (2008). He has been named USA National Coach of the Year (13 times), NCAA Coach of the Year, USOC Coach of the Year, Big Ten Coach of the Year, and inducted into the state of Indiana Swimming and Diving Wall of Fame.

Huber received his doctorate from the University of Nebraska in educational psychology with an emphasis in cognitive processing differences between elite and non-elite athletes. While fulfilling his coaching duties, he also was adjunct assistant professor part-time in the Department of Counseling and Educational Psychology as well as the Department of Kinesiology at Indiana University. He is currently on faculty as Professor of Practice in the Department of Psychological and Brain Sciences at Indiana University and is the author of *Applying Educational Psychology in Coaching Athletes*. He and his wife, Lesa Huber, PhD, also on faculty at Indiana University, reside in Bloomington.